IMAGES
of America

DETROIT
CITY OF INDUSTRY

For my loving wife, Kate

IMAGES
of America

DETROIT
CITY OF INDUSTRY

David Lee Poremba

ARCADIA
PUBLISHING

ISBN 978-0-7385-2037-7

Published by Arcadia Publishing
Charleston, South Carolina

Printed in the United States of America

Library of Congress Catalog Card Number: 2002110452

For all general information contact Arcadia Publishing at:
Telephone 843-853-2070
Fax 843-853-0044
E-mail sales@arcadiapublishing.com
For customer service and orders:
Toll-Free 1-888-313-2665

Visit us on the Internet at www.arcadiapublishing.com

Contents

ACKNOWLEDGMENTS

All of the photographs in these pages are from the Burton Historical Collection, Detroit Public Library. Most of the information and statistics come from the very extensive clippings files known as the Local History Collection.

INTRODUCTION

Detroit, the city of the straits, was founded by an entrepreneurial Frenchman who believed location was the key to a water system of transportation to the East Coast, and henceforth, to the markets of Europe. First the French, then the English saw their colonial aspirations in the Old Northwest disappear, and the Americans discovered that the city was the point of access to a tremendous amount of raw materials from the interior. When the Erie Canal made travel to Michigan easier and faster, Detroit grew from a frontier town into a manufacturing city and commercial port of the first importance in just a few decades.

By 1860, Detroit had grown to be the 19th largest city in the United States, with a diverse population of 45,000 German-, English-, Polish-, Dutch- and African-Americans. This cultural diversity brought a number of different skills to the workplace and allowed for an economic diversity that made Detroit the leading city of the Midwest.

Detroit's industries produced a wide range of products, most of which were created in such quantities that the city was the nation's leader in that category. Detroit was the nation's manufacturing leader in railroad cars, tobacco products, Bessemer steel, steel rails, stoves, ranges, electric heaters and furnaces, storage batteries, pharmaceuticals, matches, pins, and many other products.

It would seem that with each new product or idea that came to people in Detroit also came instant success, with what grew to be worldwide demand. For example, the Caille Brothers set up shop to produce a bigger, better slot machine in Detroit and had customers on a waiting list in Paris, France before the company was one year old. The Michigan Carbon Works, which recycled buffalo bones left on the nation's prairies, exported their fertilizers throughout Canada. And the pharmaceutical companies in Detroit had a worldwide market for their products.

The economic boom that carried Detroit into the beginning of the 20th century was nothing short of phenomenal for a relatively small community in a special geographic location. That boom also contributed greatly to laying the financial foundation for the automobile industry. The technology that was present from the stove and boiler industries (to name but two) made the transition to the manufacture of automobiles all that much easier. The experience, technology, finances, and transportation system were all in place in the town that would become the Motor City.

It is through these few photographs that I hope to present "Dynamic Detroit" as a prosperous, growing, and leading city in the United States prior to the birth of the automobile.

One

EARLY INDUSTRIES

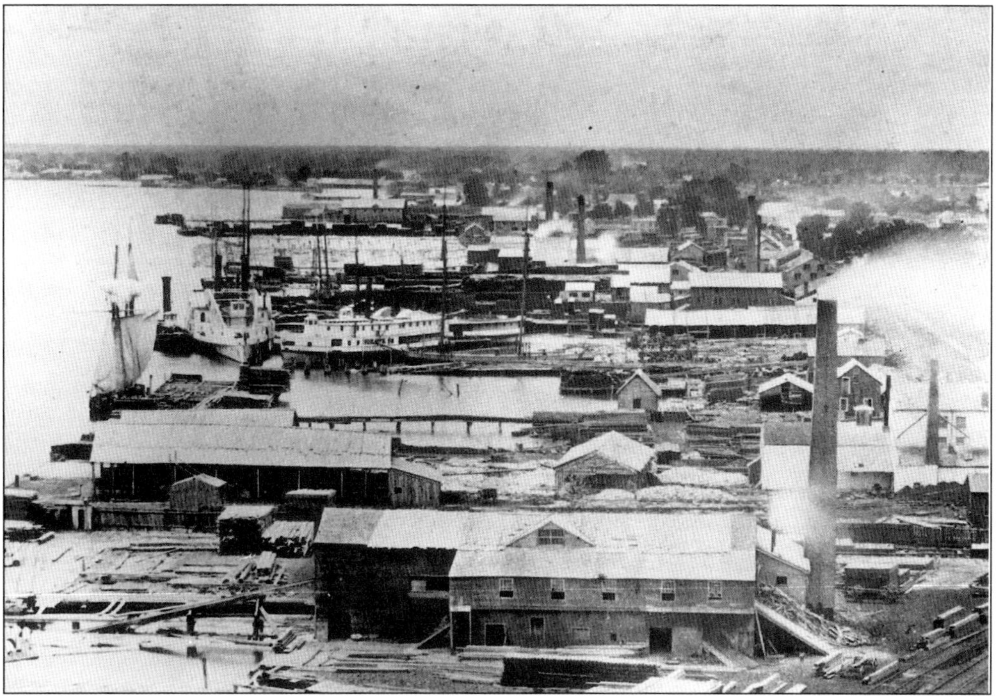

DETROIT RIVERFRONT, 1868. The riverfront is lined with warehouses to accommodate the arrival of raw materials from other parts of the state. Both sail and steam vessels are present in this photograph, tied up at different wharves just south of the city center. Lumber and iron ore shipments arrived regularly, to be used as building materials, furniture, iron and steel.

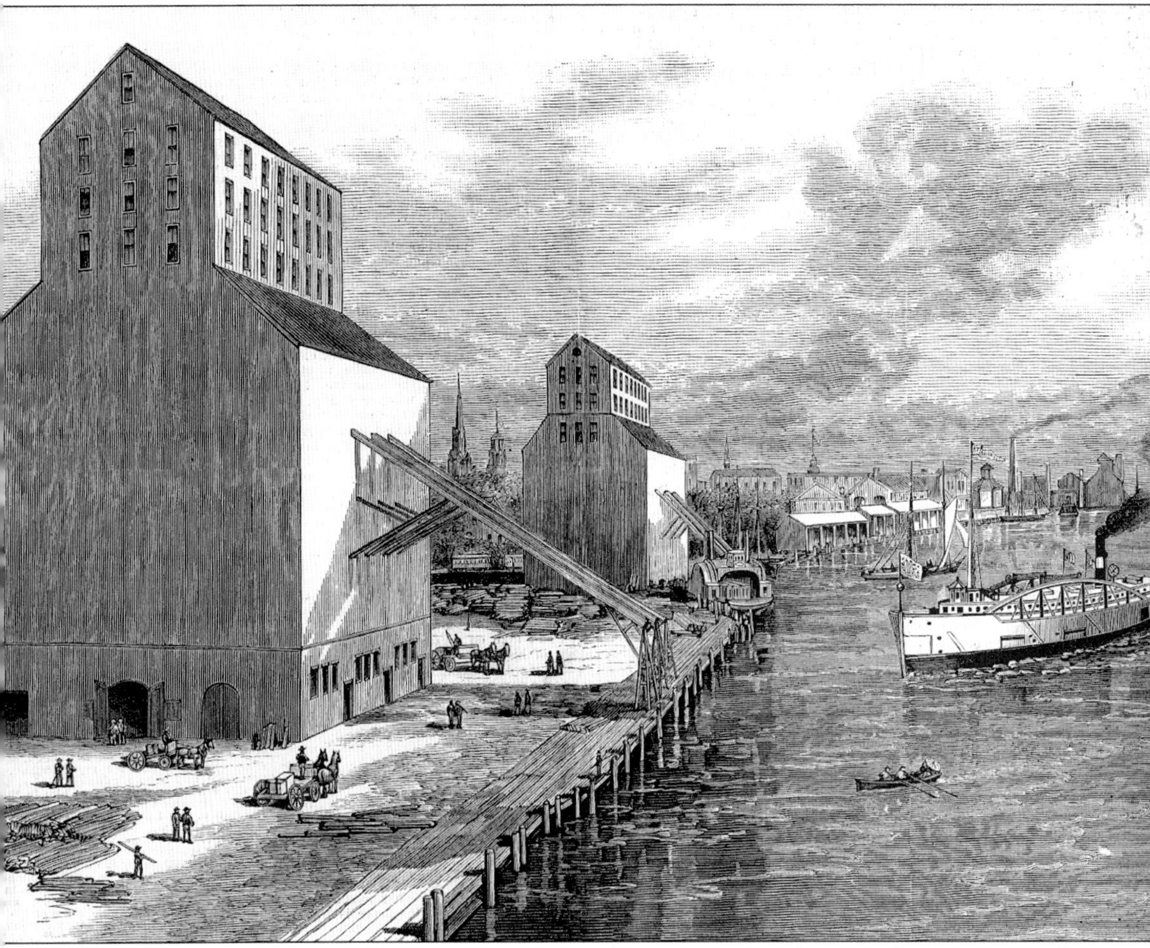

THE GRAIN ELEVATORS AT DETROIT, 1854. The new Vanderbilt grain elevator is open for business in this illustration from Frank Leslie's *Illustrated Newspaper*. These elevators would have handled products grown in Michigan and Wisconsin and transshipped to ports on the eastern seaboard of the United States and Canada. The grain arrived by wagon, and later by an ever-growing railroad system, and was loaded on sail and steam freighters. Detroit was ideally situated geographically to become a grain-shipping and receiving port and would establish a Board of Trade to handle sales and freighting of various grains, which would number in the millions of bushels each year.

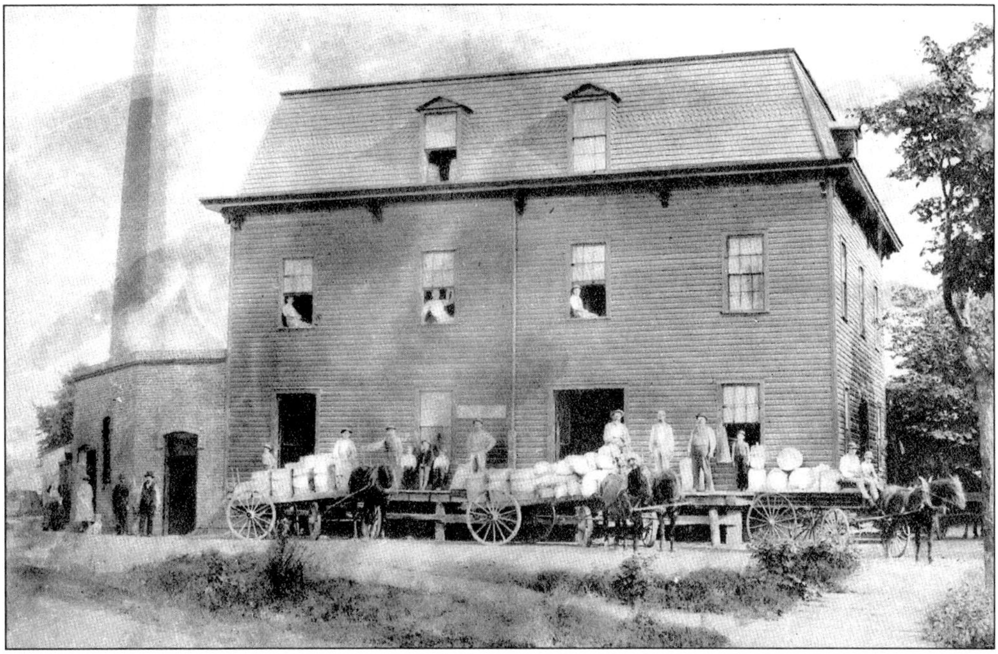

THE LOCAL FLOUR MILL. The entire work force of the Charles Appel Flour Mill takes a break from their duties to pose for this photograph during the 1860s. Area farmers brought their grain to be rolled into flour at mills like this one, which stood at 17th Street and the Michigan Central Railroad tracks.

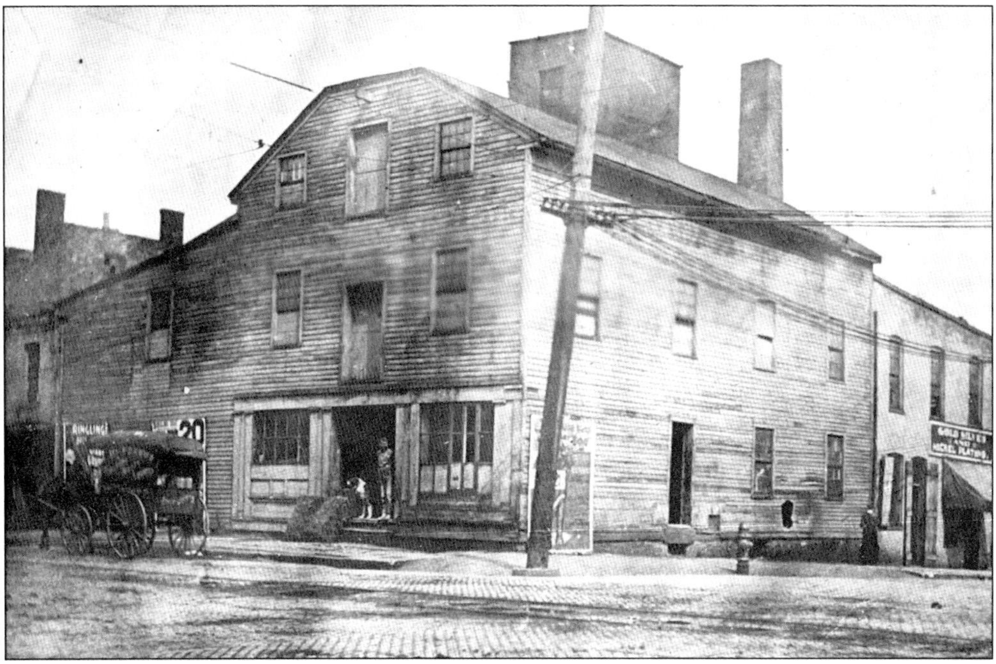

GRIST MILLS. An old grist mill on West Larned Street and Second Avenue was owned by Noah Sutton and called the old city mill. Mills date back to the founding of the city by the French and remained in operation through the 1890s. They were often powered by steam.

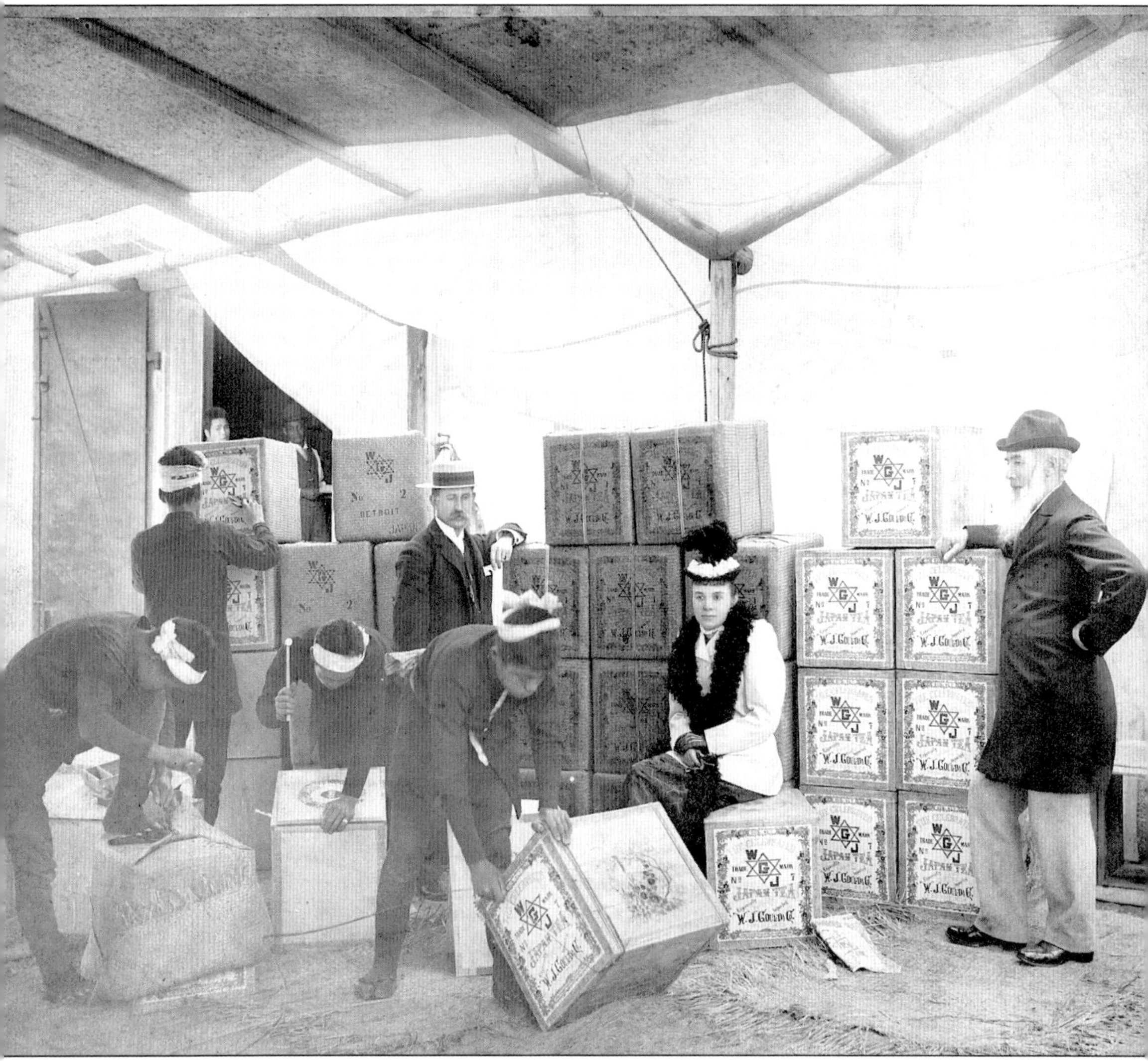

TEA IMPORTERS. The W.J. Gould Company, seen here inspecting a shipment of Japan tea, was a leading wholesale grocery house in Detroit. W.J. Gould, born in England in 1830, came to Detroit with his parents in 1836. His father and grandfather were both grocers and both had failed in their business. But it would be the son who really built up a successful business. In 1864, he went into a partnership with M.S. Fellers on Woodward Avenue, bought Fellers' interest in 1873 and moved the firm to Jefferson Avenue where he prospered. In 1880, he formed the W.J. Gould and Company along with D.D. Cady and Lewis F. Thompson. The business continued to grow and prosper and Gould served on the Boards of more than one Detroit bank, always a symbol of success.

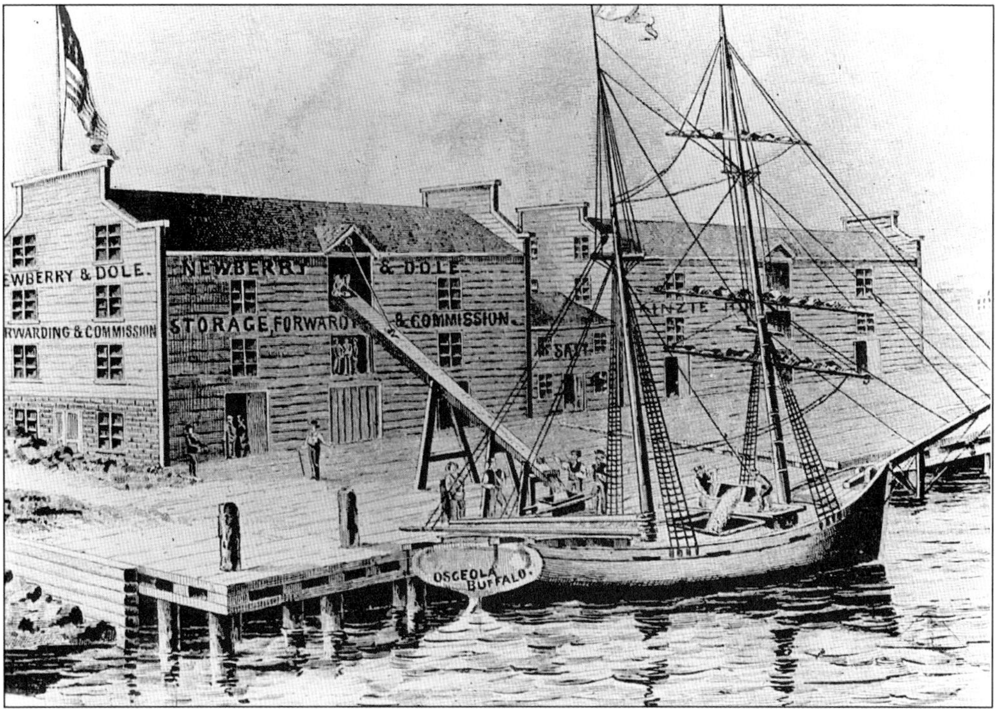

RIVERFRONT BUSINESS. This illustration depicts a section of warehouses belonging to the firm of Newberry and Dole, commission agents important to the transaction of business along the riverfront. Transshipments of goods and materials into and out of the Port of Detroit were essential to the city's growth and prosperity as a major city along the Great Lakes waterway.

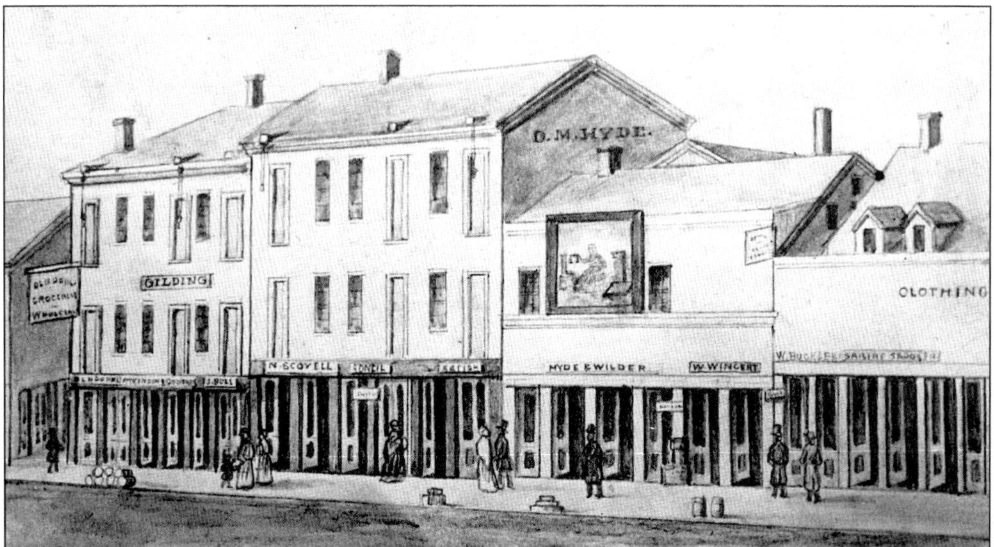

WOODWARD AVENUE, 1845. This section of Woodward Avenue between Atwater and Woodbridge Streets depicts a number of early and important businesses in frontier Detroit. Nelson Scovell operated a grocery right next to one of his competitors and a clothing store (on the extreme right), made up the block.

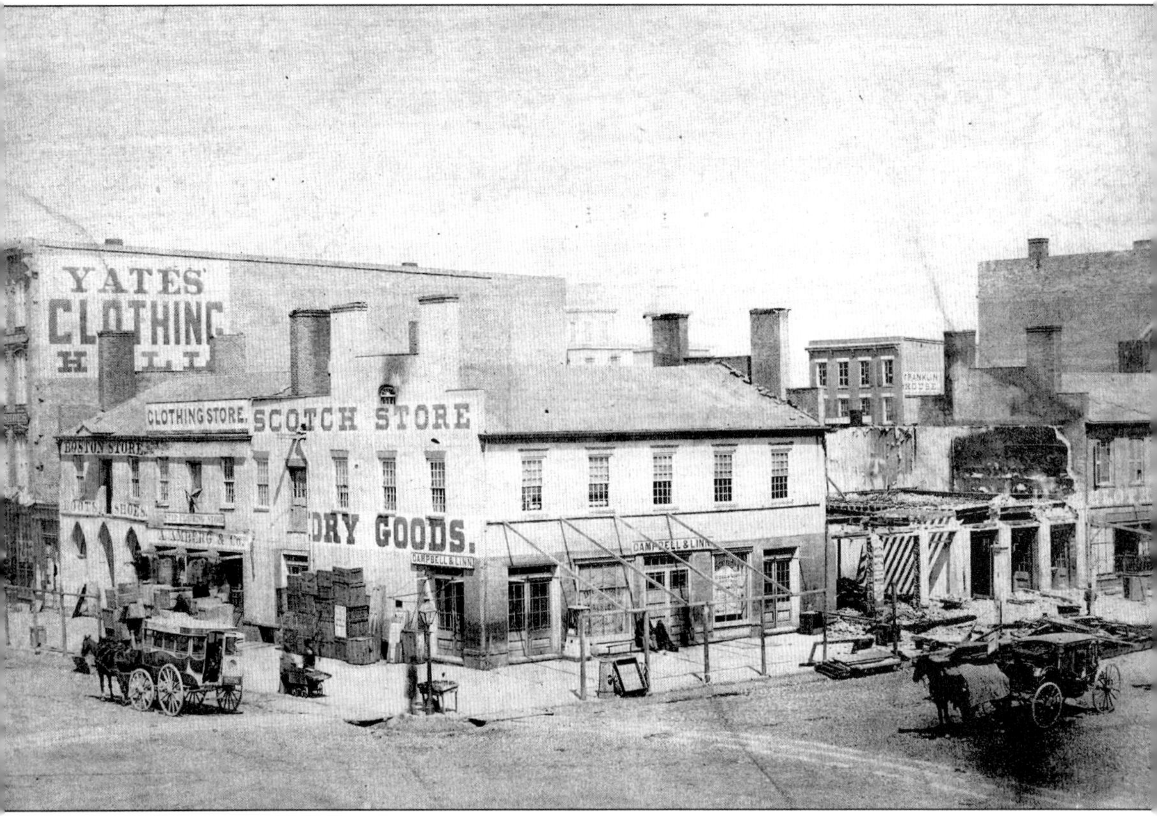

CAMPBELL, LINN AND COMPANY. At the northeast corner of Jefferson and Woodward Avenues stood the Scotch Store, an early Detroit landmark. This 1858 photograph depicts a successful business that looks as though it is about to expand a little along Jefferson Avenue. Importers and retailers of dry goods, cloaks, and shawls, Mr. Campbell and Mr. Linn started their business in the early 1840s. they carried an extensive line of staple and fancy dry goods, ranging from the latest novelties in dress fabrics, notions, trimmings, fancy goods, ladies' and gents' furnishings, gloves, laces, linens and hosiery, to a large assortment of cloaks and shawls. The firm's fortunes would continue to grow and a larger, three-story brick building would be built a little farther up Woodward. Campbell's descendents would be a part of the business until the late 1880s. The two buildings to the right of the Scotch Store were badly burned by fire.

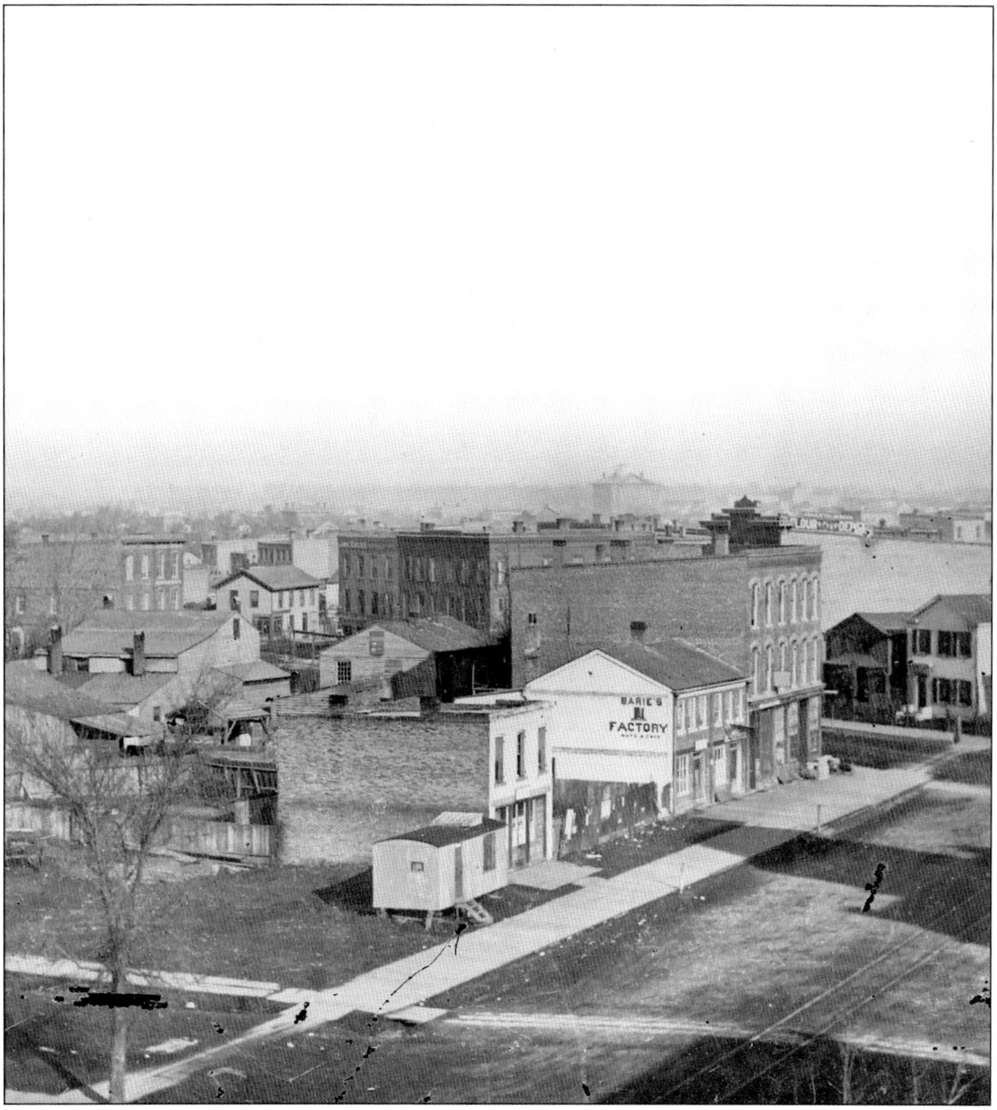

ALL BECAUSE OF THE FUR TRADE. This small stretch of downtown Detroit taken during the early 1860s shows Barie's Hat Factory, certainly one of the city's earliest industries, which could be dated back to the founding days of the French, who were the manufacturers of beaver hats for King Louis XIII. John P. Barie opened his first hat factory on Jefferson Avenue in late 1859 or early 1860 and the following year went into partnership with a fellow haberdasher named Joseph Ulrich, calling the business Ulrich and Barie. Then, in 1870, Mr. Barie was in business on his own again with a shop on Woodward Avenue. His business prospered and by the middle of that decade, he owned a second store on Michigan Avenue, just west of Woodward.

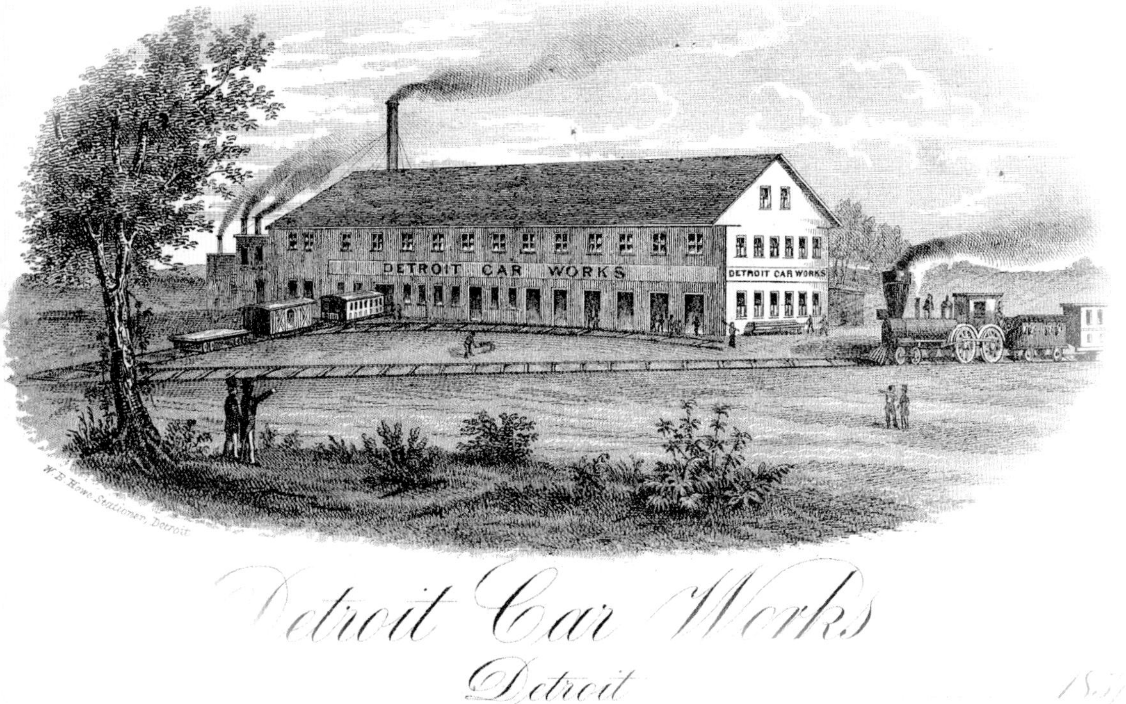

THE DETROIT CAR WORKS. In 1857, cars in Detroit meant railroad cars, the rolling stock that transported goods from one point to the other faster than ever before on a nationwide, growing network of railroads. With its access to both lumber and iron, Detroit was to become one of the country's largest manufacturers of railroad cars and railroad trucks, the wheels on which the cars rode. The Detroit Car Works was founded in 1860 by Dr. George B. Russell. In 1862, the firm had contracts worth $60,000 to build freight cars for the Michigan Southern and Cincinnati Air Line Railroads and were already building the same for the Detroit & Milwaukee and Grand Trunk Railways. Russell employed 75 men in his works at Croghan and DeQuindre Streets. The main building measured 275 by 60 feet and had two planning machines and an iron working machine.

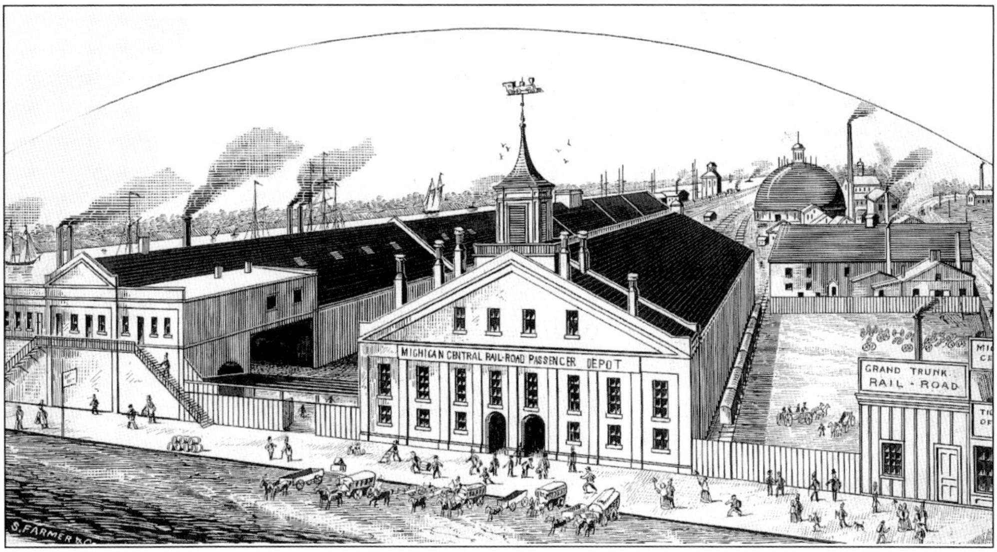

RAILROAD DEPOTS. This artists' drawing of the Michigan Central Railroad Passenger Depot near the Detroit River gives a good illustration of one of the biggest industries in the city beginning in the middle 1840s: railway transportation of people and goods. Located very near the river, goods could be off-loaded from ships directly onto railroad cars for faster delivery.

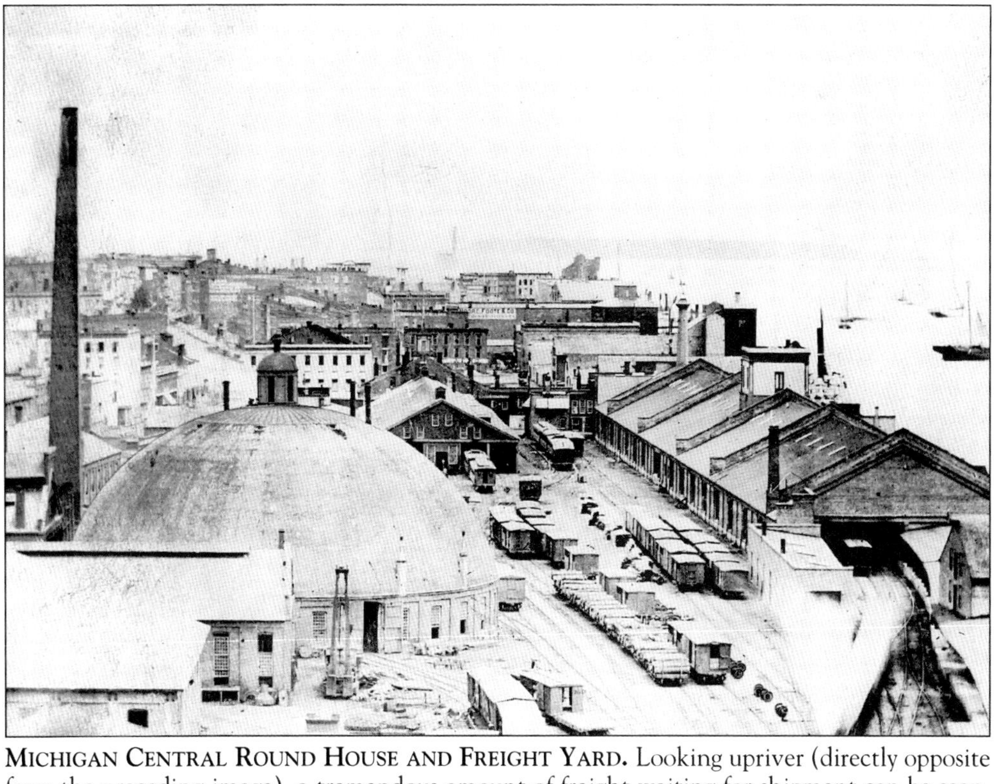

MICHIGAN CENTRAL ROUND HOUSE AND FREIGHT YARD. Looking upriver (directly opposite from the preceding image), a tremendous amount of freight waiting for shipment can be seen. The blur in the right foreground is a loaded train leaving the freight house for points south. The roundhouse was used to service and repair locomotives.

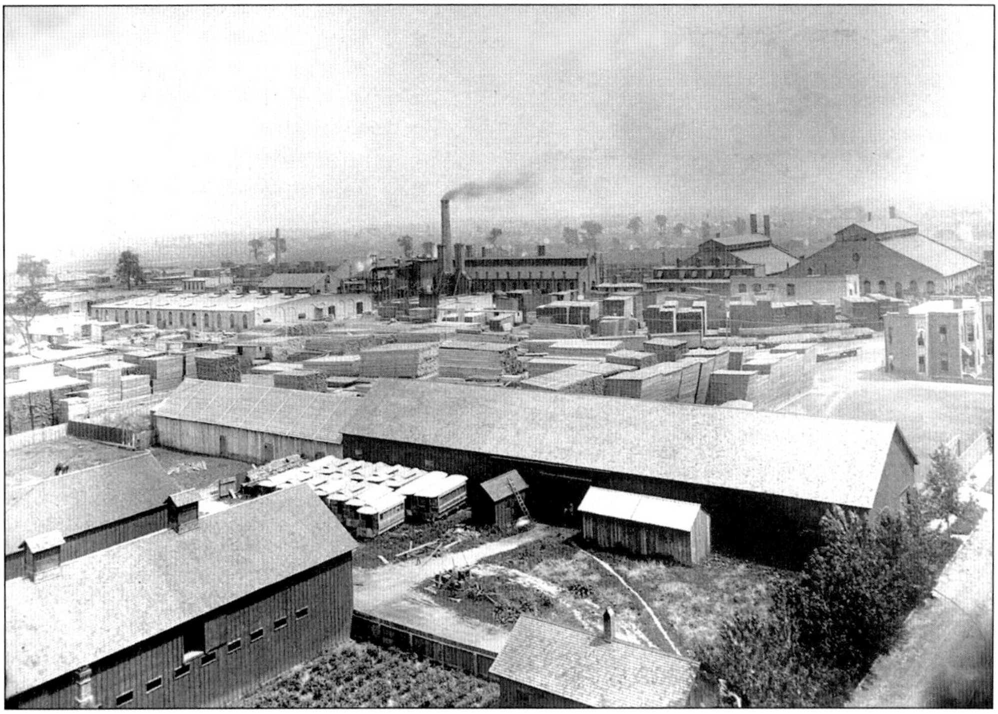

THE PENINSULAR CAR WORKS. The sprawling yards of the Peninsular Car Works at Ferry and Russell Streets illustrate the size of the business in Detroit, with its car barns and stacks upon stacks of lumber. The site covered forty acres and employed 1,500 men. Their annual output was 9,000 railroad cars. Frank J. Hecker and C.L. Freer were president and vice-president, respectively.

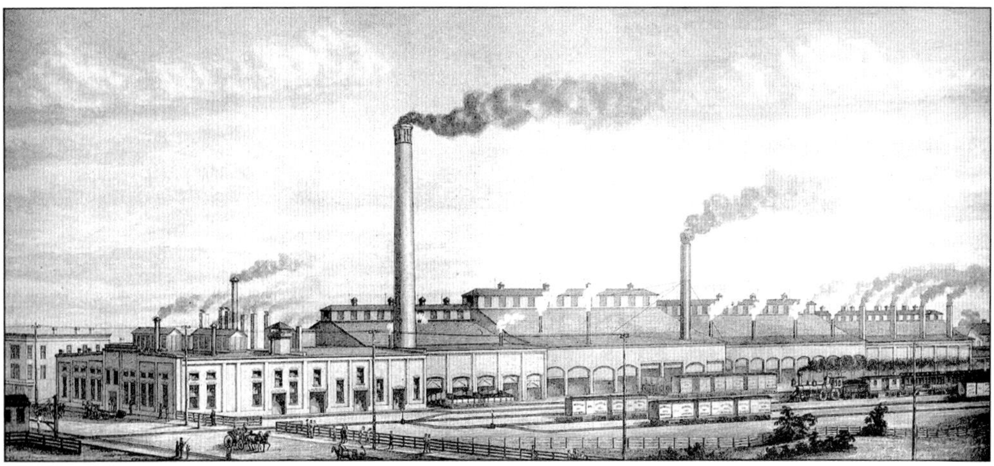

DETROIT STEEL AND SPRING WORKS. Located at Michigan and Indian Avenues, the works of this company covered two acres and employed a force of four hundred men. Established in 1879, this company produced all kinds of steel and was run day and night, selling products to dealers in steel and railcar companies all over the United States and Canada.

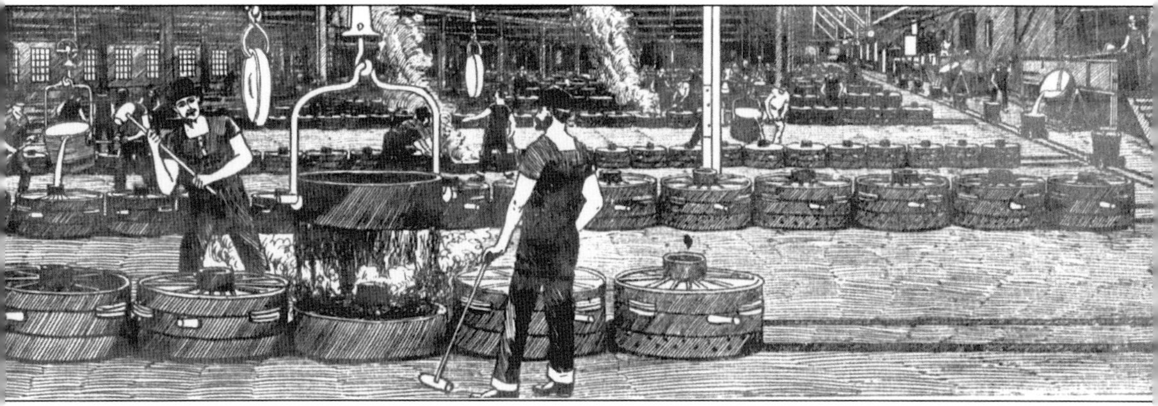

The Detroit Car Wheel Company. One of the largest manufacturers of railway car wheels and castings, the Detroit Car Wheel Company was established in 1865, with a capital stock of $12,000. Twenty years later, its capital amounted to $250,000 with an employment of six hundred workmen who turned out 30,000 tons of castings and 13,000 car wheels annually. Most of these car wheels were used by the Michigan Car Company and the remainder were sold to car manufacturers and railway corporations across the United States and Canada. The company occupied a portion of a tract of 40 acres, upon which were the Michigan Car Company and the Detroit Pipe and Foundry Company. All were owned by the same executive management. James, Hugh, and W.C. McMillan were a force to be dealt with in Detroit. James McMillan would later be elected to the United States Senate.

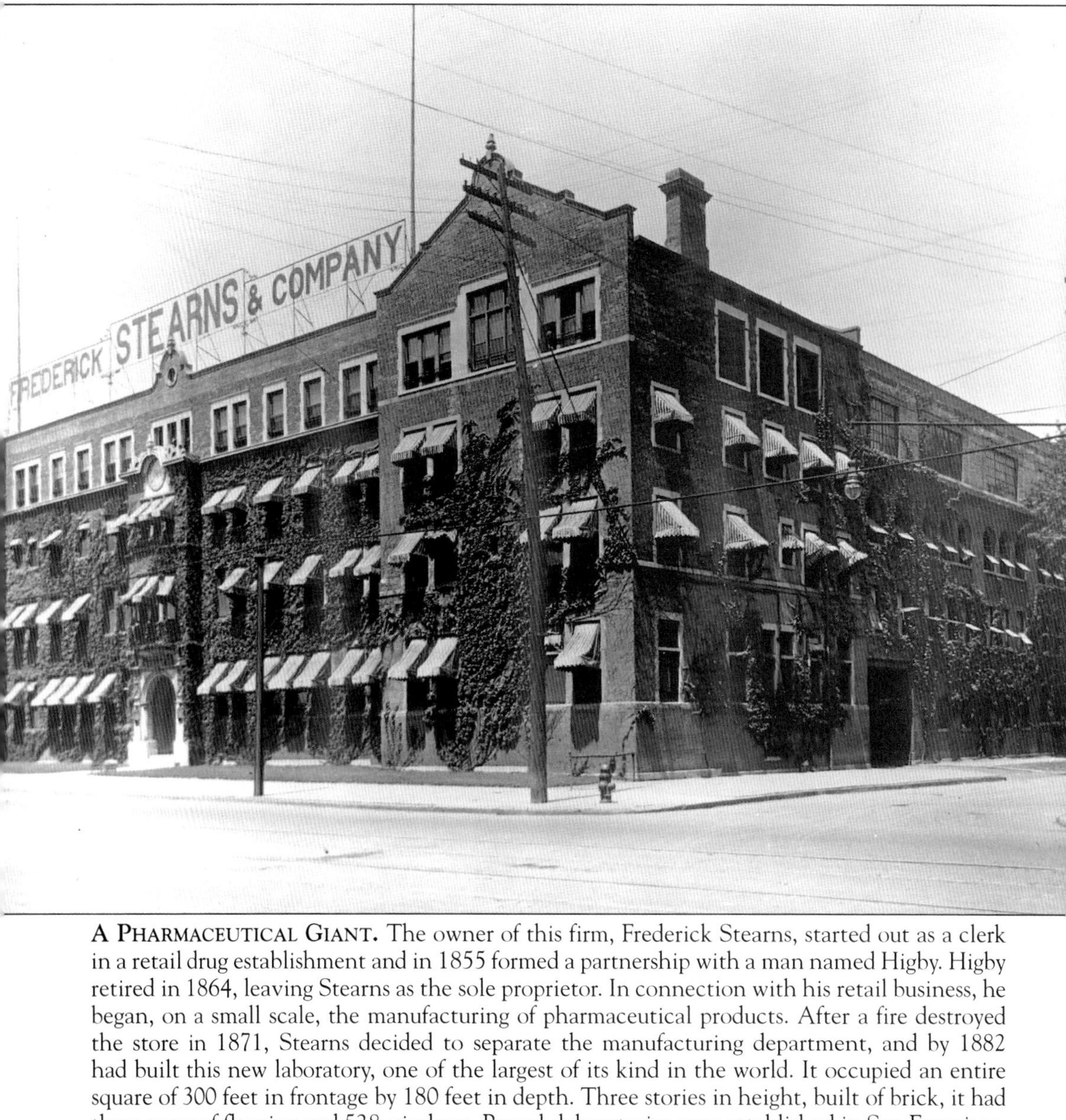

A PHARMACEUTICAL GIANT. The owner of this firm, Frederick Stearns, started out as a clerk in a retail drug establishment and in 1855 formed a partnership with a man named Higby. Higby retired in 1864, leaving Stearns as the sole proprietor. In connection with his retail business, he began, on a small scale, the manufacturing of pharmaceutical products. After a fire destroyed the store in 1871, Stearns decided to separate the manufacturing department, and by 1882 had built this new laboratory, one of the largest of its kind in the world. It occupied an entire square of 300 feet in frontage by 180 feet in depth. Three stories in height, built of brick, it had three acres of flooring and 528 windows. Branch laboratories were established in San Francisco, California, and Windsor, Ontario. An office was maintained in New York City to handle the East Coast trade.

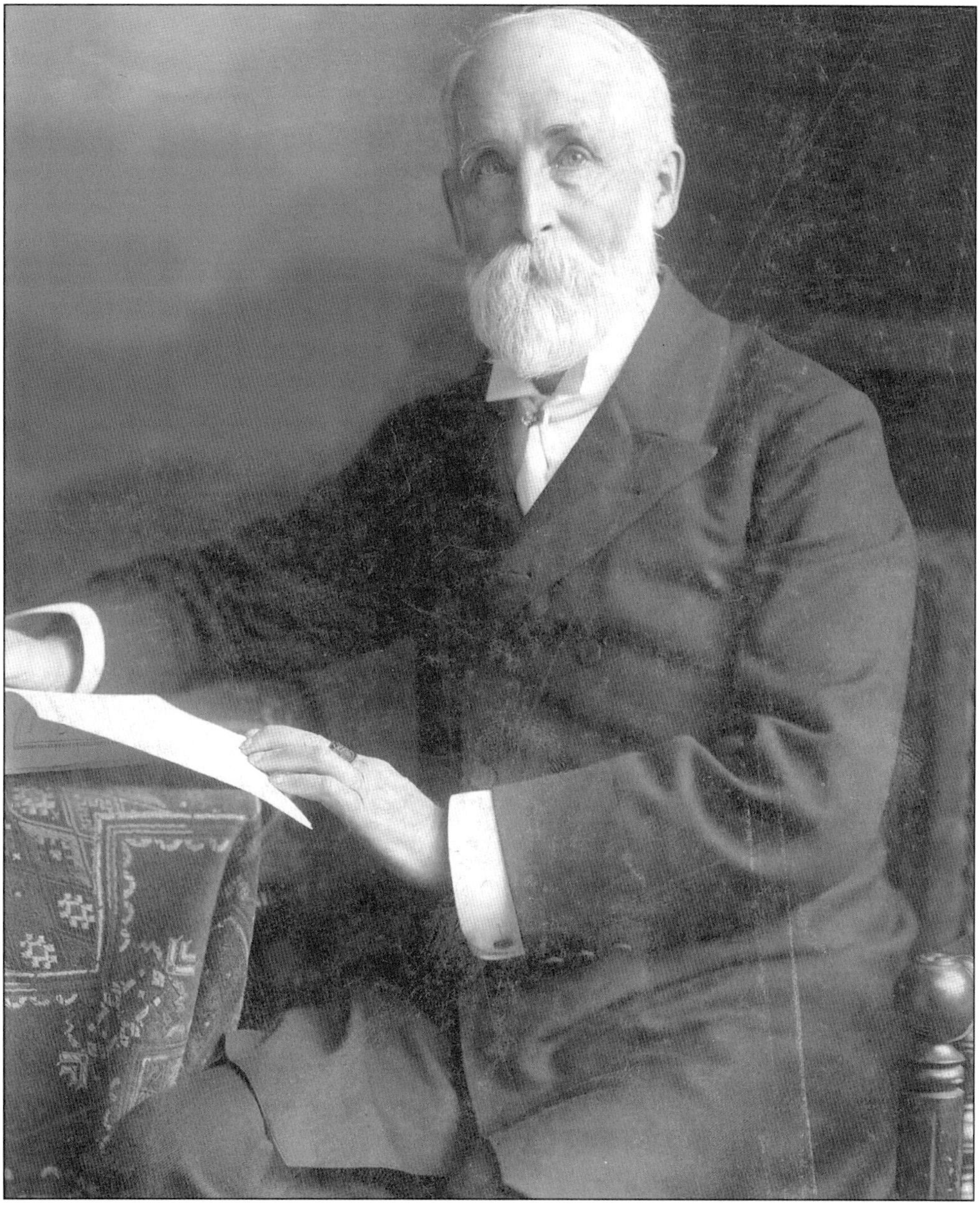

DRUG KING. Frederick Stearns came to Detroit from Buffalo, New York in 1855, where he had worked as a clerk and afterward as a partner in a retail drug establishment. By 1875, Stearns concentrated on the manufacturing of pharmaceuticals to the exclusion of all else and created an empire. In 1876, he conceived of the "New Idea" of putting up a complete line of popular remedies with the formulas displayed right on the labels to replace the secret and often deleterious compounds known as patent medicines. Probably the first instance of the actual ingredients of a product appearing on the label, the success of this idea is reflected in the fact that Stearns' drugs were sold to all parts of the world, including Australia, South America, Africa, Asia, the Middle East, and the East and West Indies. The Stearns Company manufactured all of their own paper boxes, wrappers, labels and circulars, thereby providing a less expensive product.

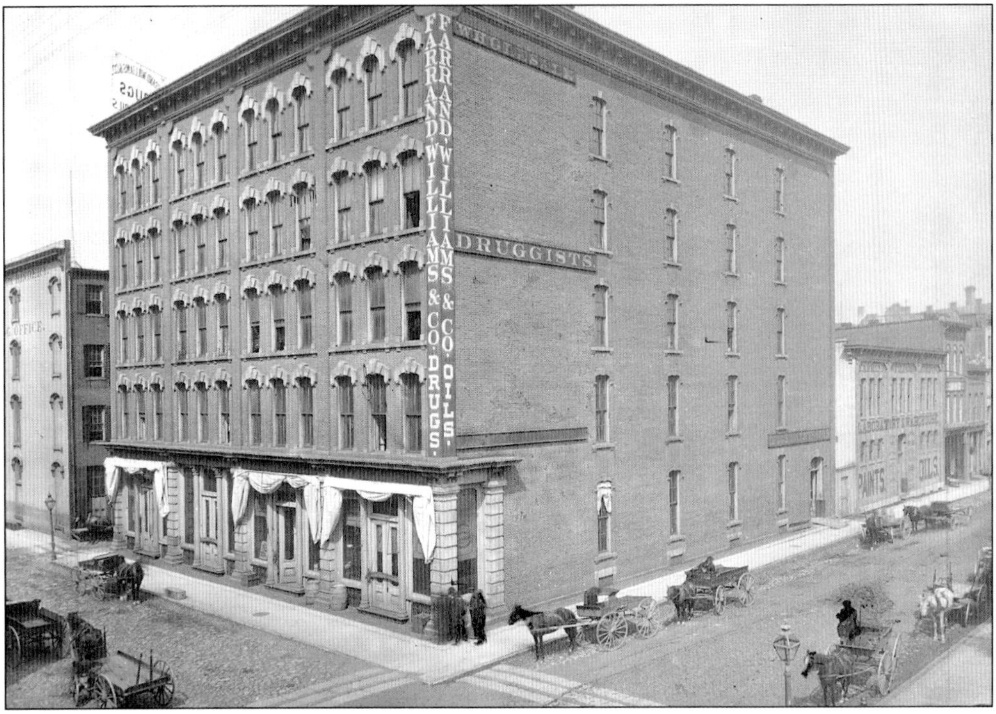

FARRAND, WILLIAMS AND COMPANY, 1881. Built in 1872 on East Larned Street, this building housed one of the city's largest importers and jobbers of drugs, chemicals, paints and oils. The Farrand Company also manufactured pharmaceutical and toilet preparations and was one of Detroit's oldest, dating back to 1820. It occupied half of the block at Larned and Bates.

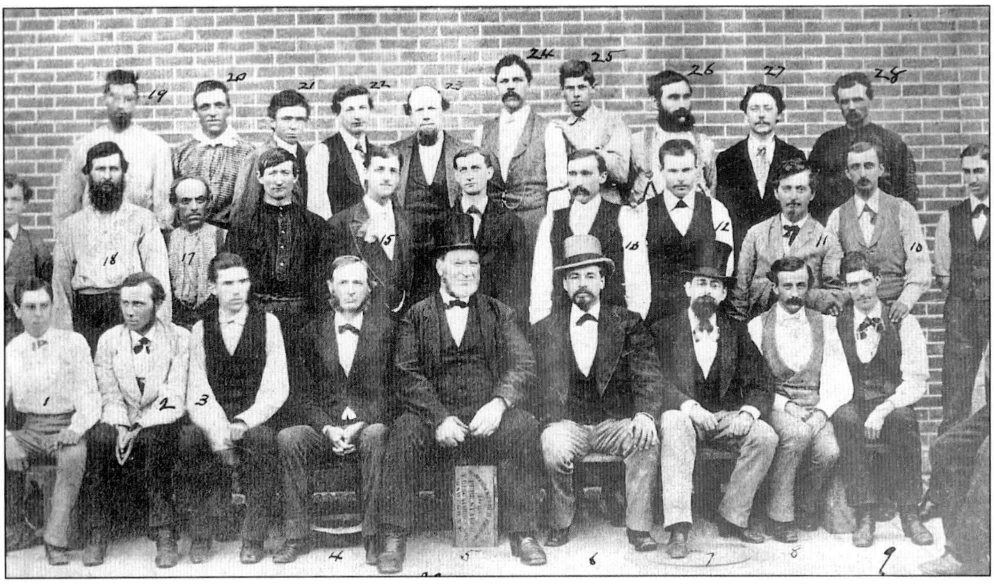

THE STAFF OF FARRAND, WILLIAMS AND COMPANY. The entire staff of the plant of the Farrand Drug Company during the 1870s. Seated fourth from the left is Jacob S. Farrand, who became a partner in the Penniman & Rice Drug Company in 1836, the forerunner of the company to bear his and Mr. Williams' names.

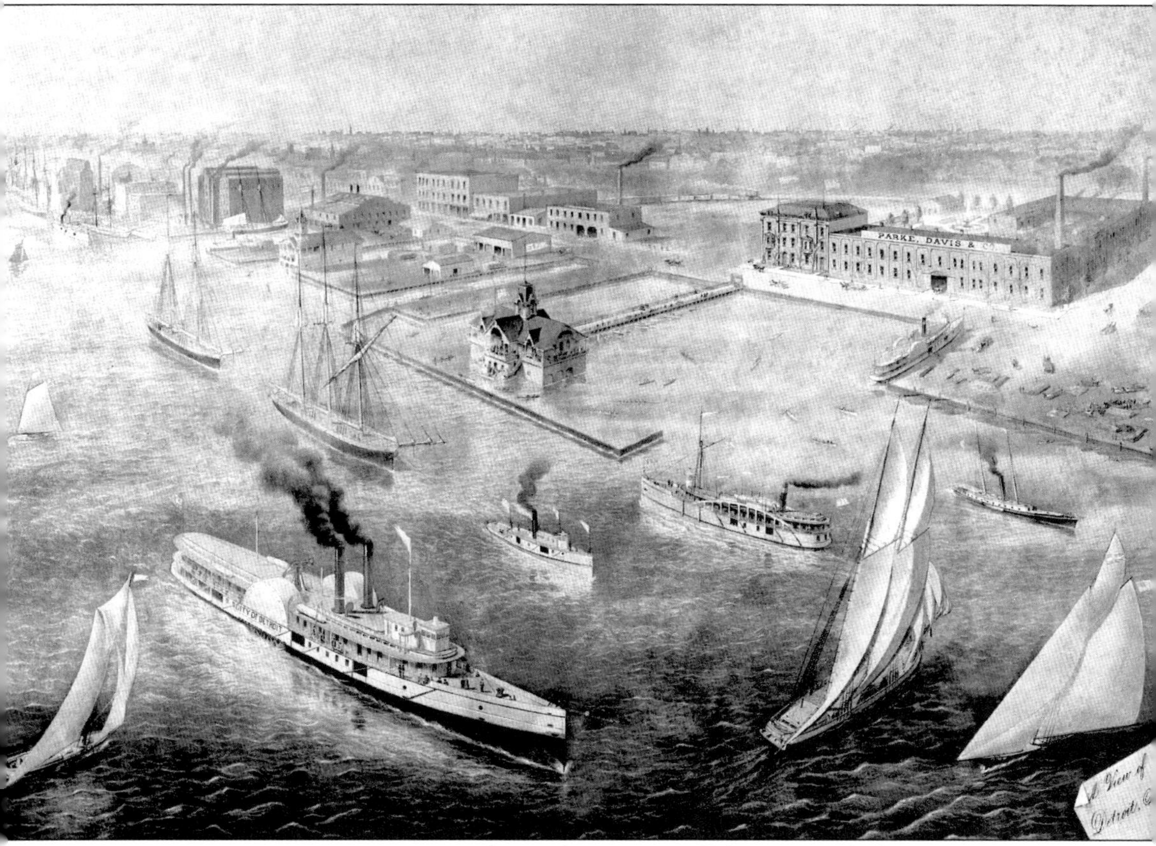

PARKE, DAVIS AND COMPANY. Perhaps the most well-known and the longest-living pharmaceutical company in Detroit is Parke, Davis & Company. Begun as a co-partnership with Doctor Samuel P. Duffield, Hervey C. Parke and drug salesman George S. Davis in 1867, the firm began manufacturing pharmaceuticals in standardized drug strengths. In two years, they were making a profit. The firm was incorporated under the name Parke, Davis & Company in 1875, beginning with a capital stock of $125,000. By 1882, it had grown to $1,000,000. In 1874, the company moved to this site along the Detroit River at Atwater Street. Repeated additions to the site resulted in a frontage of 850 feet with an average depth of 50 feet. The company also had a three-story building on the corner of Fourth and Abbott Streets, where its empty capsules were manufactured. Offices were also maintained in New York City.

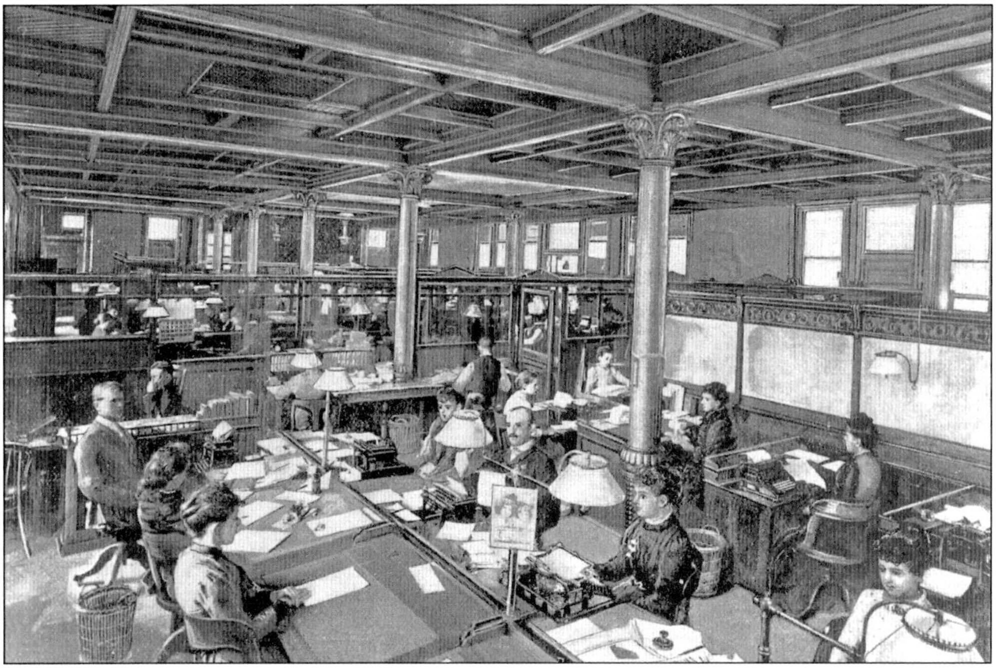

CLERICAL OFFICE, 1890S. An artist's rendering of the clerical offices at Parke, Davis & Company reveals an equal mix of men and women secretaries, even though not many women had entered the business world at this time. The second floor of an elegant four-story building along the river was devoted to correspondence, billing and shipping operations.

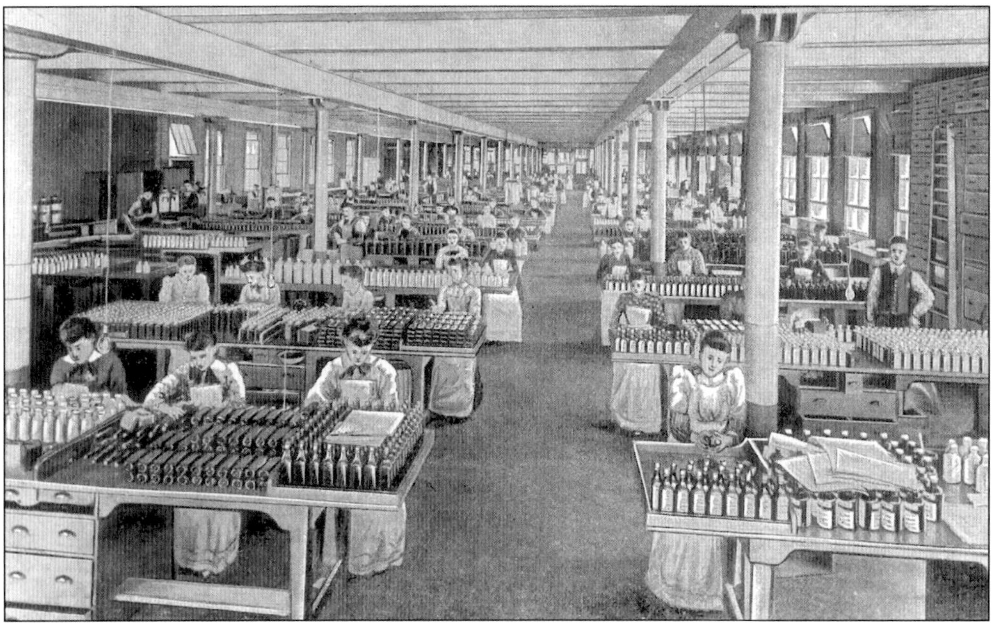

THE BOTTLING ROOM. Another rendition, this one of the bottling room, where pills and elixirs were bottled prior to shipment around the world, shows a large staff of women doing the labor, supervised by men. The ladies appear to be dressed in a standard uniform of sorts, topped off by an apron or smock to protect the clothing. Over 430 employees worked in the complex on the river.

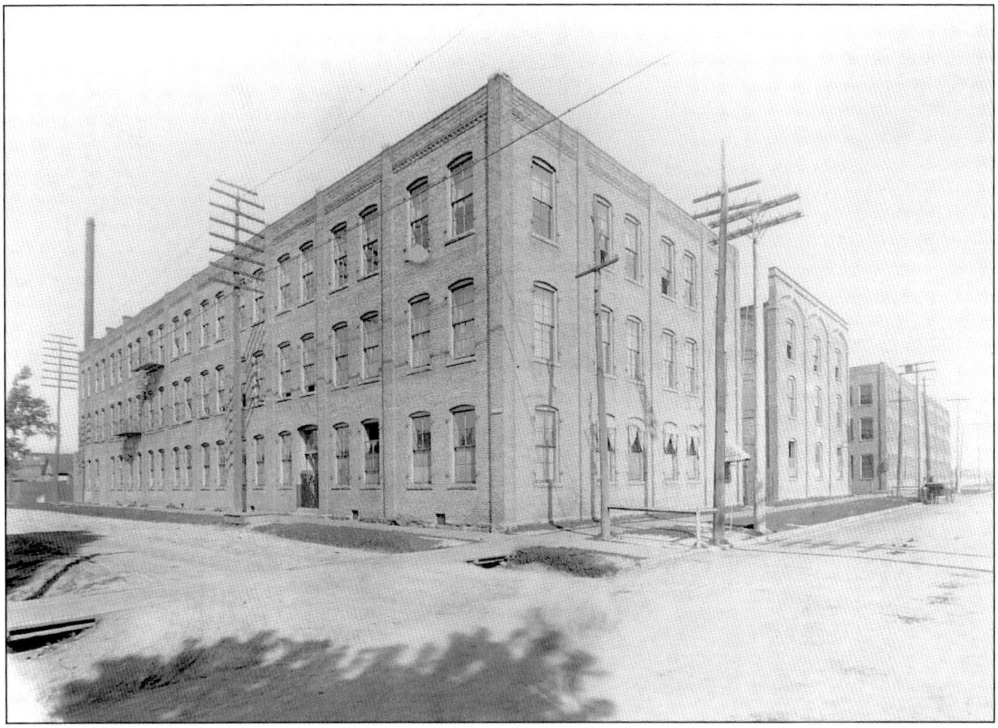

THE LABORATORIES. Parke, Davis & Company laboratories fronting on Joseph Campau Street were an integral part of the riverfront complex. The lab was where new formulas were created, as the company continually sent out expeditions throughout the world in search of new medicinal materials. The company also built a laboratory in Walkerville, Ontario in order to supply its products of Canadian manufacture.

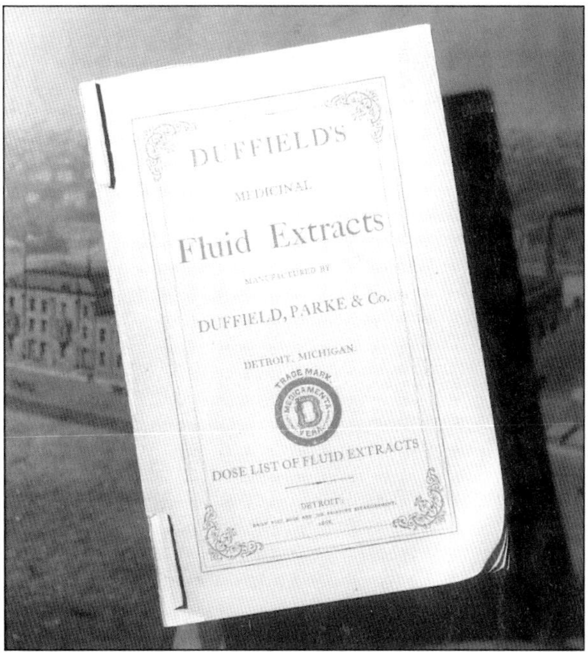

THE PUBLICATION DIVISION. Pictured here is an 1868 edition of the Parke, Davis & Company catalog which included a dose list of various fluid extracts. By the early 1880s, the company had a publication department, issuing several regular periodicals such as *The Therapeutic Gazette*, *Medical Age*, *The American Lancet*, "*Medical Index*" and *Druggists' Bulletin*. The department also handled all of the in-house printing, employing a force of over thirty men.

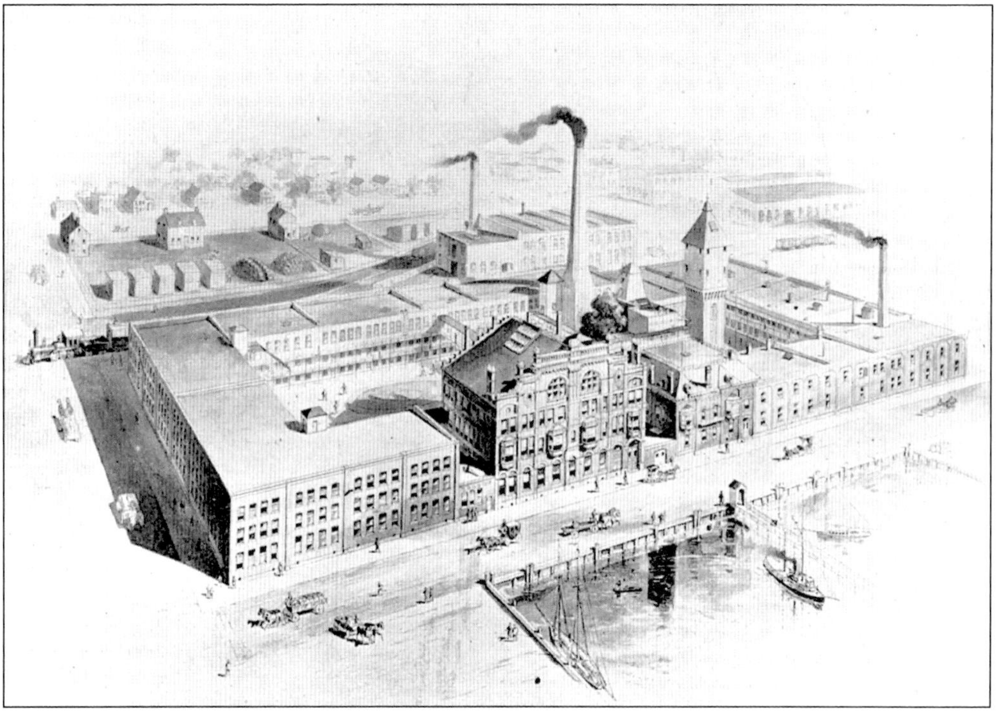

THE DRUG GIANT. This bird's eye view of the Parke Davis site shows the extent of the company's growth prior to 1890. The company had access to the river with its own wharves and its own railroad spur with which it could keep supply even with demand. Parke, Davis & Company employed well over 500 people in Detroit.

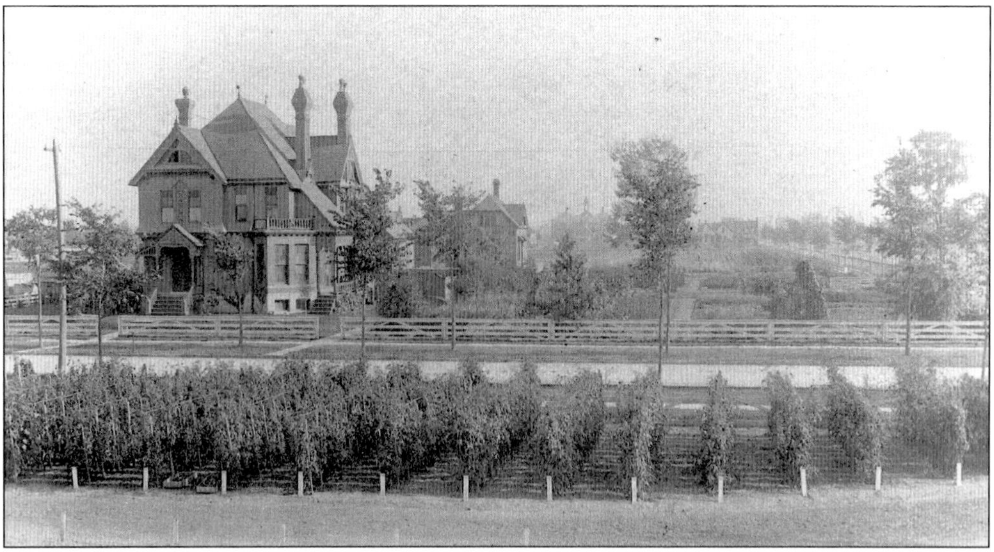

TEST GARDEN FOR SEEDS. On East Ferry Avenue, between St. Antoine and Hastings, were located the test gardens belonging to the D.M. Ferry Seed Company. This tract of land was one of the earlier gardens the company owned, having been founded in 1856 by the firm of M.T. Gardner & Company. Thirty years later, Ferry owned and operated the Greenfield Seed Farm, several hundred acres on Grand River Avenue, just outside the city limits.

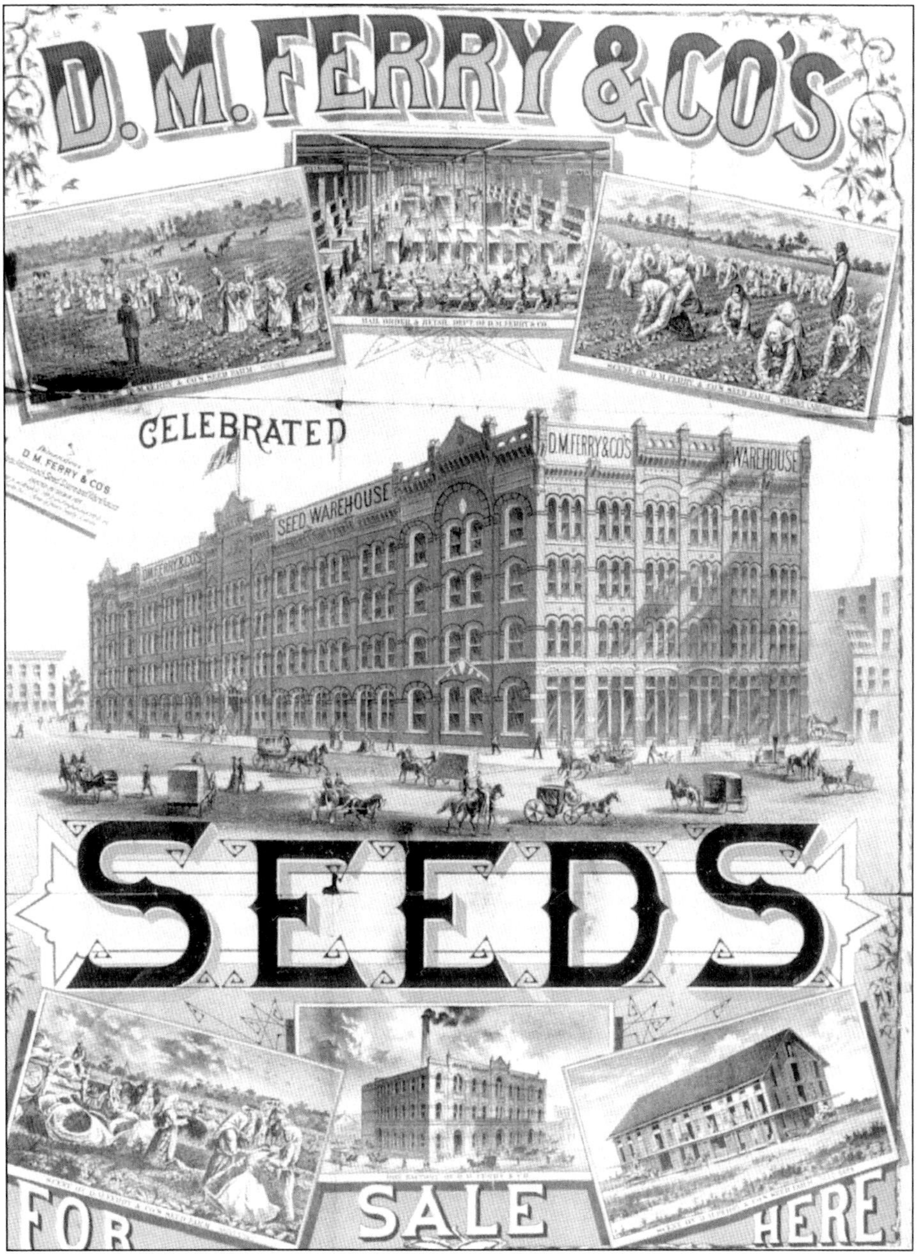

Mammoth Seed Warehouse. This 1882 poster advertises the D.M. Ferry & Company's SEEDS. The gigantic seed warehouse was built in 1879 at Brush and Monroe Streets and occupied the entire block. Incorporated under the Ferry name in 1879, the company employed over 1,500 people during the busy season. These included those employed in the warehouse, the seed growers and the box factory at Brush and Croghan Streets. On New Years' Day, 1886, this warehouse and its contents were destroyed by fire, a loss amounting to one million dollars in 1886 currency. Undaunted, the company rented as many buildings as it could to house its remaining products while a new, larger warehouse was built on the site. It would be a six-story brick building with all of the latest modern improvements, such as iron doors, elevators, and stairways, making it practically fire proof.

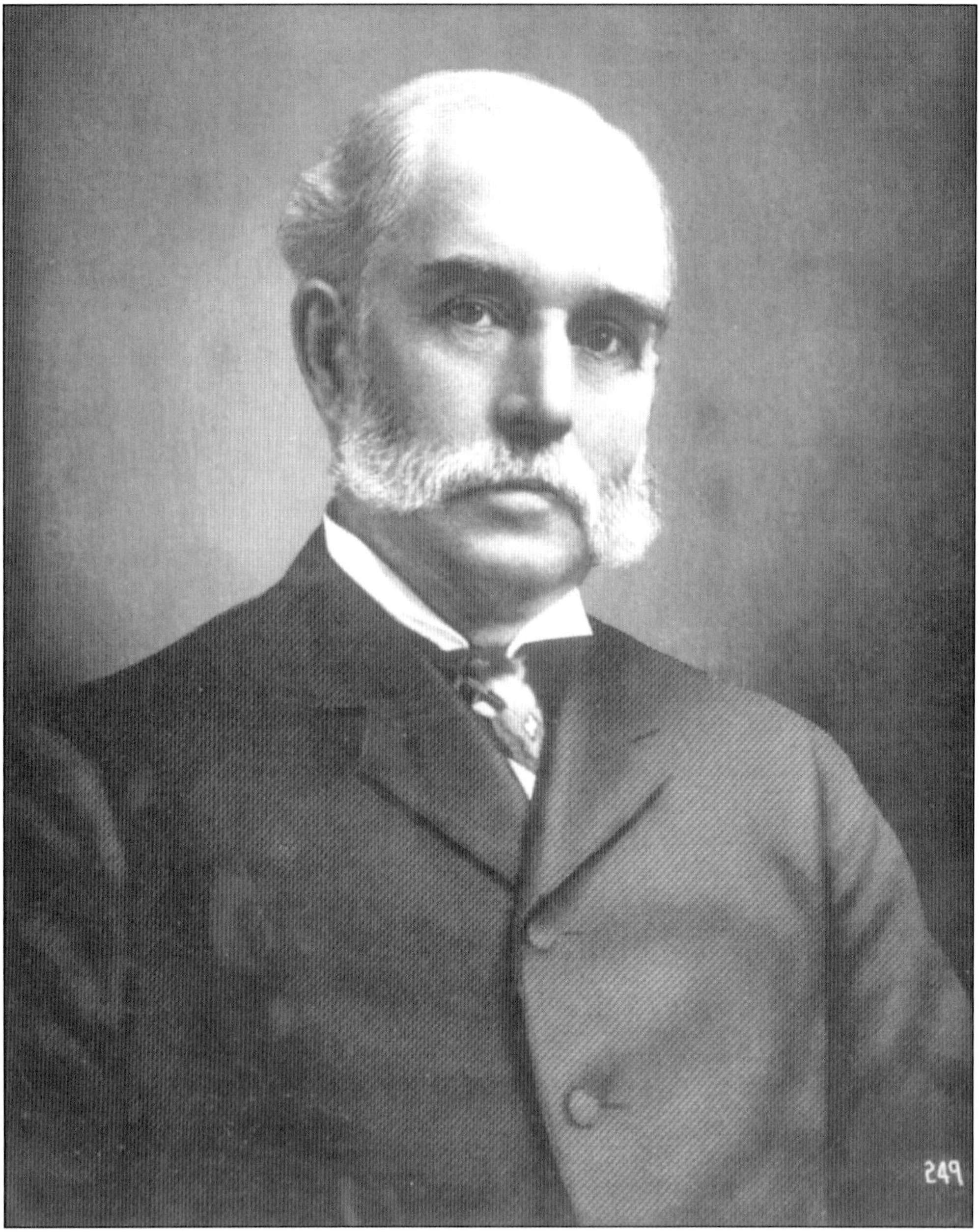

Dexter Monroe Ferry. The son of a wagon maker and blacksmith, Dexter Monroe Ferry was born in New York State in 1833 and moved to Detroit in 1852. He worked in a book and stationary store, first as an errand boy, clerk, salesman, and finally as a bookkeeper. He left the bookstore to join Mr. M.T. Gardner and Company to package seeds. His idea for seeds in connection with Detroit farms stemmed from his realization that all of the important seed companies were in the east, far from Michigan farms. His first seed farm was at Michigan and Merriman Roads in Wayne, Michigan. Later he had a 300-acre farm in Greenfield Township. Ferry married Addie E. Miller in 1867 and they had a son, D.M. Ferry, Jr., in 1872. Upon his success in the seed business, he supported many institutions in the city, including the Detroit Institute of Arts, Harper and Grace Hospitals, and the Detroit Board of Education.

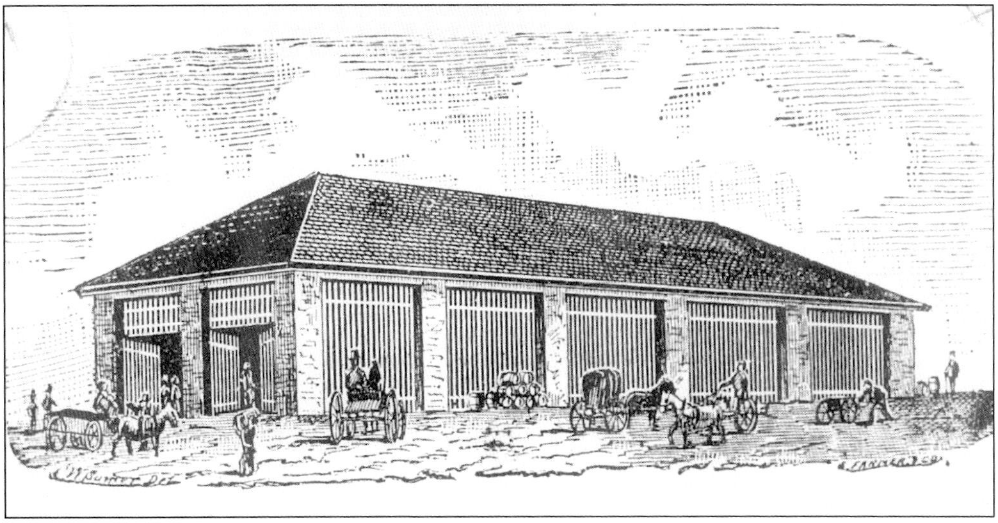

THE WOODWARD AVENUE MARKET. Among the very early businesses in Detroit were the open air markets, located in various portions of the growing metropolis. This illustration shows the old Woodward Avenue market, located to the south of Campus Martius. Built of brick, it was supported by fourteen pillars and allowed sellers to bring in everything from vegetables and poultry to craft goods to sell.

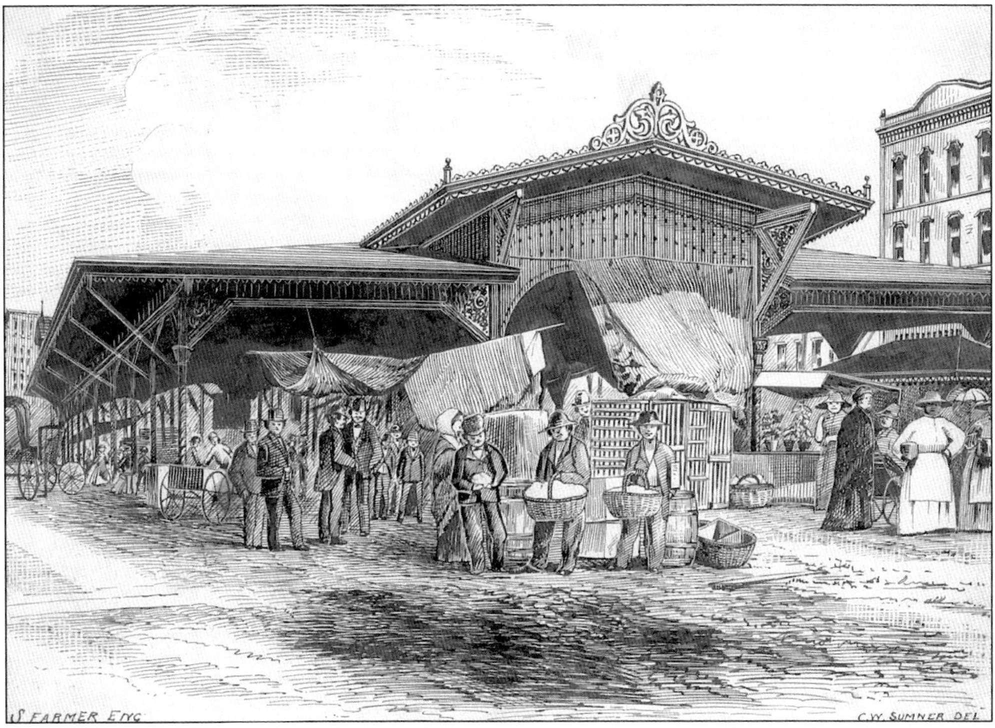

CENTRAL MARKET VEGETABLE STALLS. A beautiful illustration of Market day in Detroit, c. 1868, shows Detroiters at the vegetable stalls in Central Market at Cadillac Square. This was an open-air market where city dwellers could purchase not only green goods for their tables, but house plants as well.

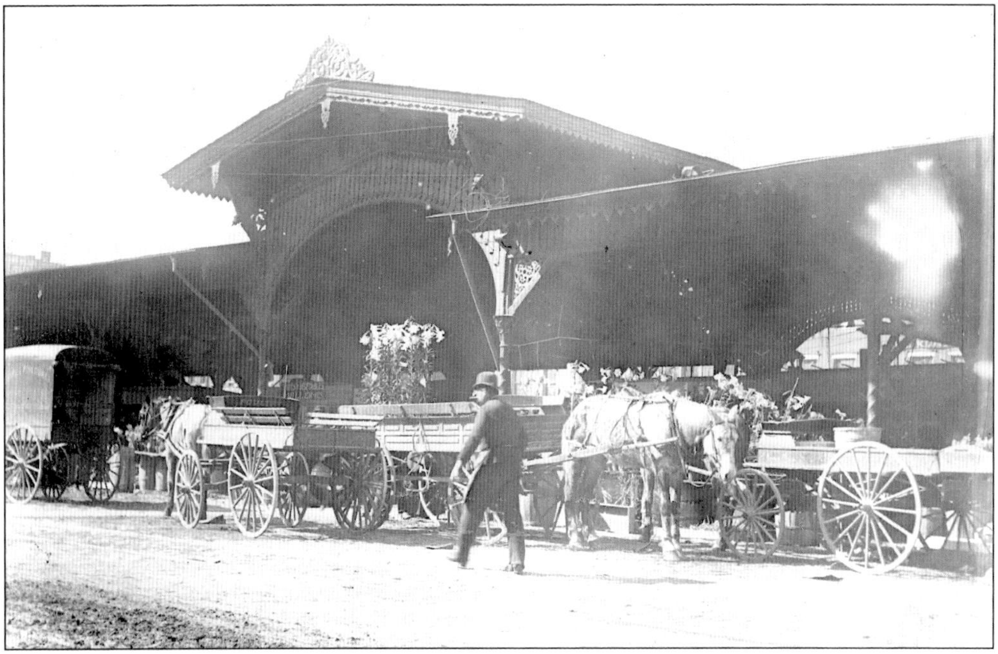

CENTRAL MARKET, 1880S. From the looks of the empty wagons, it would appears to be delivery day at the market in this photograph taken sometime after the 1870s. Farmers from the outlying districts traveled to the big city to dispose of their produce. The market would later expand to include other goods and services as well.

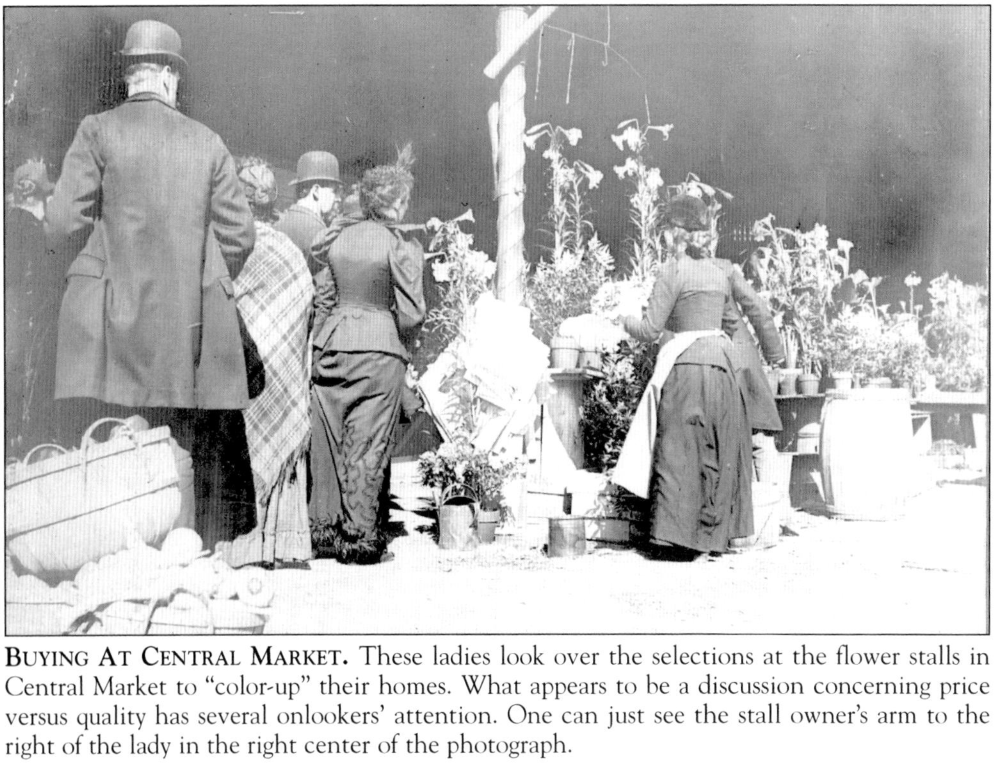

BUYING AT CENTRAL MARKET. These ladies look over the selections at the flower stalls in Central Market to "color-up" their homes. What appears to be a discussion concerning price versus quality has several onlookers' attention. One can just see the stall owner's arm to the right of the lady in the right center of the photograph.

FRESH MILK. One of Detroit's dairy producers poses for a picture in an alley near the market district with her handler/owner. As the city center developed from a residential to a business area, fewer people kept livestock on their lots at all. The need for fresh produce was filled at the market.

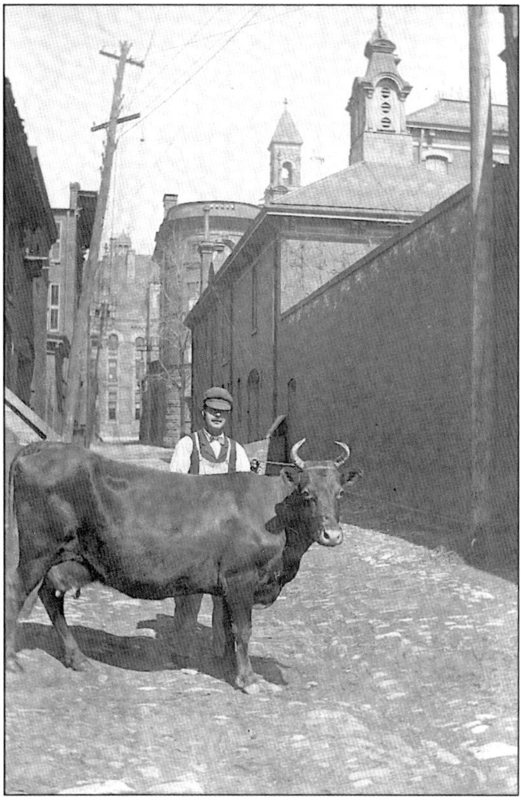

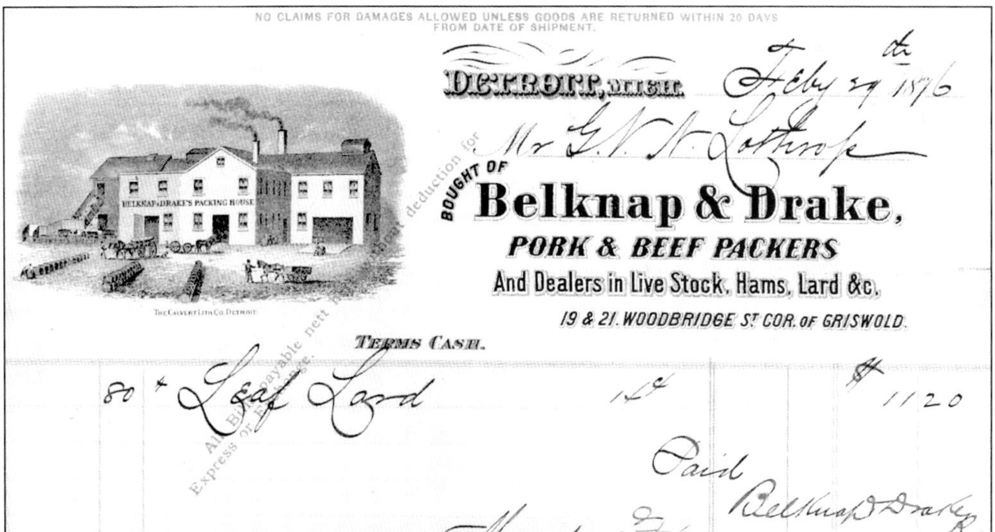

EARLY MEAT PACKERS. An invoice for eighty pounds of leaf lard at a cost of $11.20 also illustrates the packing house of Belknap & Drake, pork and beef packers, located at Woodbridge and Griswold Streets. Printed by the Calvert Lithograph Company of Detroit, these artifacts provide illustrations for a time from which no photograph survives.

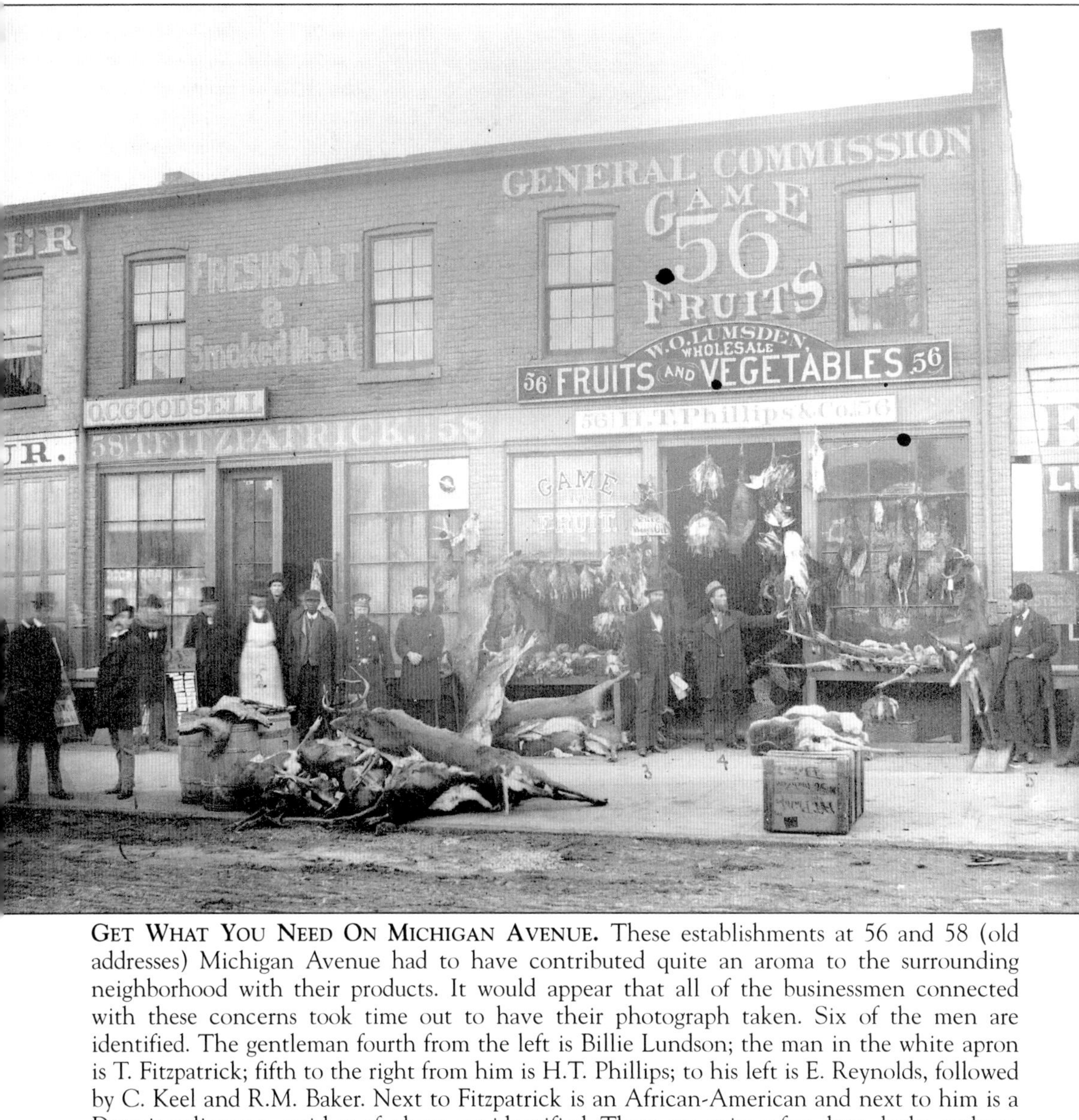

Get What You Need On Michigan Avenue. These establishments at 56 and 58 (old addresses) Michigan Avenue had to have contributed quite an aroma to the surrounding neighborhood with their products. It would appear that all of the businessmen connected with these concerns took time out to have their photograph taken. Six of the men are identified. The gentleman fourth from the left is Billie Lundson; the man in the white apron is T. Fitzpatrick; fifth to the right from him is H.T. Phillips; to his left is E. Reynolds, followed by C. Keel and R.M. Baker. Next to Fitzpatrick is an African-American and next to him is a Detroit policeman, neither of whom are identified. There are quite a few deer, ducks, turkeys, and pheasants available to buy, all at least partially dressed out. Mr. Phillips also sold pure bear oil. At least on this day, there is not a woman in sight.

Two

MACHINE INDUSTRIES

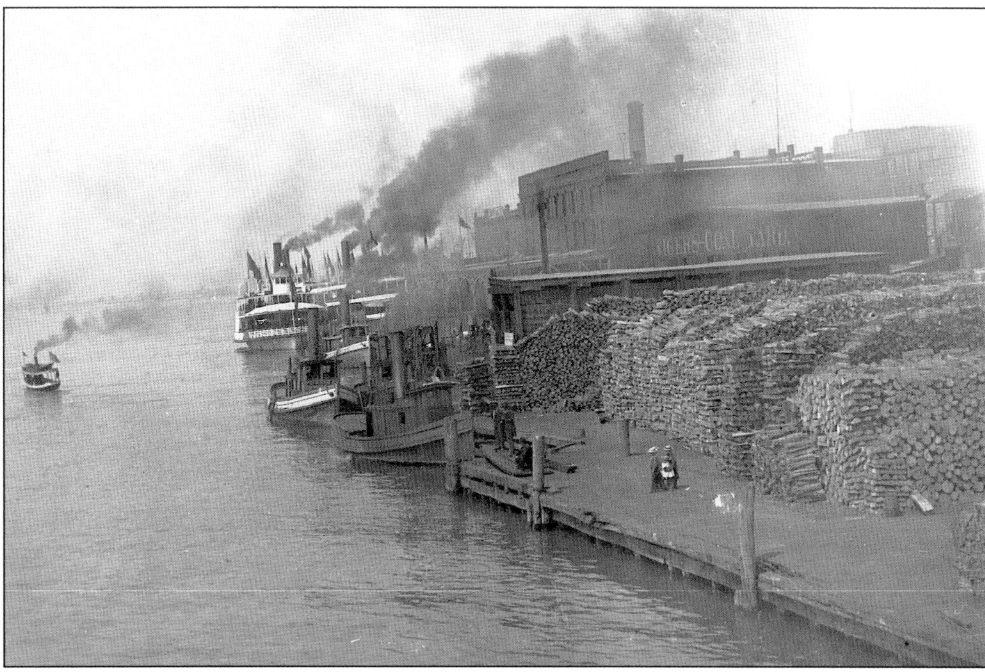

RIVERFRONT INDUSTRY. Engine exhaust darkens the sky along the Detroit riverfront from the coal and wood fired boilers of vessels arriving and departing from the port. The large stacks of wood belong to the A.E. Viger Coal & Wood Company, which had its offices on Atwater Street. Established in 1865, Viger's business had grown steadily by the 1880s, when this photograph was taken. Adequate docks, covered coal sheds and facilities for rail and sail fit the bill.

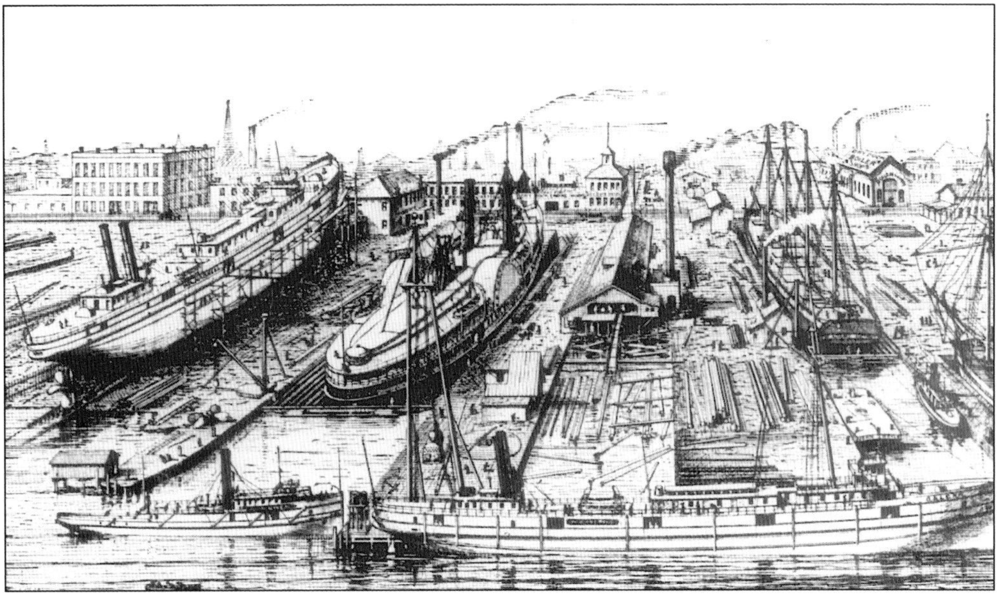

Detroit Dry Dock Company. The dry docks and repair yards of the leading corporation in its line on the Great Lakes stood at the foot of Orleans Street in Detroit. Established in 1852, the company had grown steadily and expanded with an iron ship yard in Wyandotte. In 1887 they built four steamers with a gross tonnage of 8,000 tons.

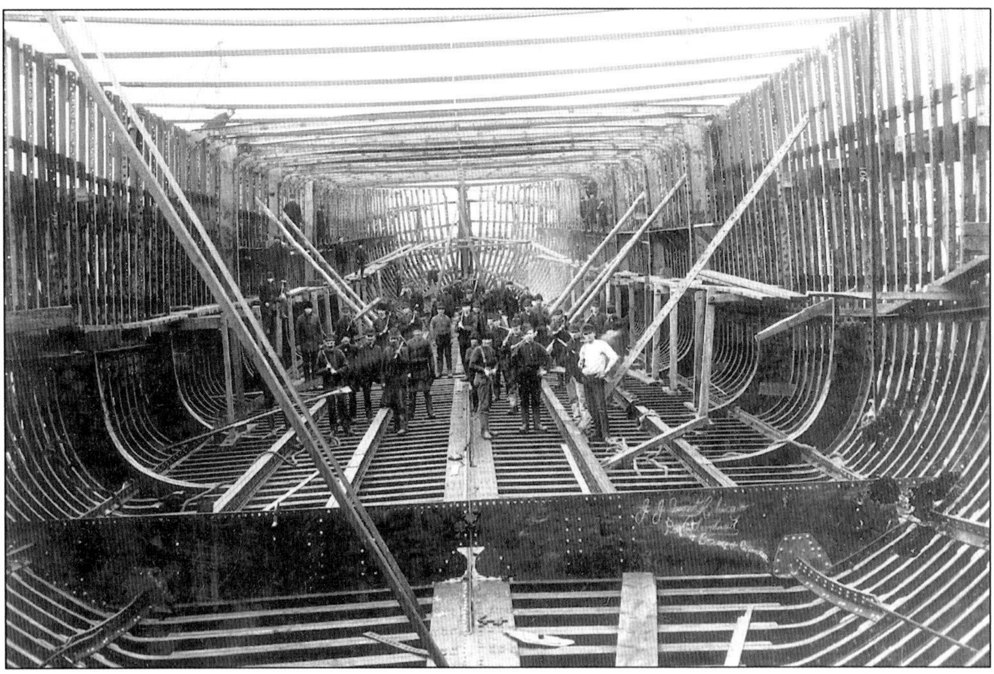

Shipbuilders. Some of the 300 shipbuilders employed by the Detroit Dry Dock Company stand on the ribs of their current project. They built and repaired all kinds of steamers and vessels for the Great Lakes trade. Some of the more famous were: *City of Cleveland*, an elegant side-wheel steel passenger vessel; and the large side-wheel iron steamer *Michigan Central*, which was capable of carrying twenty-four freight cars.

COFFEE, TEA OR SPICE. Mr. W.A. King keeps a hand on his latest shipment of coffee and fine teas with his assistant and possibly his wife beside him. Able to fill orders large and small, the aroma from his products would draw customers from near and far. He was located on Cadillac Square, just behind the Russell House.

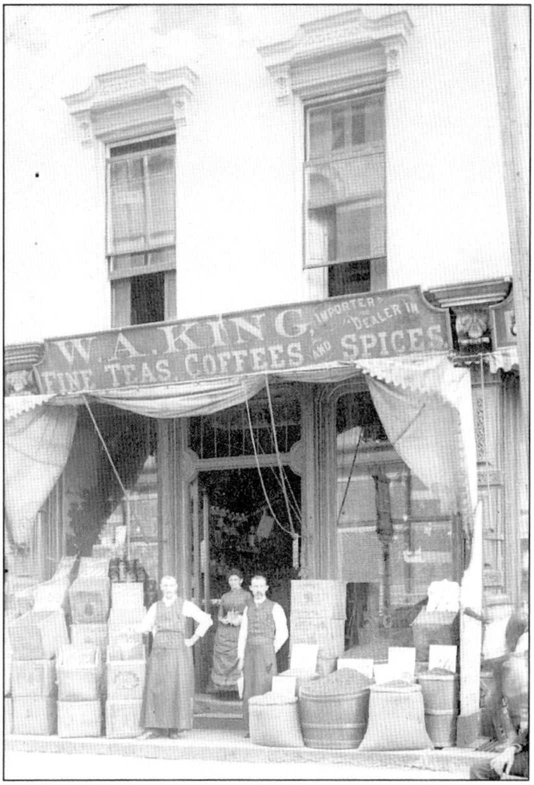

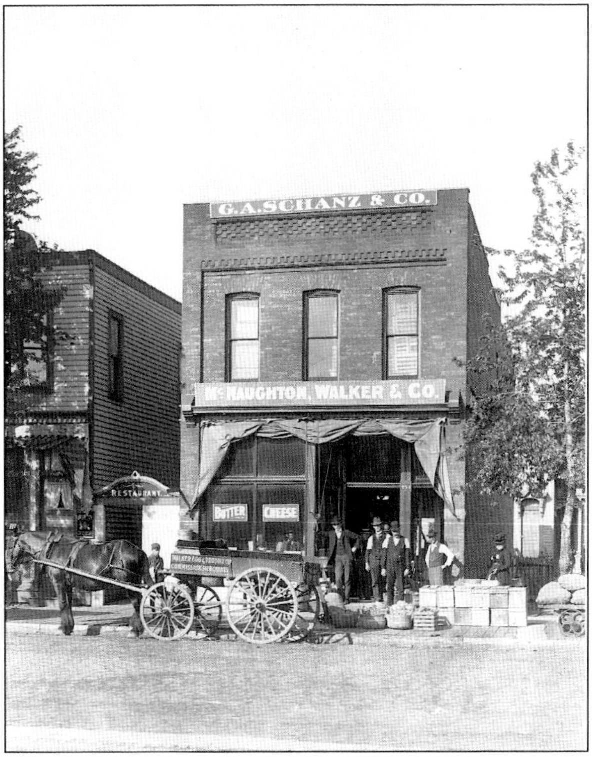

WHOLESALE PRODUCE. Duncan R. McNaughton and John Walker were the largest dealers in the city in butter, eggs, cheese, and beans, which they handled in railroad car-sized lots. Located on Woodbridge Street, their trade extended east to New York, south to New Orleans, northwest to Minneapolis and southwest to St. Louis and Kansas City.

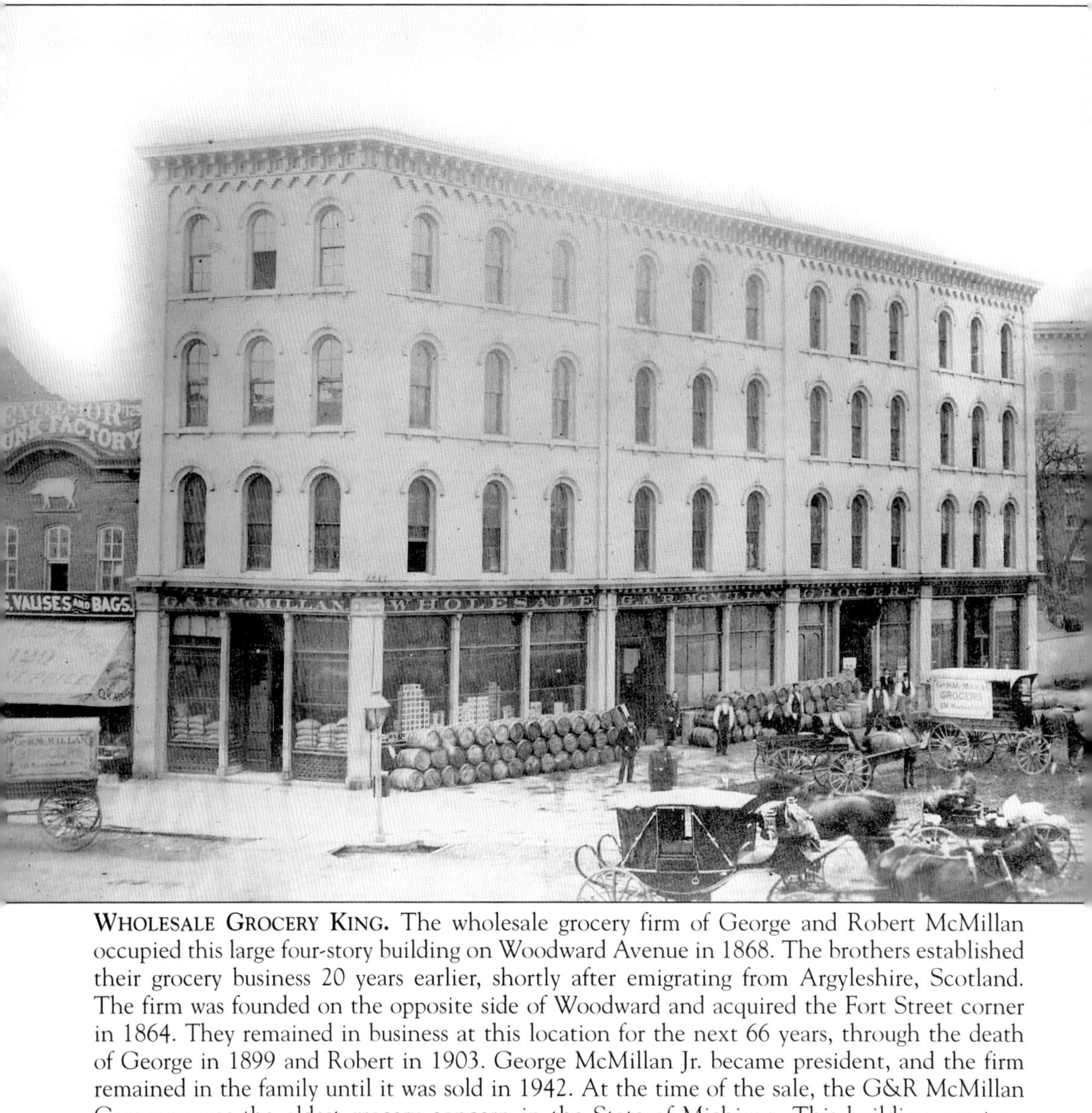

WHOLESALE GROCERY KING. The wholesale grocery firm of George and Robert McMillan occupied this large four-story building on Woodward Avenue in 1868. The brothers established their grocery business 20 years earlier, shortly after emigrating from Argyleshire, Scotland. The firm was founded on the opposite side of Woodward and acquired the Fort Street corner in 1864. They remained in business at this location for the next 66 years, through the death of George in 1899 and Robert in 1903. George McMillan Jr. became president, and the firm remained in the family until it was sold in 1942. At the time of the sale, the G&R McMillan Company was the oldest grocery concern in the State of Michigan. This building was torn down in 1931 after the firm had moved away from the city center, which was developing quickly into an all-business environment.

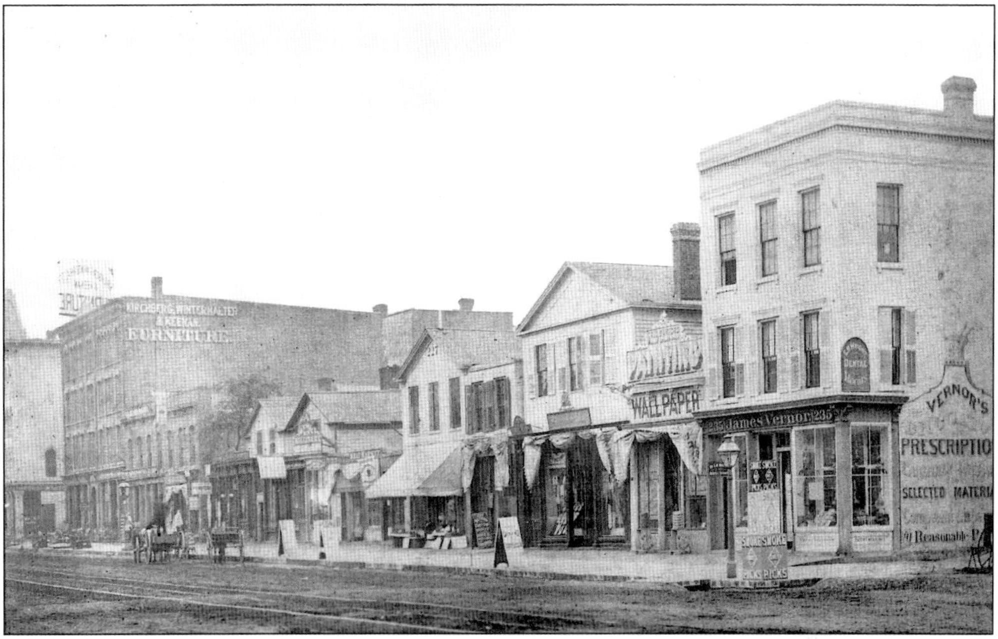

SMALL BEGINNINGS. This section of Woodward Avenue between Grand River and Clifford boasts the usual collection of businesses. On the extreme right of the photograph is the drug store owned by the first registered pharmacist in Michigan, James Vernor. A Civil War veteran, he discovered an excellent formula for making ginger ale and soon forgot about dispensing prescriptions.

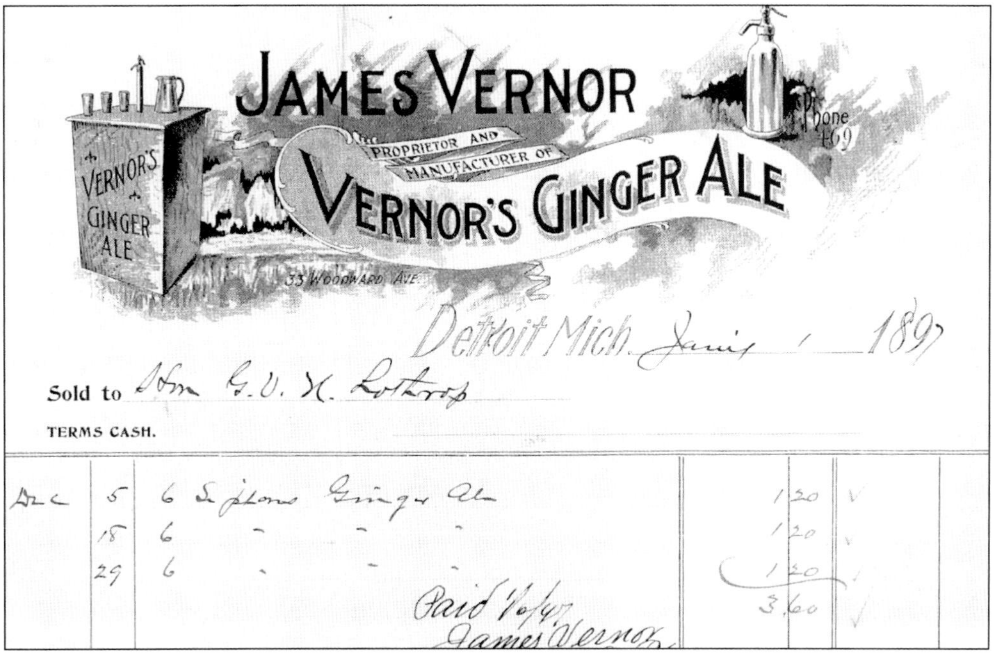

JAMES VERNOR
PROPRIETOR AND MANUFACTURER OF
VERNOR'S GINGER ALE
Phone 469
VERNOR'S GINGER ALE
33 WOODWARD AVE.
Detroit Mich. Jan 1 1897
Sold to Hon G. V. N. Lothrop
TERMS CASH.

Dec	5	6 Siphons Ginger Ale	1	20
	18	6 " "	1	20
	29	6 " "	1	20
		Paid 1/6/97 James Vernor	3	60

A DETROIT LEGEND. Thirty years after discovering his formula for making ginger ale, James Vernor's company was a going concern in the soda pop industry. The proprietor and manufacturer of Vernor's Ginger Ale had built a processing and bottling factory at the foot of Woodward Avenue near the river. This invoice reflects the sale of several siphons of ginger ale.

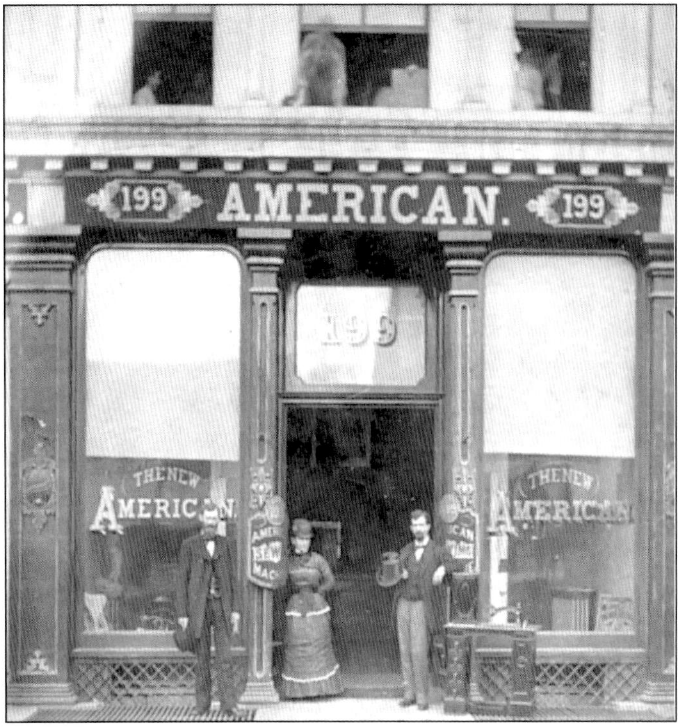

AGENTS FOR THE NEW AMERICAN. A new business concern in Detroit around 1875 was the American Sewing Machine Company, located on Woodward Avenue. Mr. C.G. Hampton stands to the left of the other two salesmen. Although not a home grown product, these machines certainly filled a need in the home.

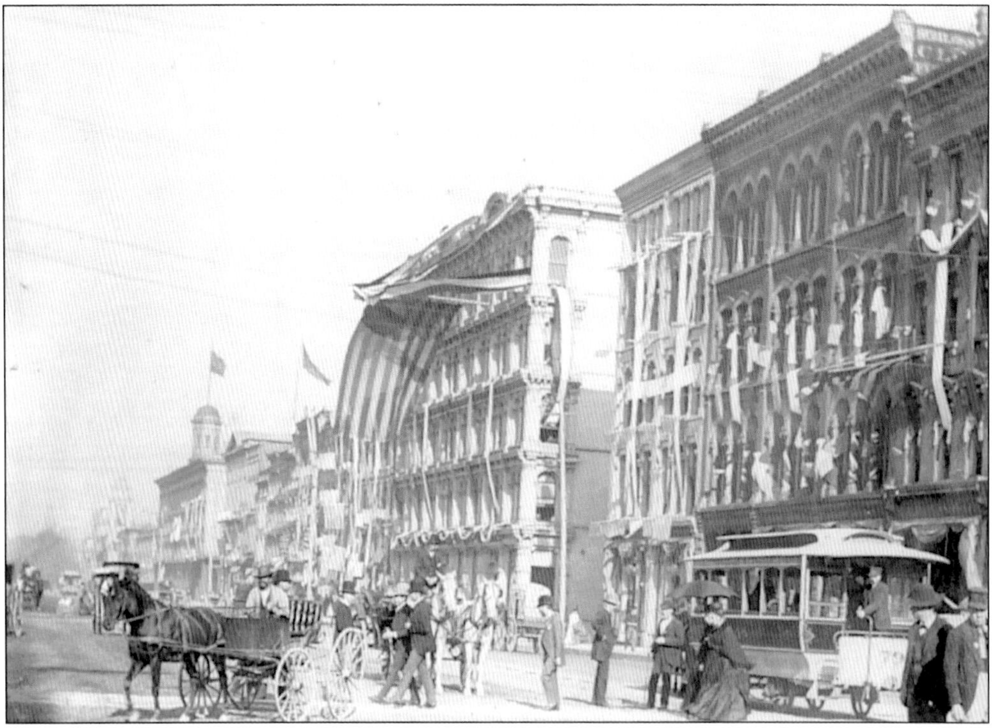

JEFFERSON AVENUE, 1870S. Bunting adorns several businesses and one huge American flag waves slowly in the breeze on Jefferson Avenue between Woodward Avenue and Bates Street. Business was good, evidenced by the number of people in business attire on this pleasant day in Detroit.

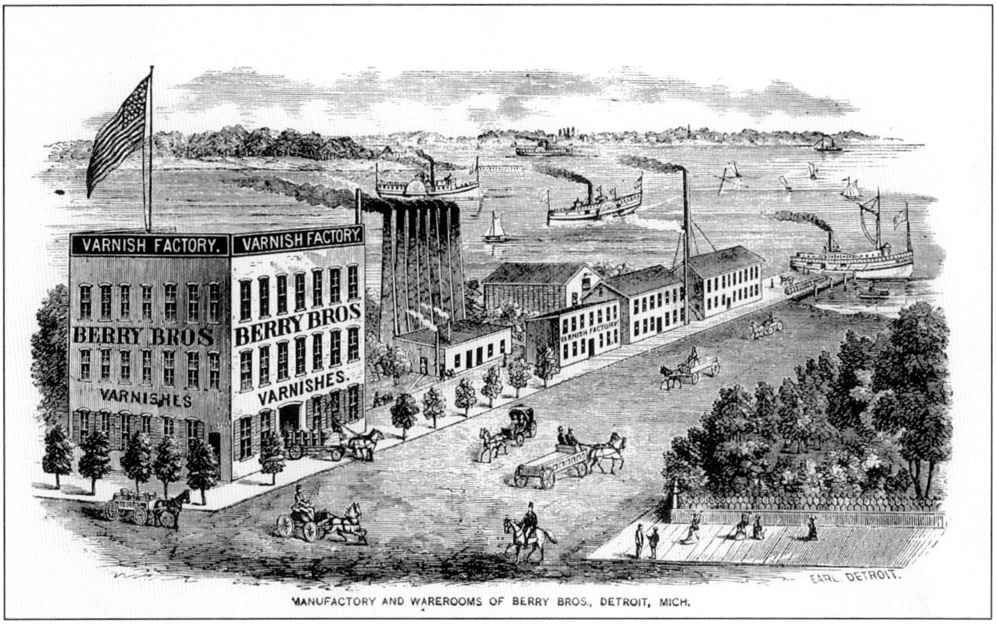

BERRY BROTHERS. An artists' illustration of the varnish factory of brothers Thomas and Joseph Berry at Leib and Wight Streets in Detroit shows the cluster of buildings that make up one of the largest makers of varnish in the world. Established in 1858, the firm had excellent facilities for shipping its products by rail and sail.

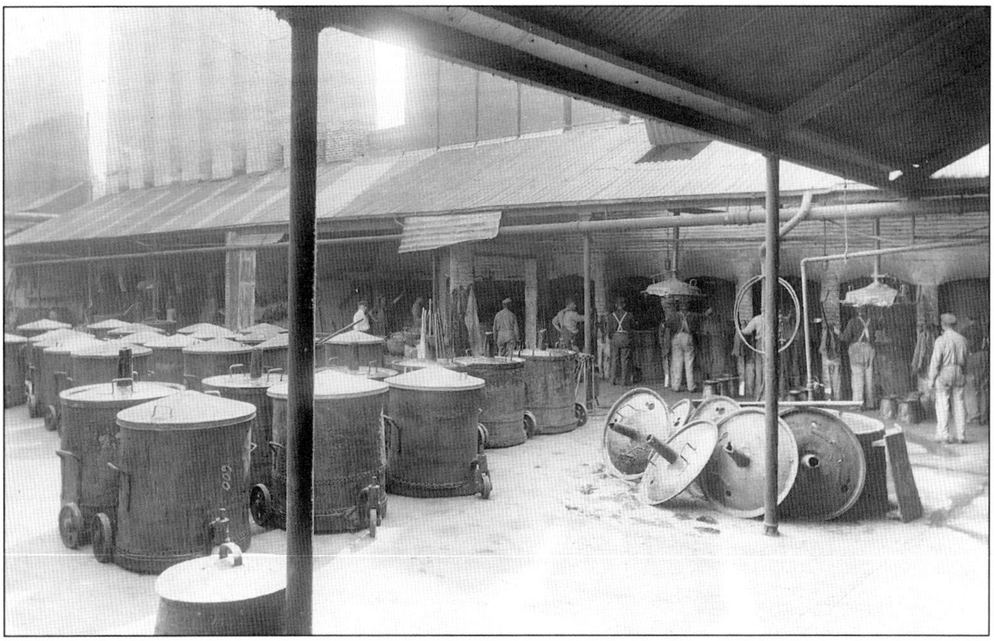

VATS OF VARNISH. An interior photograph of the Berry Brothers facilities shows the containers used to store and transport the varnish. By the 1880s, Berry Brothers Varnish was shipped to customers around the world, including Europe, the Sandwich Islands and Australia, South America, and Mexico. The firm was so busy that it had its own Western Union Telegraph Company branch and operator located in its offices.

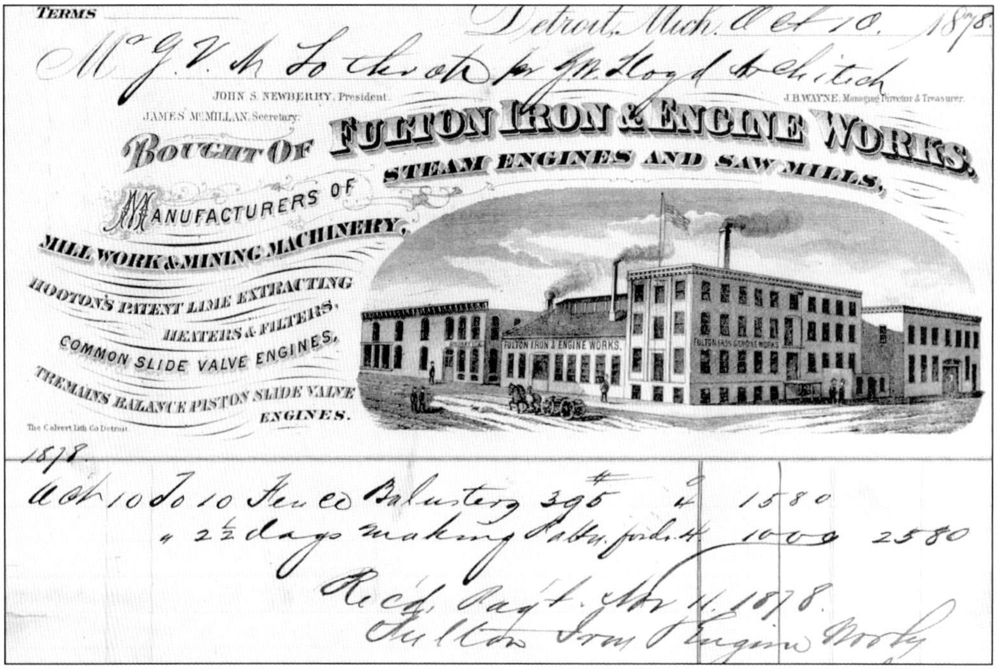

THE FULTON IRON & ENGINE WORKS. Located on Brush Street and founded in 1852, this is another business for which James McMillan served as president. A force of 125 skilled mechanics was employed in the facility, which also turned out railroad castings, brass work, and a superior line of blacksmiths' specialties. The firm did a tremendous amount of business in California and Nebraska.

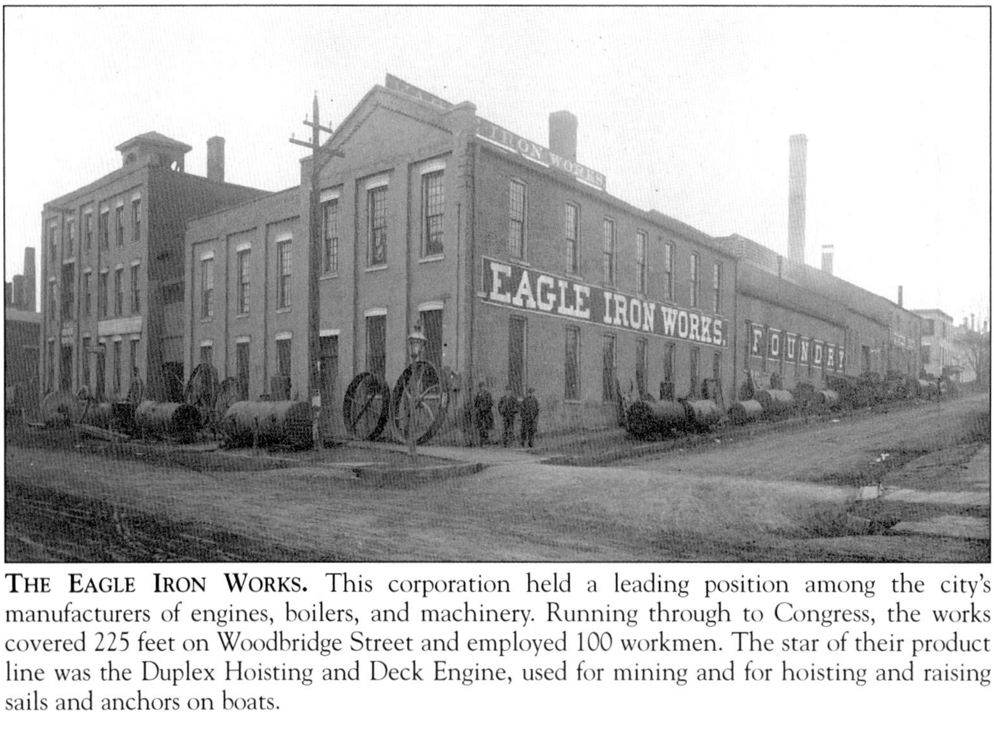

THE EAGLE IRON WORKS. This corporation held a leading position among the city's manufacturers of engines, boilers, and machinery. Running through to Congress, the works covered 225 feet on Woodbridge Street and employed 100 workmen. The star of their product line was the Duplex Hoisting and Deck Engine, used for mining and for hoisting and raising sails and anchors on boats.

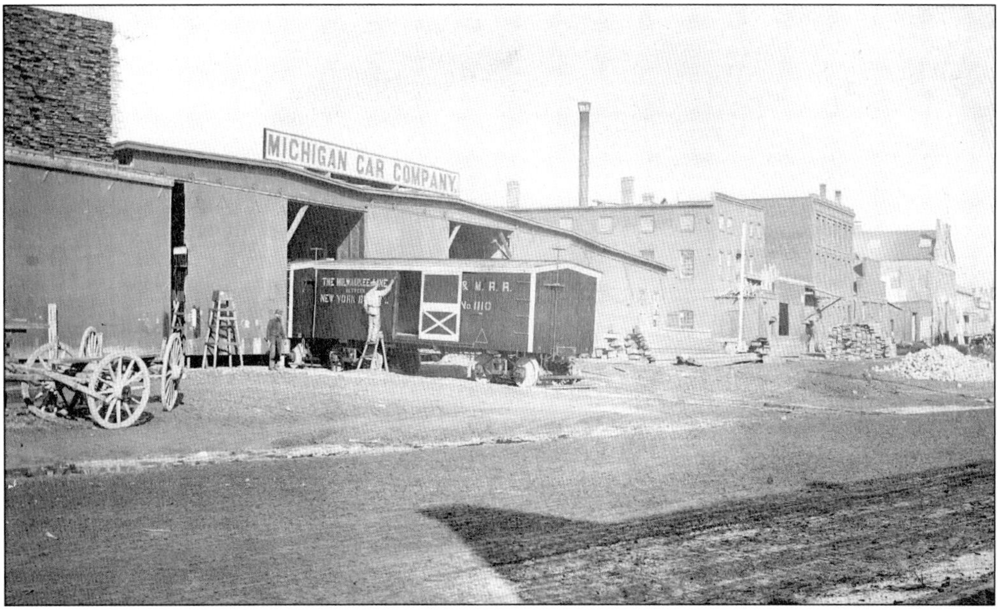

The Michigan Car Company. Out of its construction sheds at the Grand Trunk Railway Junction comes a railroad freight car for which the company was noted. Incorporated in 1864, just 20 years later the company employed over 2700 men. The company was famous for two of their very successful beef and dairy cars, the "Wickes" and the "Tiffany".

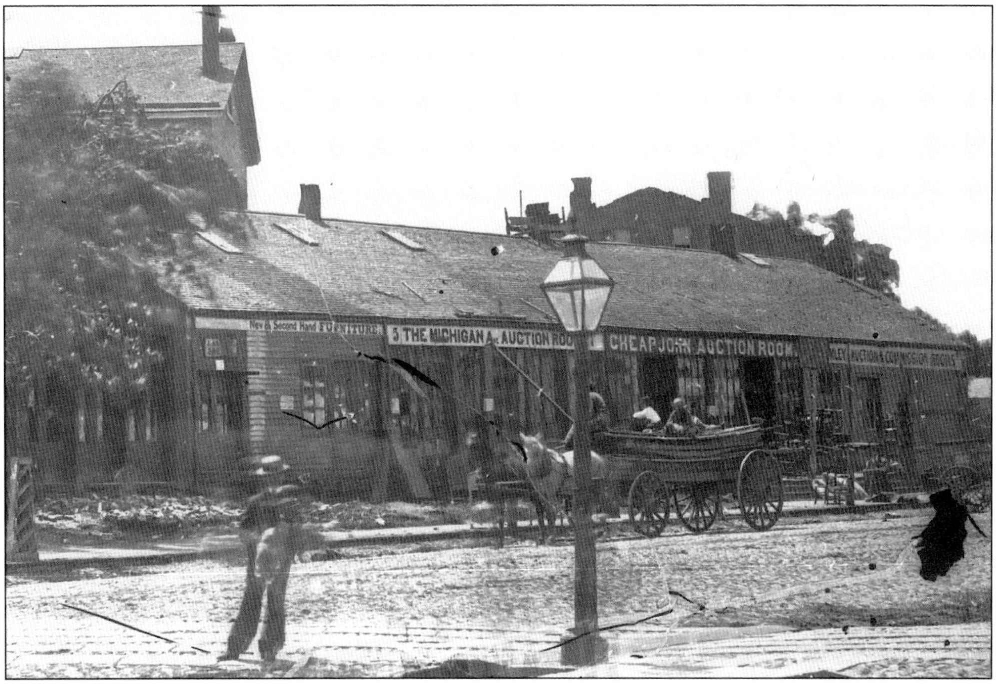

Michigan Avenue. Once the early site of the passenger depot of the Michigan Central Railroad, this section of Michigan Avenue now contains a string of second-hand shops and auction rooms. With the abundance of a multitude of different products, there has to be somewhere to dispose of used items.

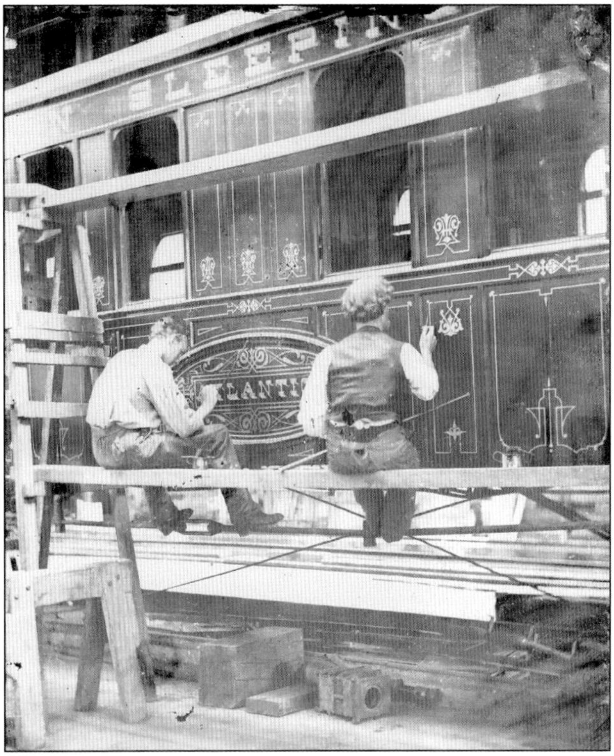

THE PULLMAN SLEEPER. A rare interior photograph of the assembly area of the Pullman Palace Car Company shows workmen applying decorative trim to the railcars. Taken by the famous Detroit photographer Jex Bardwell, it offers a glimpse of 19th century working conditions.

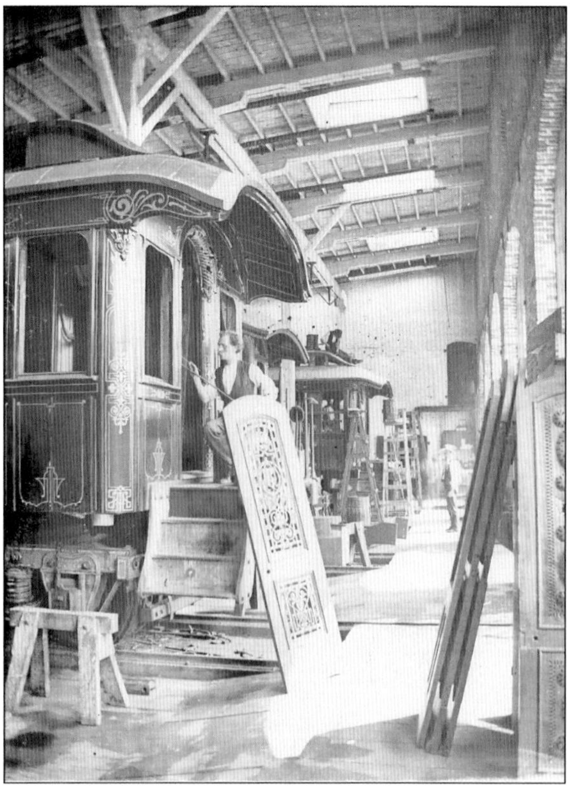

THE PULLMAN PALACE CAR COMPANY. Another Bardwell photograph shows a different section of the work force painting (or varnishing) the door trim on a sleeper. George Pullman did not produce his cars in Detroit for long as, we would imagine, because competition was rather stiff in the railcar city. He moved his operation to Chicago, Illinois.

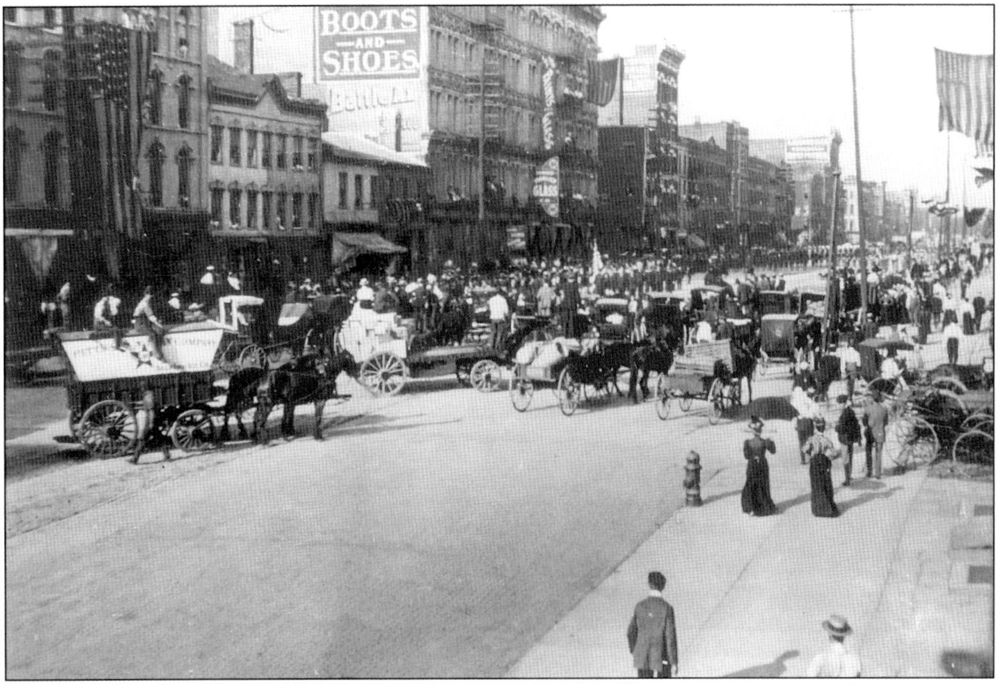

TIME OUT FOR A PARADE. Detroiters were always partial to parades and didn't need much of a reason to hold one. This scene on Woodward Avenue shows a bit of a traffic jam of horse-drawn vehicles near the end of the route. Some of the vehicles have business advertisements on them.

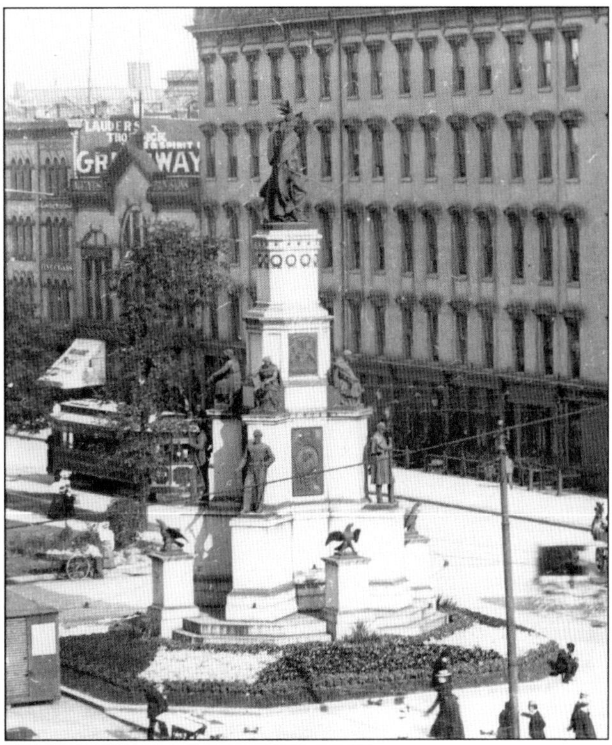

BUSTLING METROPOLIS. The Soldiers' and Sailors' Monument is surrounded by colorful beds of flowers, undoubtedly done in red, white and blue, in this photograph of Campus Martius. Behind the monument is the Russell House, one of Detroit's more noted hotels. There are some push cart vendors around the square, which is not too far from the Central Market.

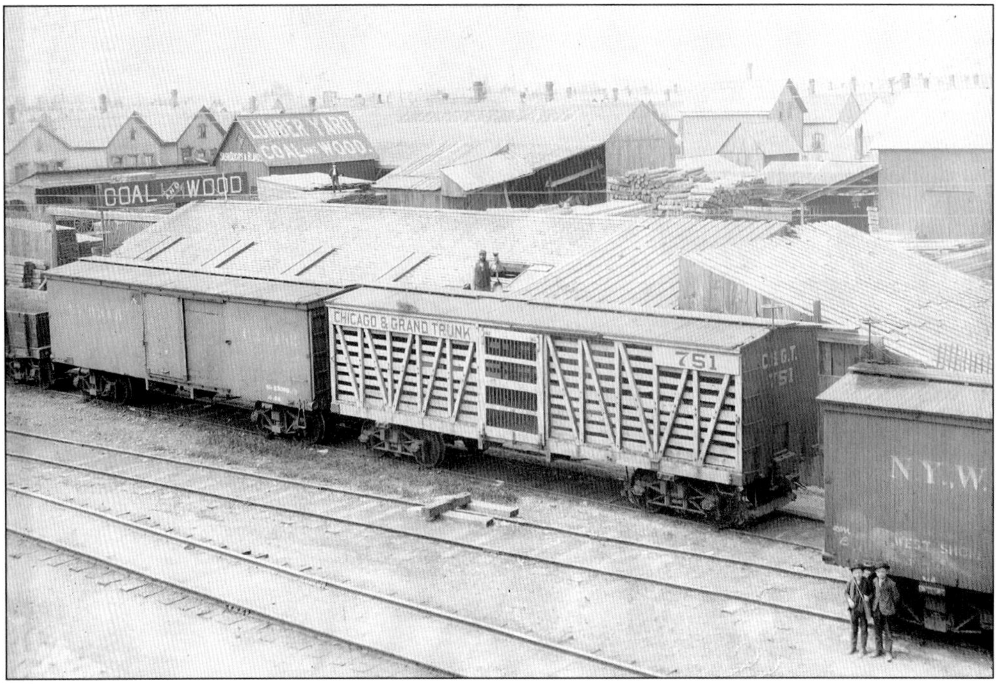

TROWBRIDGE LUMBER YARD. A workman stands up through the roof of one of the coal sheds, probably getting ready to either load or unload the freight car in front of him. Two young boys are caught in the photograph (lower right), as young men were often drawn towards train yards.

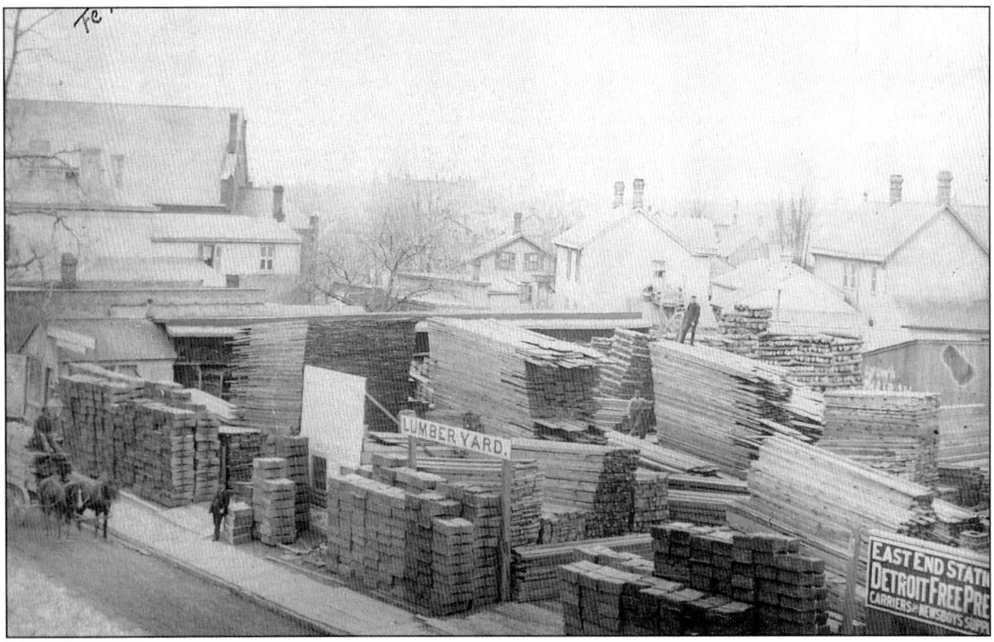

LUMBER TO BUILD A CITY. The other end of the Trowbridge yard on Gratiot Avenue contains a tremendous amount of sawn lumber ready for shipment. A workman standing on top of the wood (right center) gives a sense of scale to the stacks of wood. The East End Station of the Detroit Free Press is right next door.

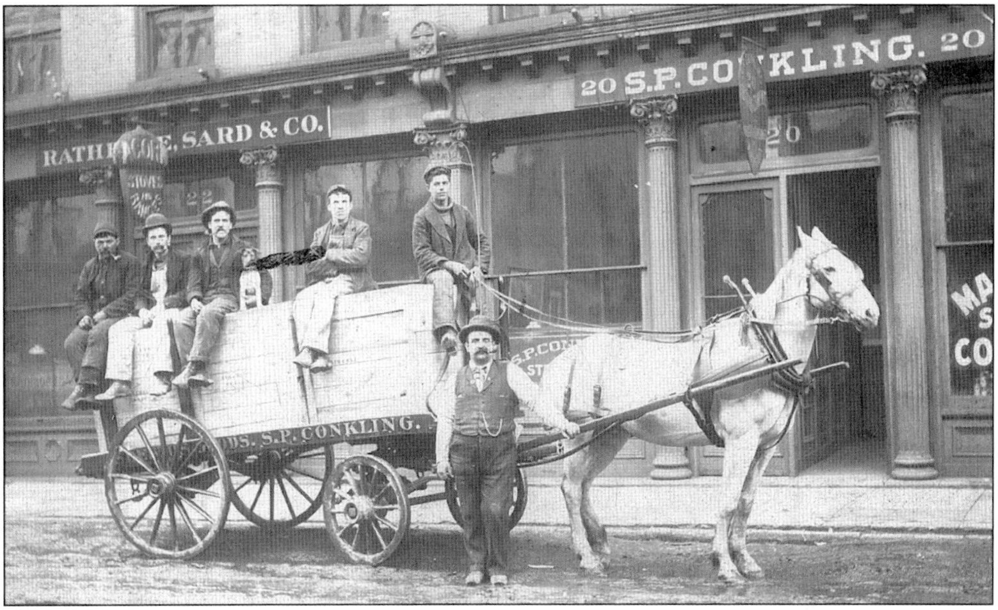

CONSTRUCTION CONTRACTOR. Mr. S.P. Conkling stands next to one of his delivery wagons while his employees pose, ready to go to work in this 1880s photograph. A local contractor, Conkling's business probably took care of a bit of the residential construction going on in the evolving and expanding city.

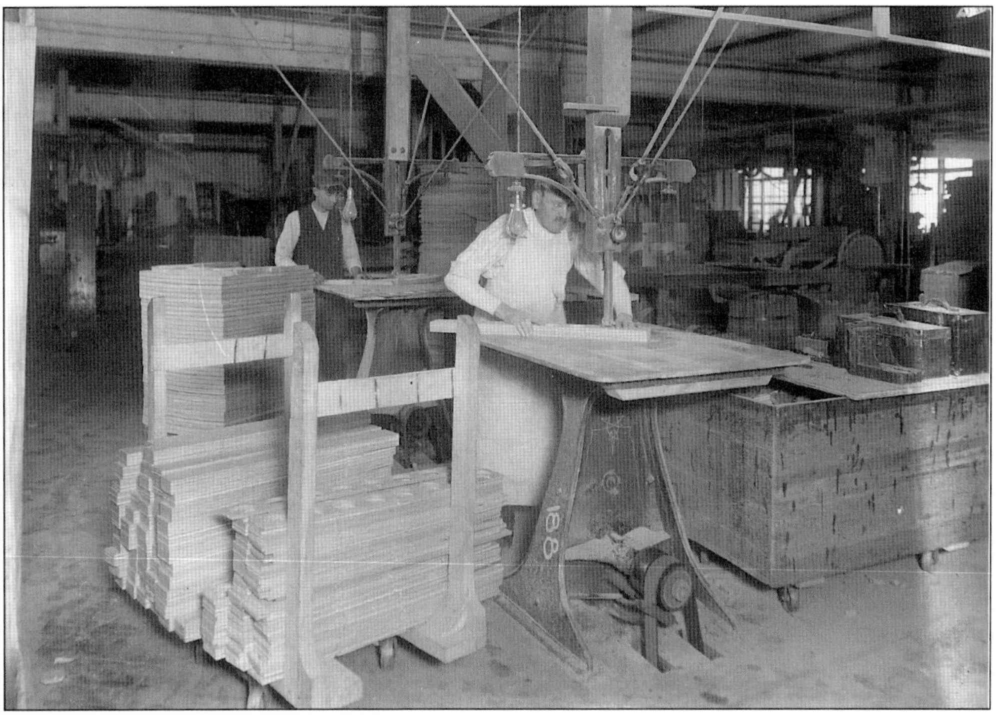

SEAMON AND COMPANY. The machines in this wood finishing business are run by a drive belt system powered by a steam engine located beneath the shop floor. These men are operating jig saws and appear to be scrolling designs into the wooden boards.

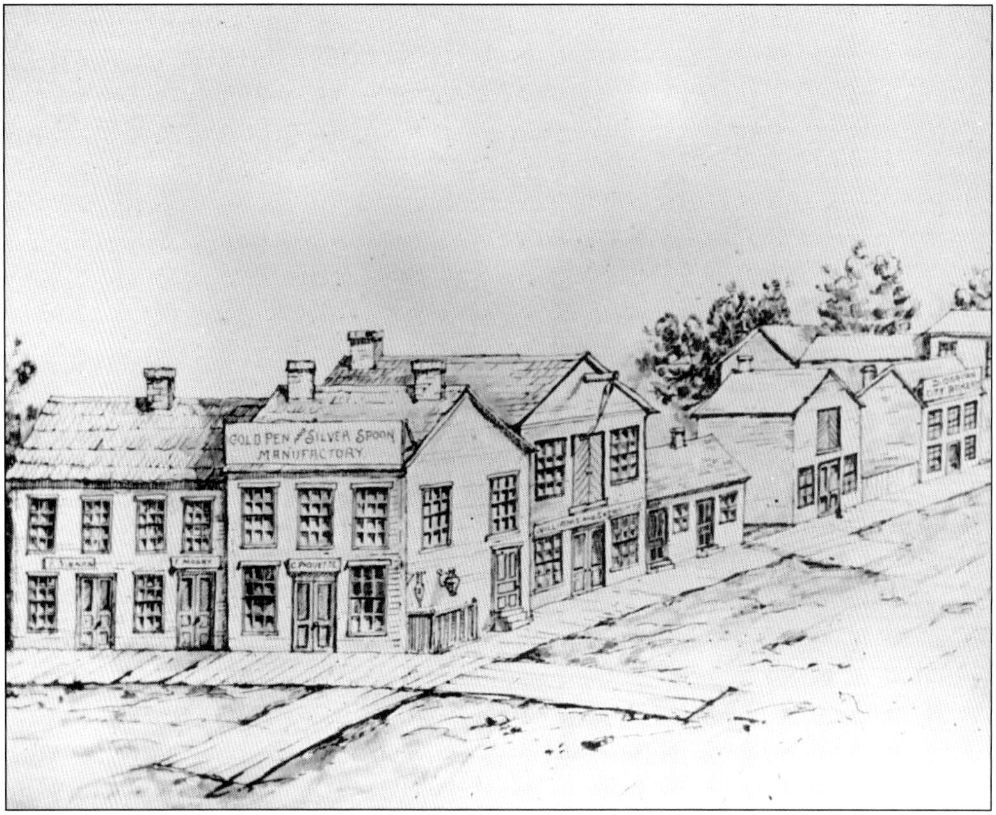

SPECIALIZED INDUSTRY. An artists' drawing shows the Gold Pen & Silver Spoon Manufactory in Detroit around 1875. A Mr. C. Piquette appears to be the proprietor of this small, specialized business. Around the corner is the City Bakery. As the city's economy prospered and wealth grew, specialized items like these were more affordable.

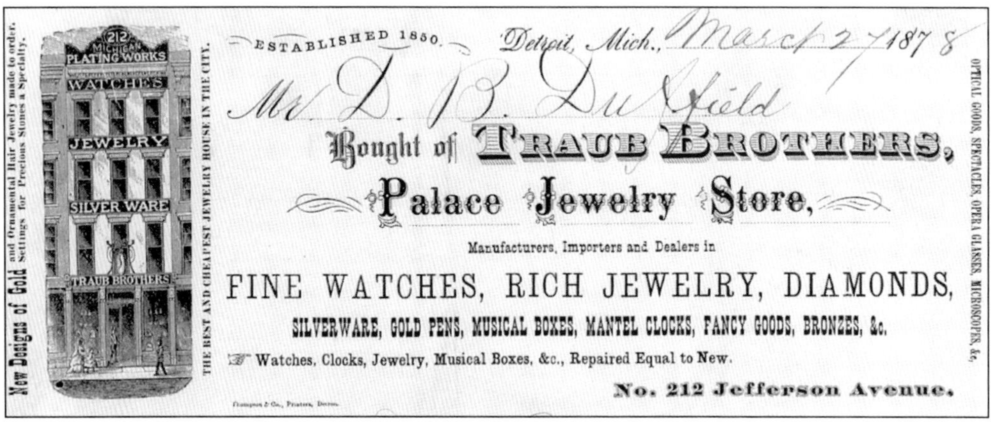
New Designs of Gold and Ornamental Hair Jewelry made to order. Settings for Precious Stones a Specialty.

212 MICHIGAN PLATING WORKS

WATCHES

JEWELRY

SILVER WARE

TRAUB BROTHERS

THE BEST AND CHEAPEST JEWELRY HOUSE IN THE CITY.

ESTABLISHED 1850. Detroit, Mich., March 27 1878

Mr D. B. Duffield

Bought of TRAUB BROTHERS,

Palace Jewelry Store,

Manufacturers, Importers and Dealers in

FINE WATCHES, RICH JEWELRY, DIAMONDS,

SILVERWARE, GOLD PENS, MUSICAL BOXES, MANTEL CLOCKS, FANCY GOODS, BRONZES, &c.

☞ Watches, Clocks, Jewelry, Musical Boxes, &c., Repaired Equal to New.

No. 212 Jefferson Avenue.

OPTICAL GOODS, SPECTACLES, OPERA GLASSES, MICROSCOPES, &c.

THE PALACE JEWELRY STORE. Established in 1850 and operated by the Traub Brothers, the Palace offered all types of fine merchandise, including optical goods, spectacles, opera glasses, microscopes, and new and used musical boxes. The building was also home to the Michigan Plating Works, which could bronze your baby shoes.

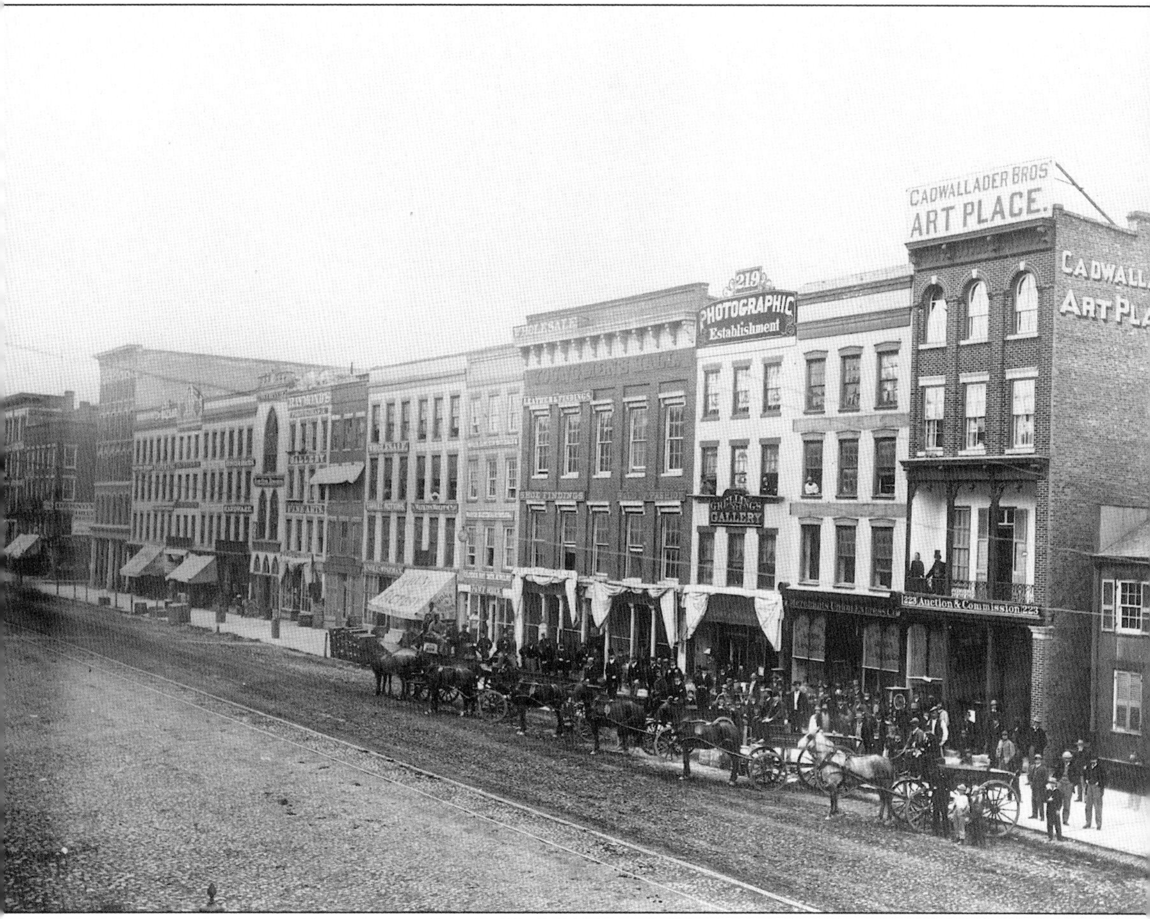

EARLY STRIP MALL. The north side of Jefferson Avenue between Bates and Randolph Streets offered a variety of goods and services to the discriminating customer. The Cadwallader Brothers operated an art gallery and held auction and commission sales. There were two photographers' galleries in this block, one was run by Grellings and the other by Raymond, who also offered fine arts. The fourth building from the right was the Young Men's Hall, which now contained a wholesale leather and shoe store and a Hall of Fashion. Next to the Trunk Factory (white awning in the middle of the photograph), was Wiseman's wholesale Yankee notions store. Further down the avenue was the inevitable clothing store at the One-Cent Bazaar. The diversity of manufacturing in Detroit enabled a variety of different retail businesses to flourish in strips located in the downtown area.

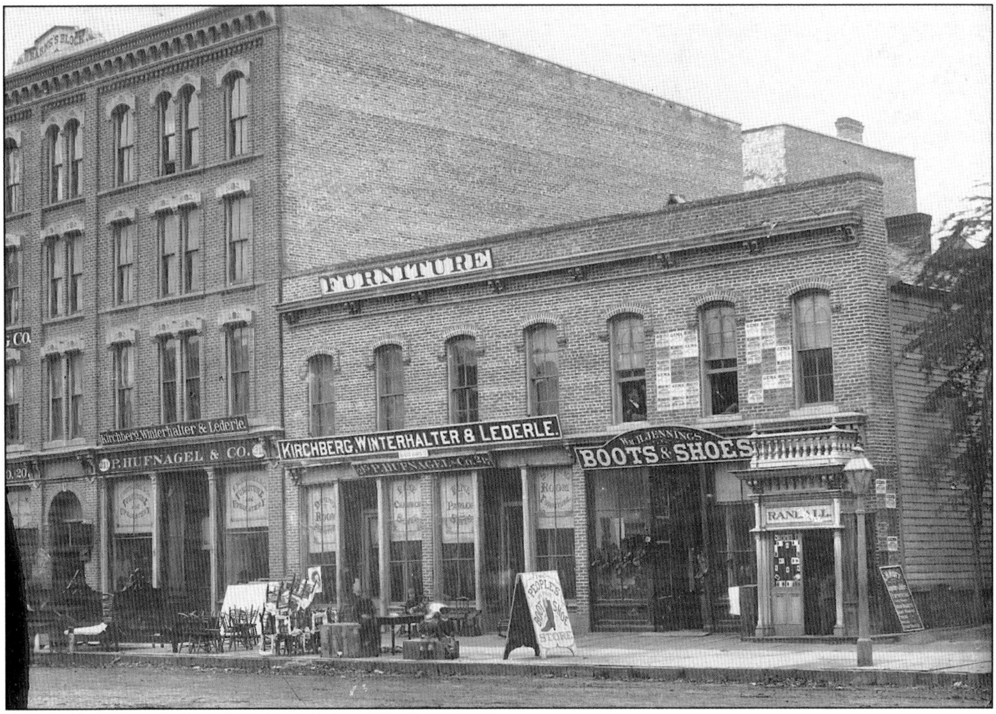

THE BARNES BLOCK. Dominated by Barnes Hall, the west side of Woodward Avenue north from Grand River contains the William H. Jennings shoe store and the P. Hufnagel and Company furniture store. Kirchberg, Winterhalter & Lederle was a law firm. Hufnagel's sold dining and sitting room furniture and fine chamber pieces and chamber suites. In the building next door, he had an upholstery business.

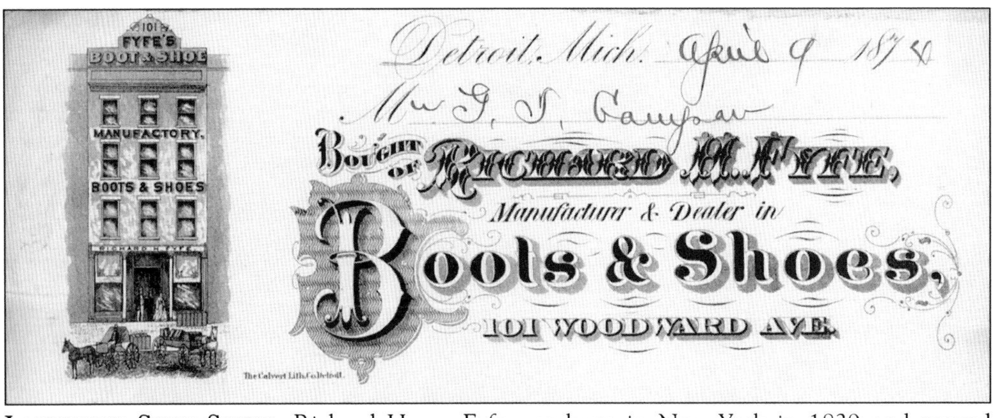

LANDMARK SHOE STORE. Richard Henry Fyfe was born in New York in 1839 and moved to Michigan while still an infant. Raised in Hillsdale County, he came to Detroit in 1857 and worked in a shoe store owned by T.K. Adams. In 1865, Fyfe bought the business from Adams' successors and began the business that would grow to be the largest retail shoe store in the world.

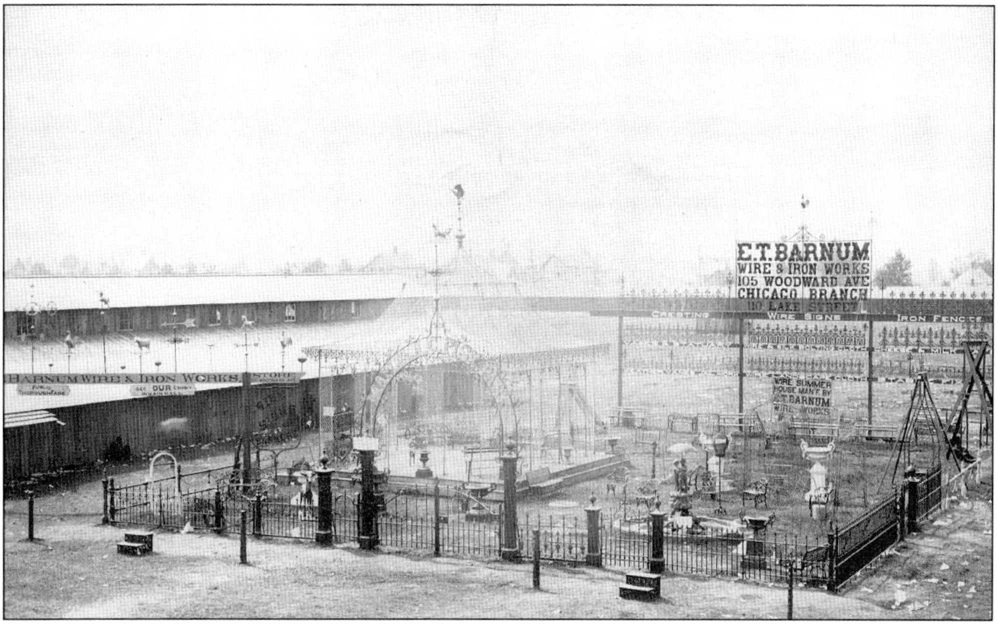

State Fair Exhibit. The E.T. Barnum Wire & Iron Works exhibit at the Michigan State Fair shows off the wrought iron products of this manufacturer. Eugene T. Barnum started his business in a small store on Woodward Avenue in 1866, making just a few ornamental wire work items. Twenty years later, he had an office on Jefferson Avenue and a huge factory on Grand River.

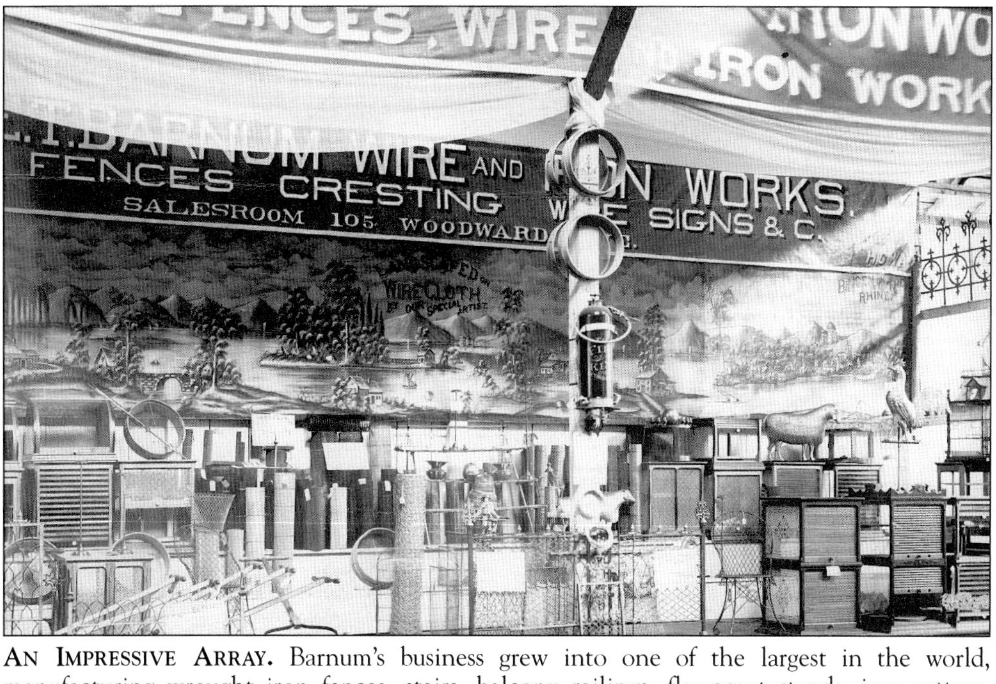

An Impressive Array. Barnum's business grew into one of the largest in the world, manufacturing wrought iron fences, stairs, balcony railings, flowerpot stands, iron settees, chairs, vases, lawn furniture for private residences and parks, cemetery fences, and even cells and other jail work. Barnum employed 700 people plus clerks and salesmen.

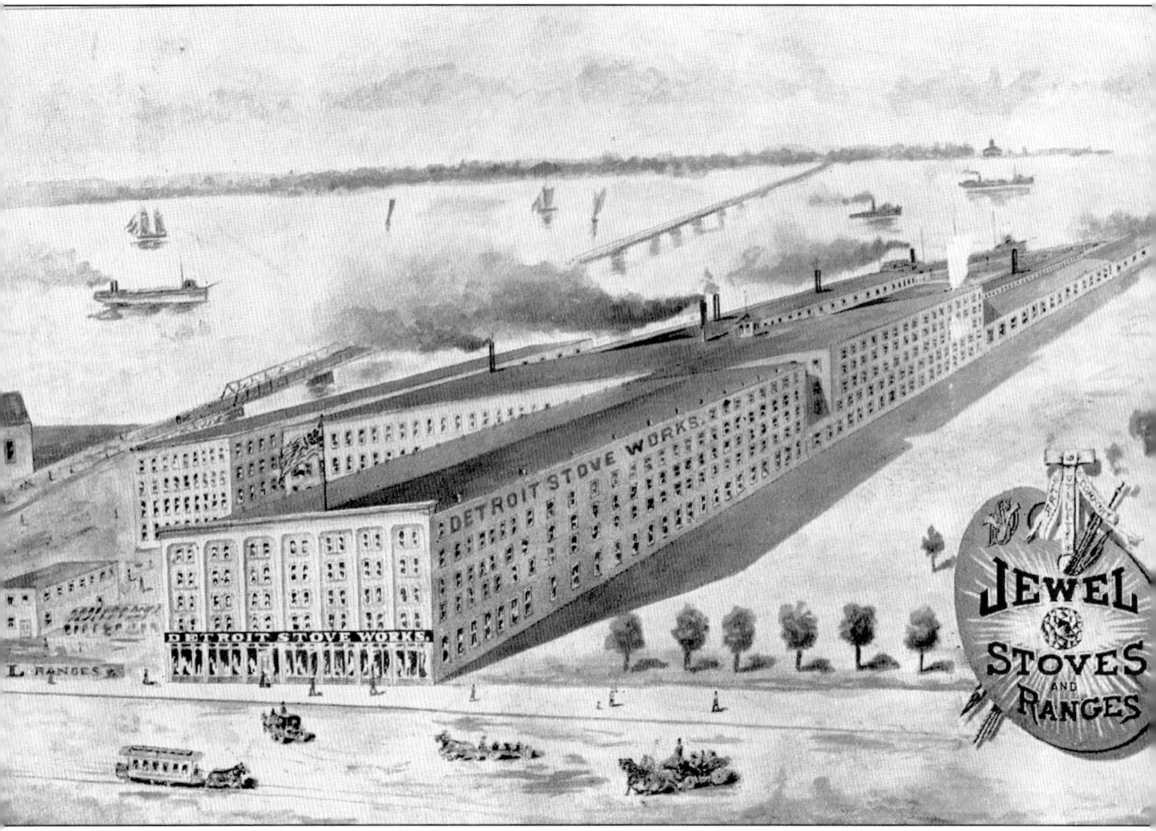

THE NATION'S LEADER. This massive factory complex on Jefferson Avenue belonged to the Detroit Stove Works, first established in 1864 by Mr. W.H. Tefft. The Detroit company was the first stove foundry located in the Old Northwestern part of the United States. The factory pictured here ran through to the Detroit River and covered ten acres of land. The building had a multitude of windows in an attempt to give each workman ample light to correctly do his job. The stove works had its own pattern and blacksmith's shops, japanning rooms, stock shed, tool room, a cinders mill and a five-story warehouse in addition to the buildings devoted to actually building the stoves. The total floor space in this complex amounted to some 350,000 superficial feet. The works employed 1,400 men, and the Jewel logo was known throughout Europe, with agents in Germany, England, Belgium, France, and Austria. There were also branches in Chicago, St. Paul, and Buffalo.

WOODWARD AVENUE, 1876. Stoves made in Detroit were initially sold through retail dealers such as Mr. E.W. Stoddard, who carried a line of Jewel stoves and ranges in his "Housekeeper's Emporium" on Woodward Avenue, some of his line can be seen on the sidewalk in front, used to entice customers inside.

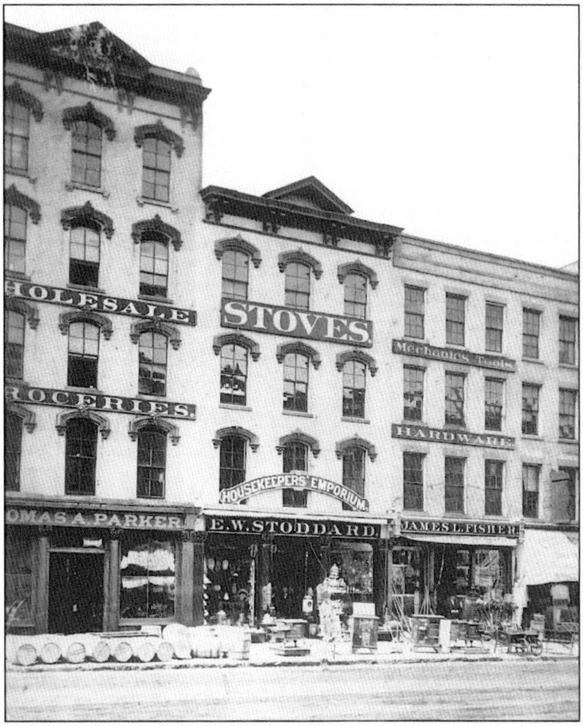

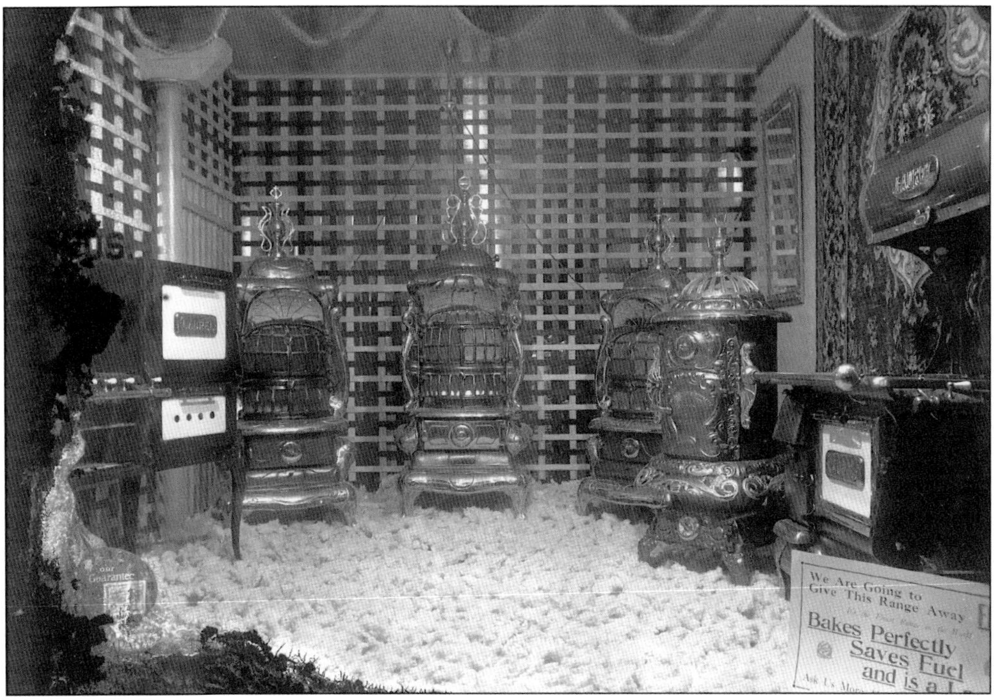

THE ART STOVE COMPANY SHOWROOM. In competition with the Detroit Stove Works was the Art Stove Company, which also manufactured a line of stoves and ranges. In the photograph are four different stoves flanked on both sides by the company's ranges, called Laurel ranges, and used for cooking. They would later merge with the Michigan Stove Company.

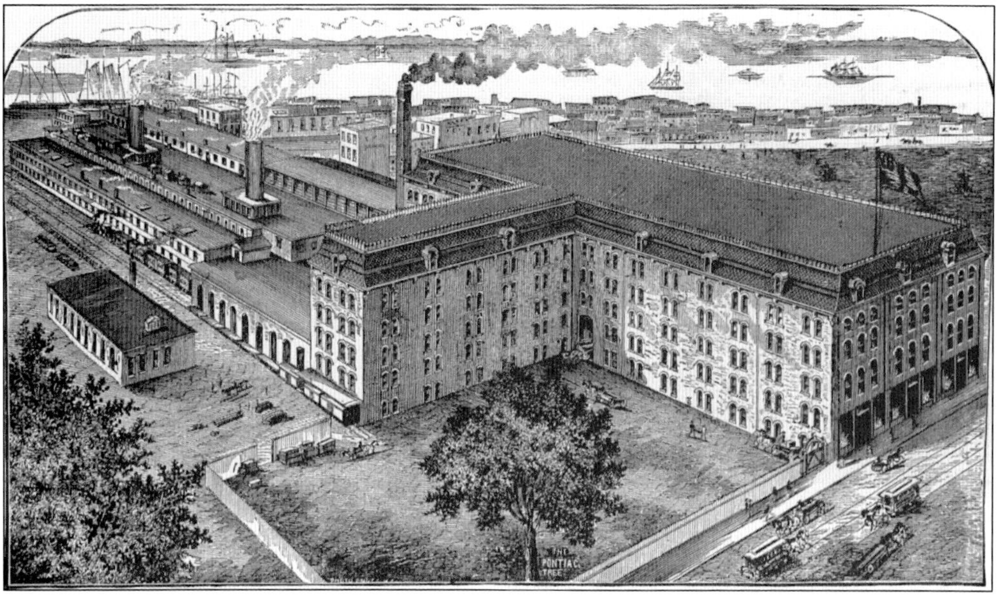

ANOTHER STOVE GIANT. The other major stove producer in Detroit was the Michigan Stove Company, also located in a massive complex on Jefferson Avenue at the corner of Adair Street. Established in 1871, these buildings were constructed over time, from 1872 to 1883. The main building was a five-story brick structure, employing from 1,200 to 1,500 workmen who produced Garland stoves and ranges.

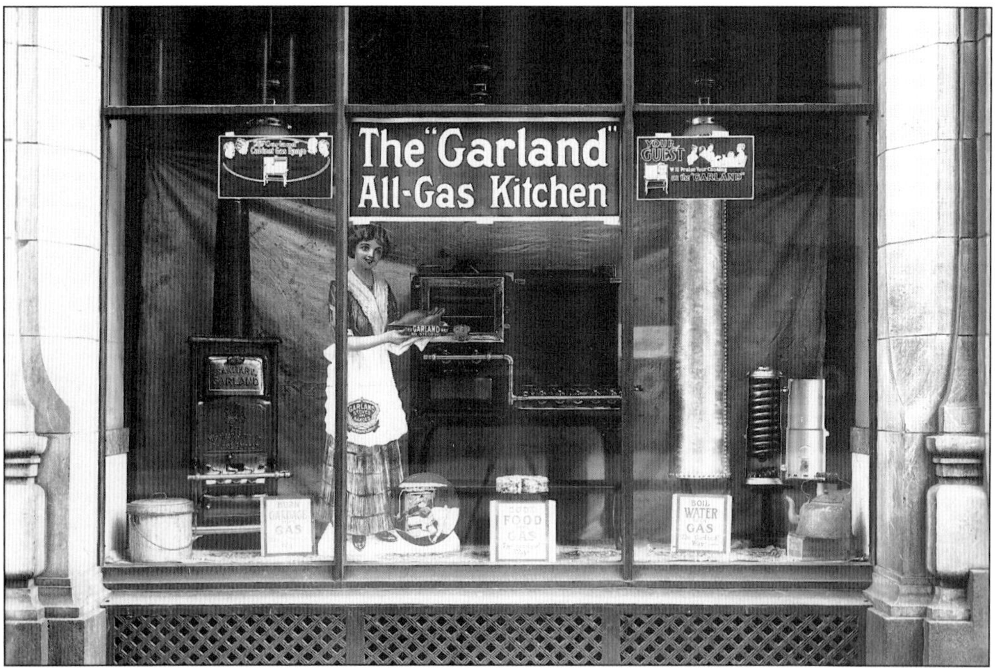

THE KITCHEN OF THE FUTURE. The "Garland" line of kitchen appliances promised less work for the lady of the house in her "all-gas kitchen." One could burn garbage, cook food and boil water with gas "The Garland Way." The Michigan Stove Works produced 60,000 stoves and ranges annually.

NO IDLE THREAT. Both wife and daughter appear to be admonishing the man of the house, who is relaxing in smoking jacket and slippers and trying to read the newspaper in this 1880s advertisement featuring the Garland logo. The Garland line was constructed in accordance with scientific requirements for securing the best results.

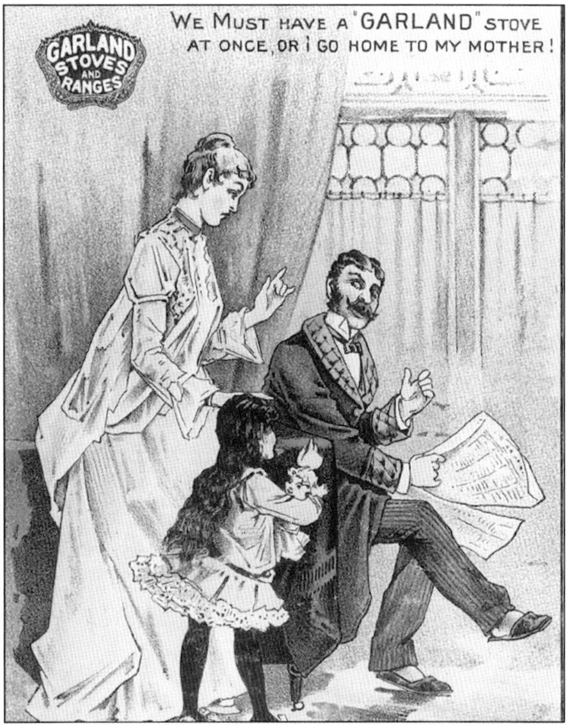

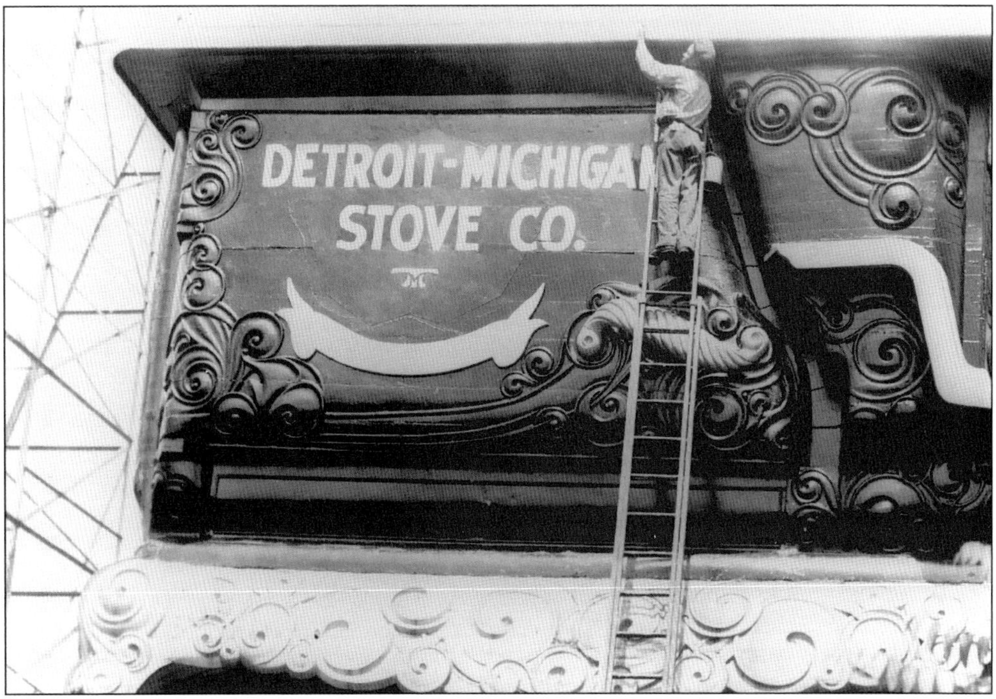

THE GIANTS MERGE. This famous Detroit landmark, long located opposite the Belle Isle Bridge, was made of wood to advertise the company's products at the Columbian Exposition in Chicago, Illinois in 1893, shortly after the merger of the Michigan and Detroit Stove Works. The city of Detroit took the lead in stove production from New York City.

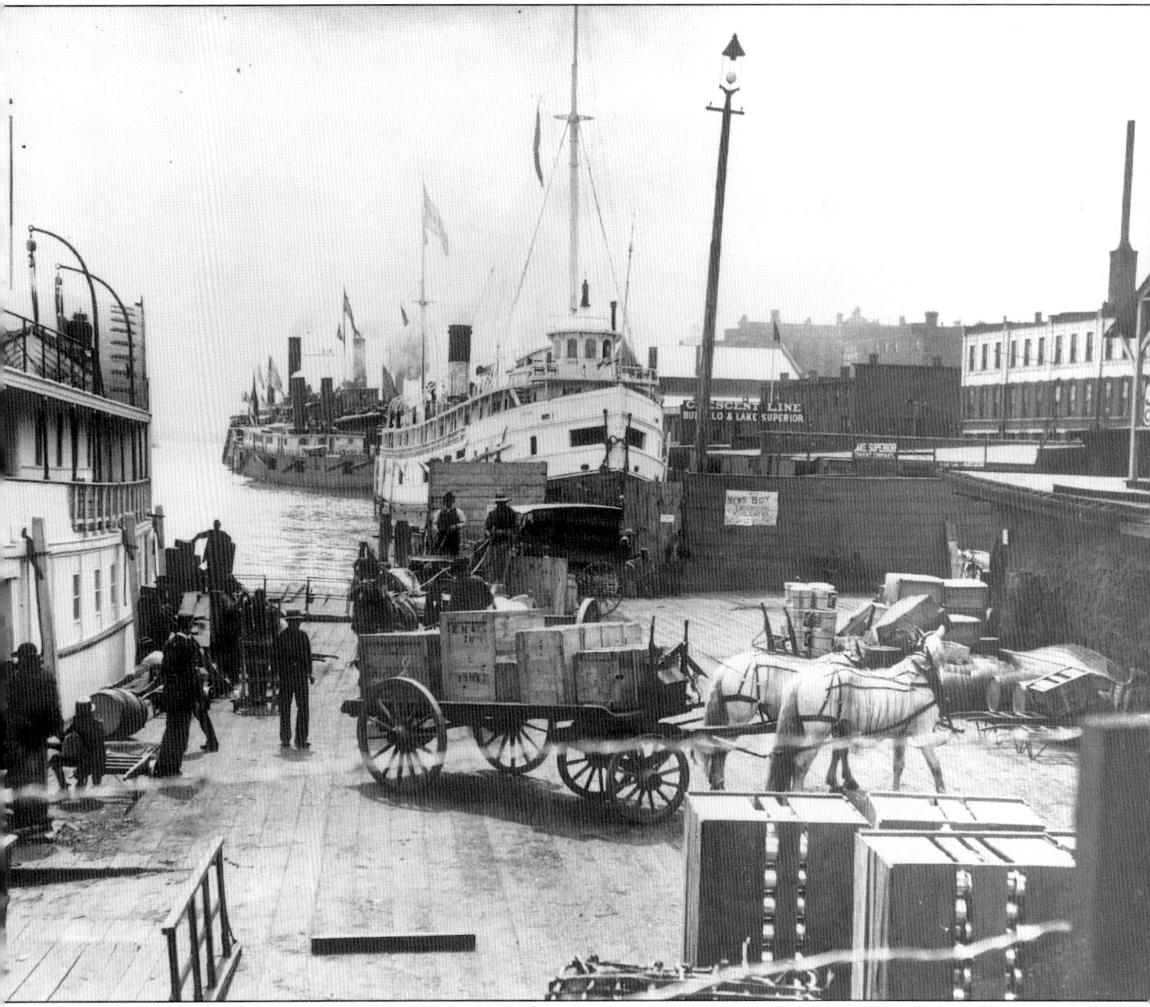

THE BUSY RIVERFRONT, 1890. Freight wagons wait to load goods and materials from river steamers in this 1890 photograph of the docks near the foot of Woodward Avenue. The harbor formed by the Detroit River was the largest and safest on the Lakes. It had more room to handle vessels than the harbors of Buffalo, Erie, Cleveland, Milwaukee, and Chicago combined.

Three

Neighborhood Industries

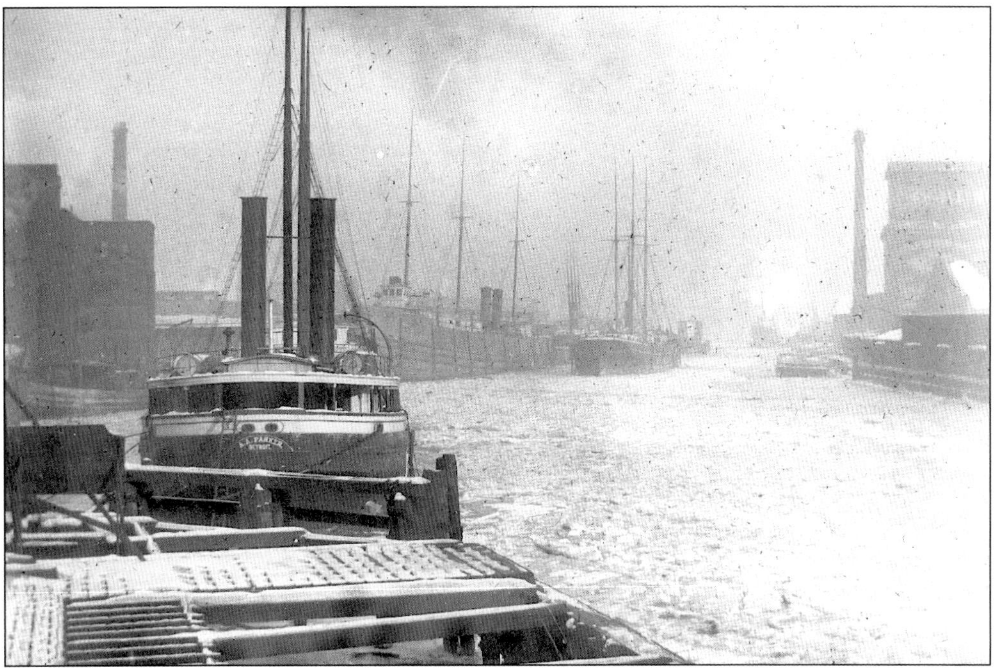

The Seaport in Winter. Lakes vessels docked in Detroit just before the close of the navigation season, which was normally during early December, depending on the weather. For the first 150 years of its existence, Detroit has depended on the river and lakes for communication and commerce. The advent of the railroad system made communication and commerce a year-round occurrence.

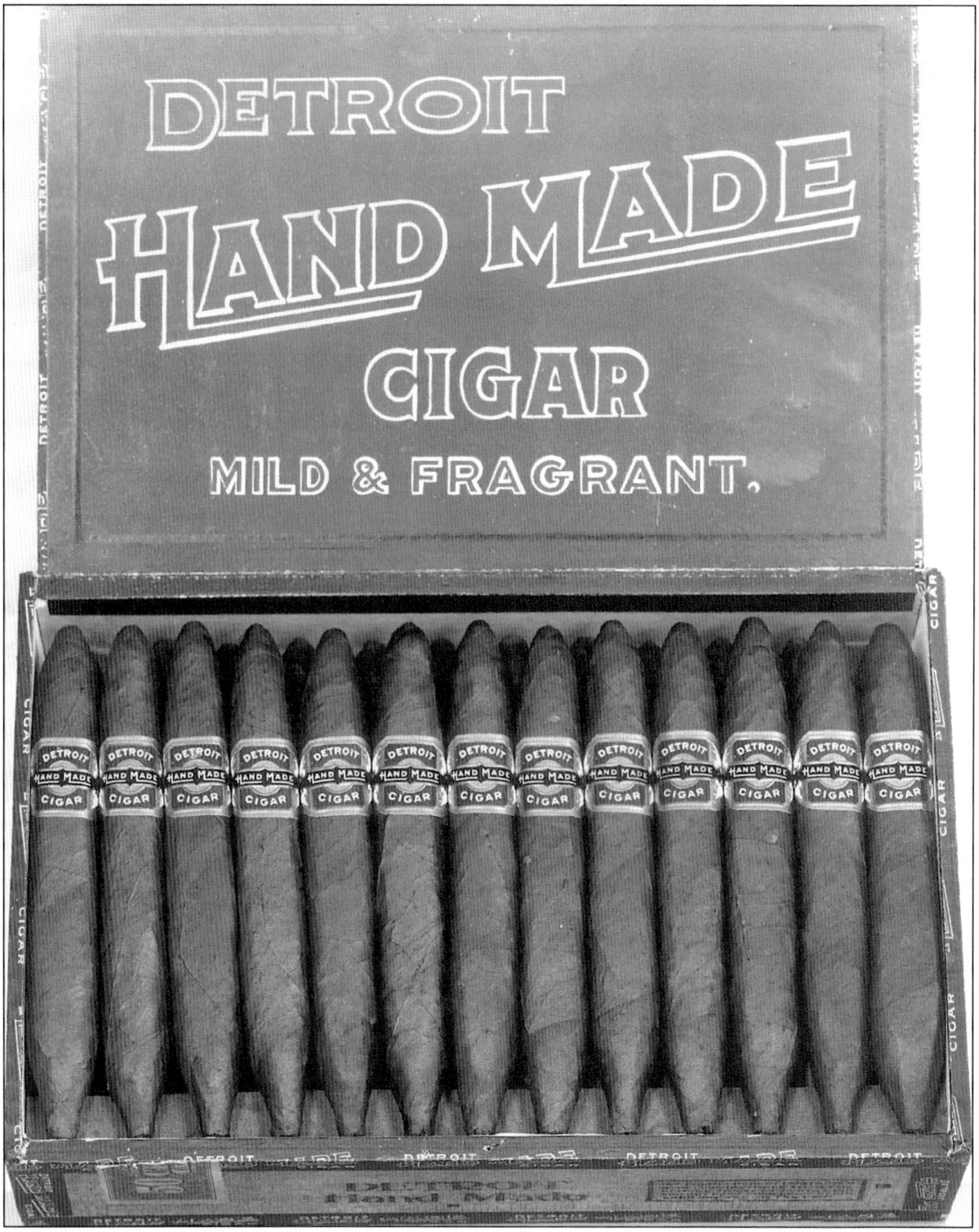

HAVANA OF THE NORTH. Probably the least known fact in Detroit history is that the city was once one of the largest producers of cigars and other tobacco products in the country, so much so that Detroit came to be called the "Havana of the North" by 1901. The very first tobacco factory was established in Detroit around 1840 by George Miller, who operated out of small two-story wooden building on Woodward Avenue near Jefferson. Tobacco was stored on the second floor and the cutting machines were located in the basement. The arrival of German and Jewish immigrants who had learned cigar-making techniques in Europe helped spawn the industry before the Civil War. That conflict added to the growth of the industry, as soldiers traded tobacco products and certain brands became more popular than others. Detroit's home-made cigars, called "seegars," gained a national reputation.

BANNER TOBACCO COMPANY. By 1880, there were several large tobacco companies in Detroit, among the 73 companies listed in the city directory. At the corner of Bates and Jefferson stood the Banner Tobacco Company, makers of Banner, Oriole, Prairie, and Antelope chewing tobacco, and Chic, Royal, Snowflake, Belle and Uncle Ben smoking tobacco.

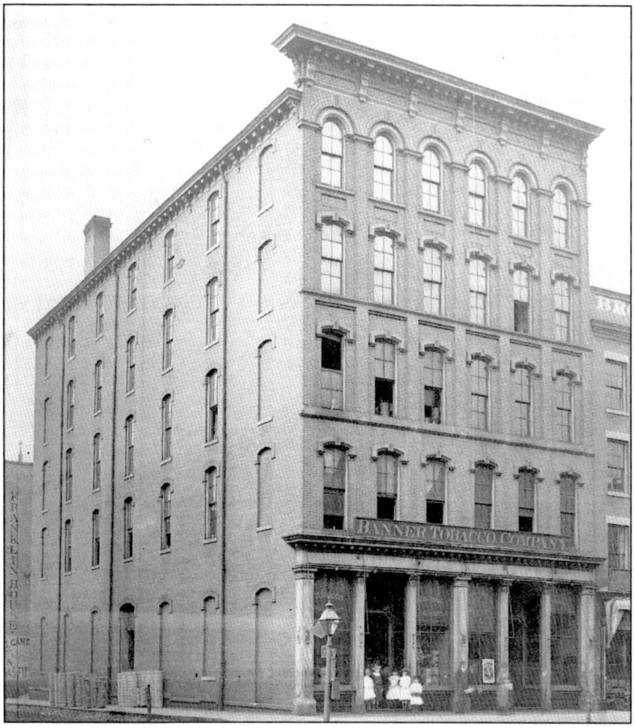

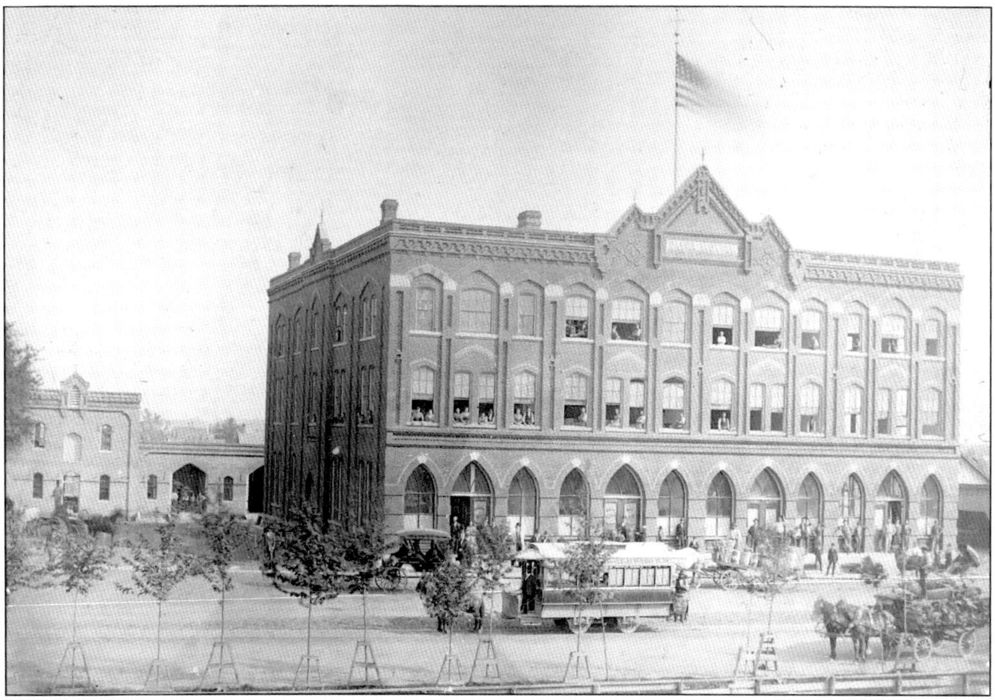

DANIEL SCOTTEN TOBACCO COMPANY. Daniel Scotten had taken over George Miller's business and moved it into this factory on West Fort Street near West Grand Boulevard. By the 1890s, Scotten employed 1,200 workers, had a weekly payroll of $8,000, and saw $4 million in annual sales. The city had 189 tobacco producers in 1890.

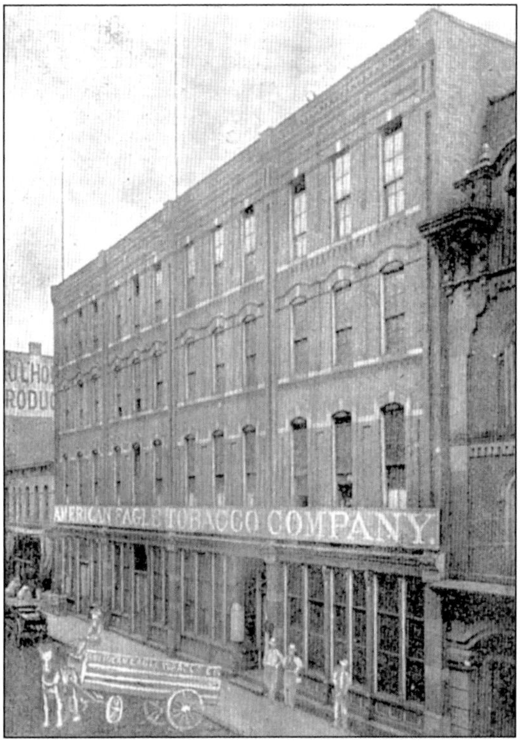

AMERICAN EAGLE. On Atwater Street, built in 1883, the American Eagle Tobacco Company produced American Eagle, Oriental, Dew Drop, Plum, Sugar Cured, and Double S chewing tobacco, as well as Eagle Cavendish and Fawn smoking tobacco. Mr. M.S. Smith, President, employed 300 people in his factory, making over 20 different brands of tobacco.

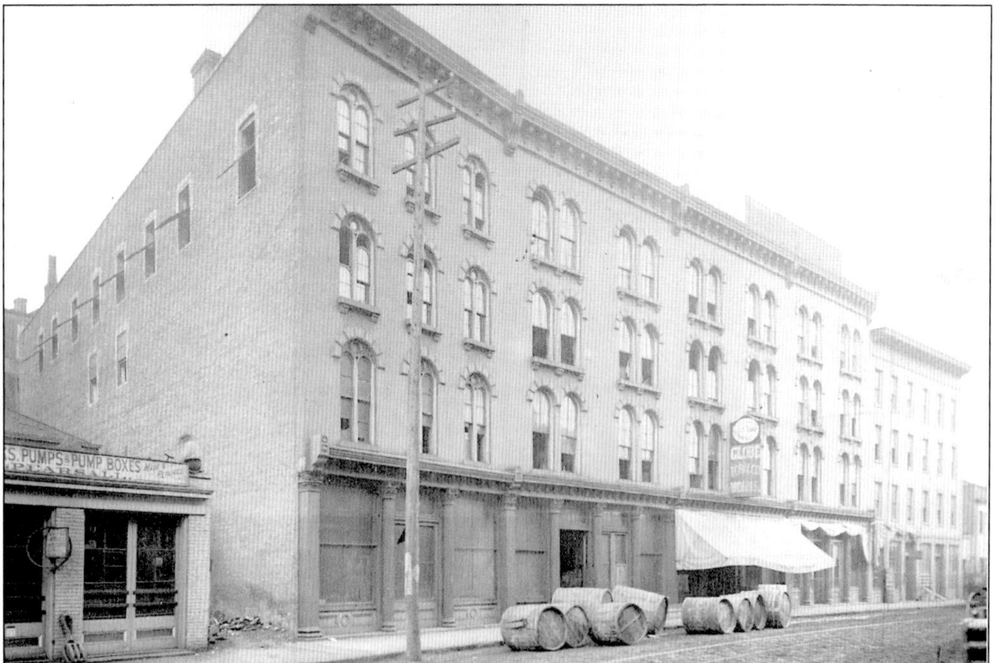

ATWATER, EAST OF BATES STREET. Another of the largest tobacco companies in Detroit was the Globe Tobacco Company, producing Globe chewing tobacco and Nerve and Fearless smoking tobacco. Incorporated in 1871, Globe employed 190 people who produced 5,000 pounds of cigarettes and 3,000 pounds of chewing tobacco every day.

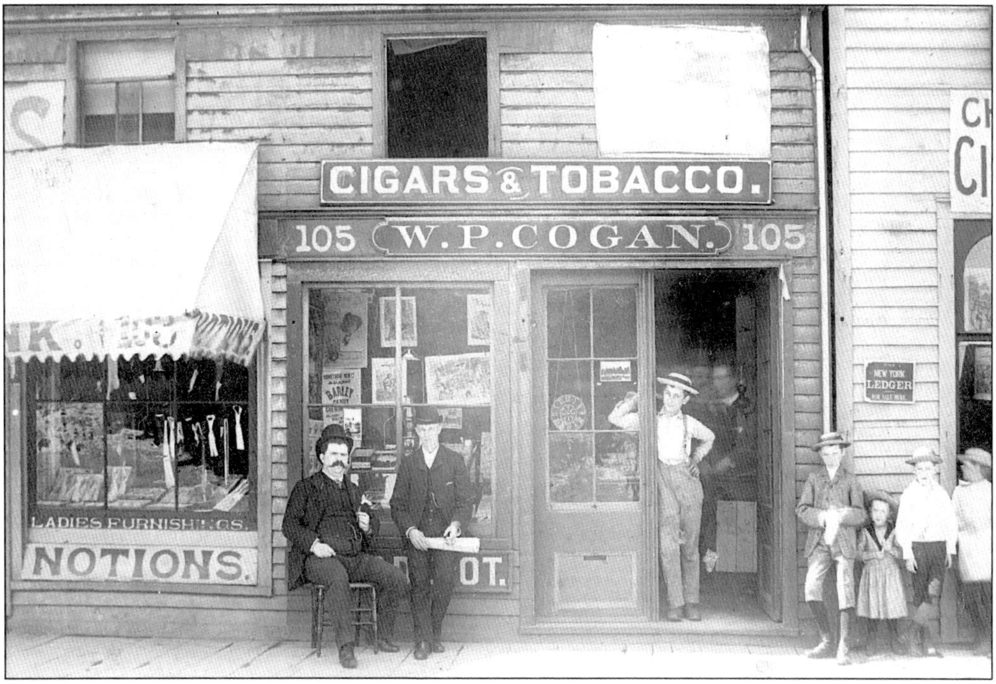

COGAN'S CIGAR AND TOBACCO STORE. Located at 105 Michigan Avenue, William P. Cogan handled some of the city's homemade tobacco products. With some six million pounds of raw tobacco imported into Detroit each year, Cogan had no trouble keeping his inventory totals up. Posing for this picture are the proprietor and his sons.

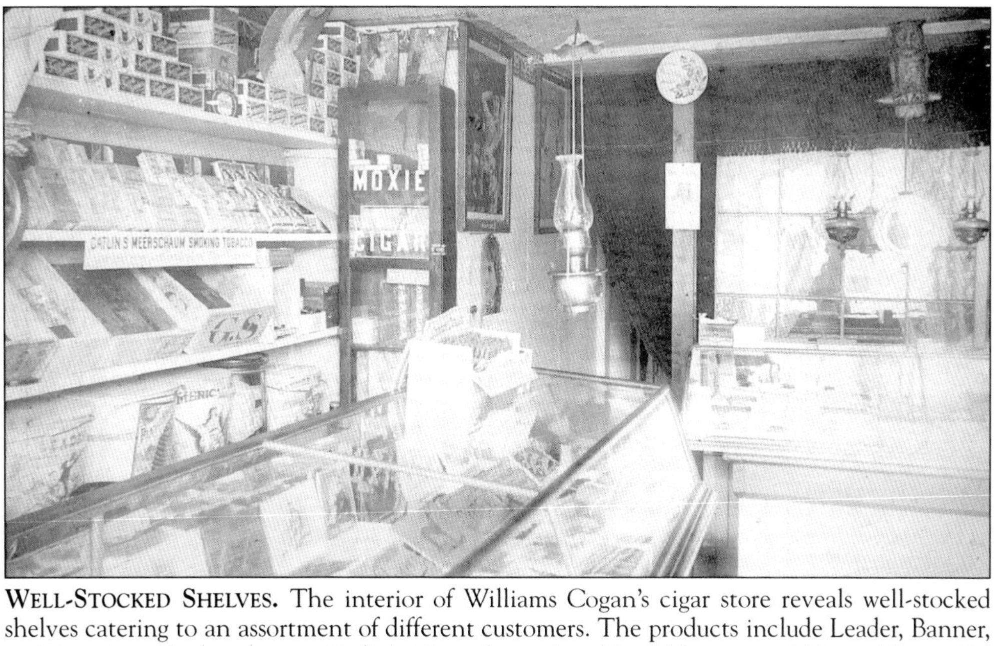

WELL-STOCKED SHELVES. The interior of Williams Cogan's cigar store reveals well-stocked shelves catering to an assortment of different customers. The products include Leader, Banner, and American Eagle tobacco, Catlin's Meerschaum Smoking Tobacco, and Moxie Cigars. On the wall to the left of the lamp is a large poster of a current stage actress, a typical decoration in these establishments.

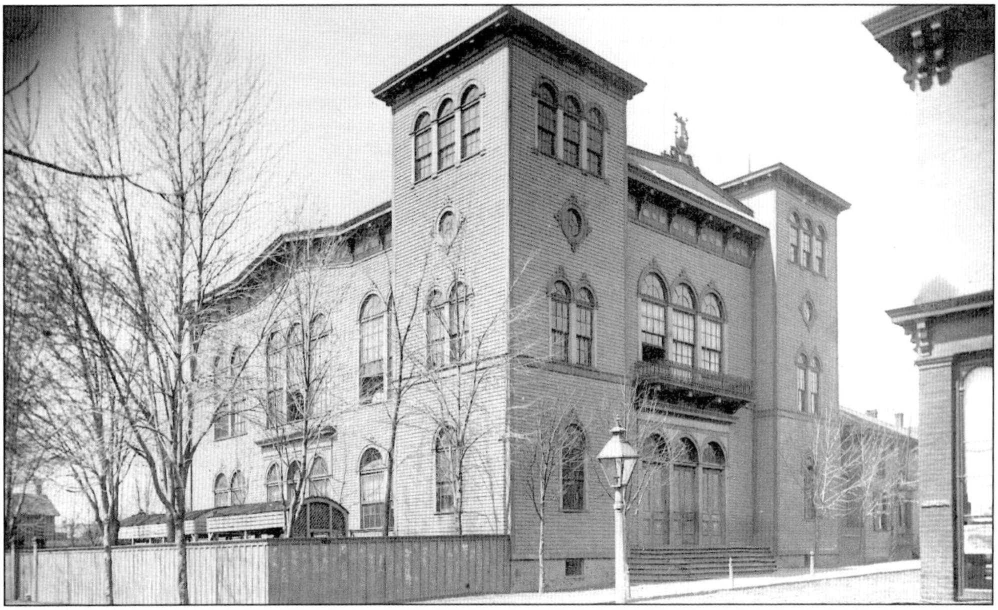

ARBEITER HALL. On the corner of Catherine and Russell Streets stood the Arbeiter (or workmen's) Hall. The beer garden, on the left of the photograph, was a social gathering place for east side Germans to quaff lager. German immigrants to Detroit helped settle the east side of the city and assisted in establishing the cigar-making and brewing industries in Detroit.

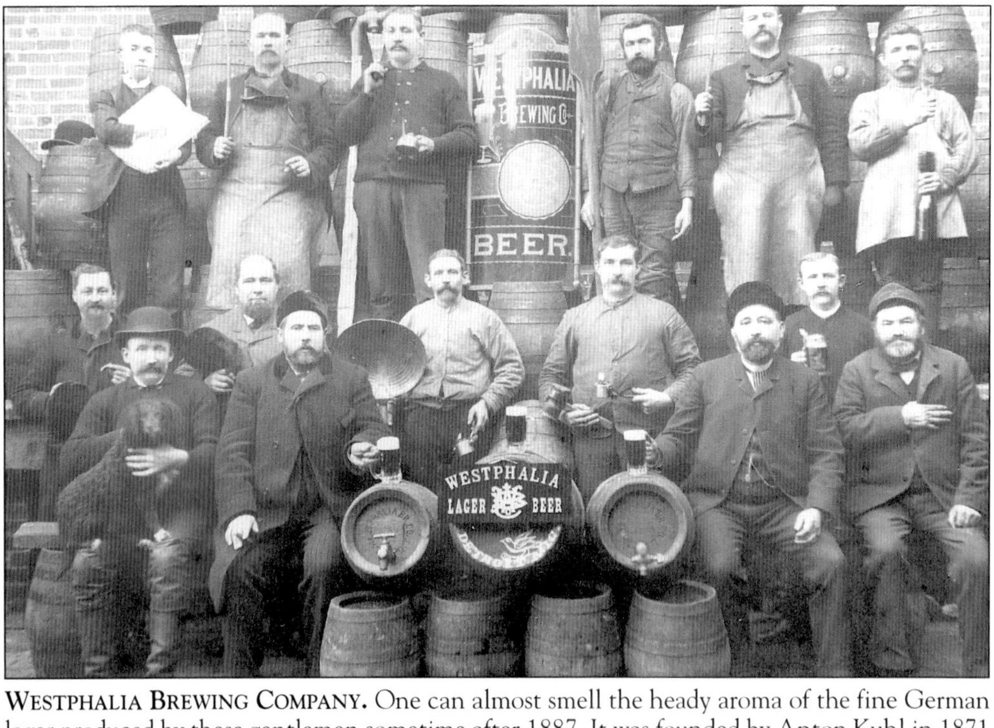

WESTPHALIA BREWING COMPANY. One can almost smell the heady aroma of the fine German lager produced by these gentlemen sometime after 1887. It was founded by Anton Kuhl in 1871 and run by his widow, Anna, until she sold it to Joseph Nagel in 1887. He changed the name to Westphalia and operated the brewery for eight years.

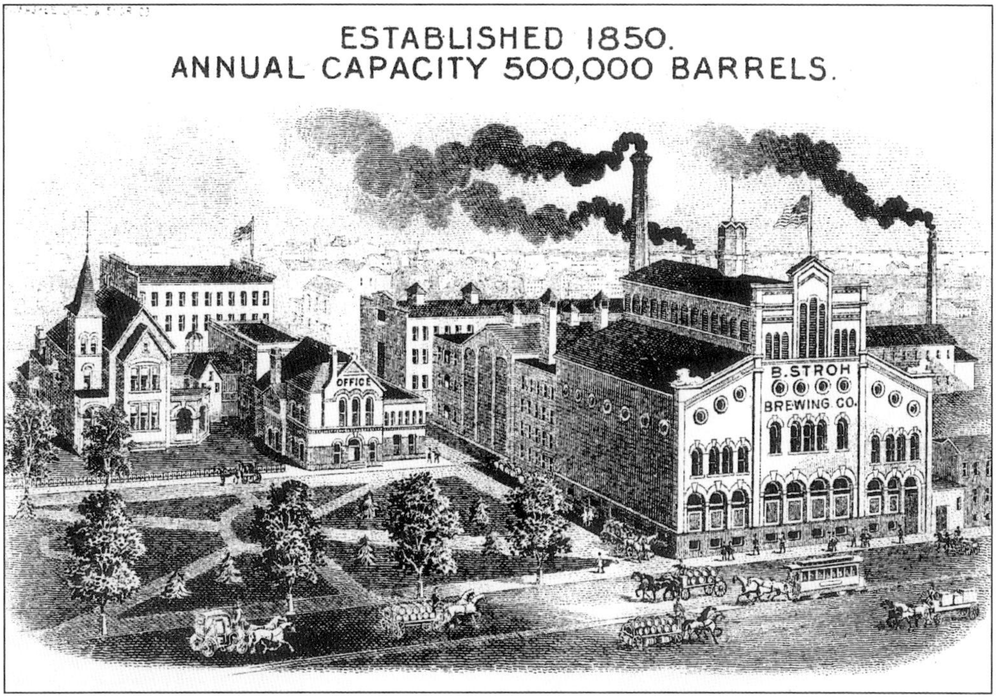

DETROIT'S FAMOUS LABEL. This late 1890s advertisement illustrates the famous Stroh's brewery on Gratiot Avenue. Bernard Stroh settled in Detroit in 1850 and opened a brewery shortly thereafter. By the turn of the century, Stroh's was the largest brewery in Detroit, with an annual capacity of 300,000 barrels.

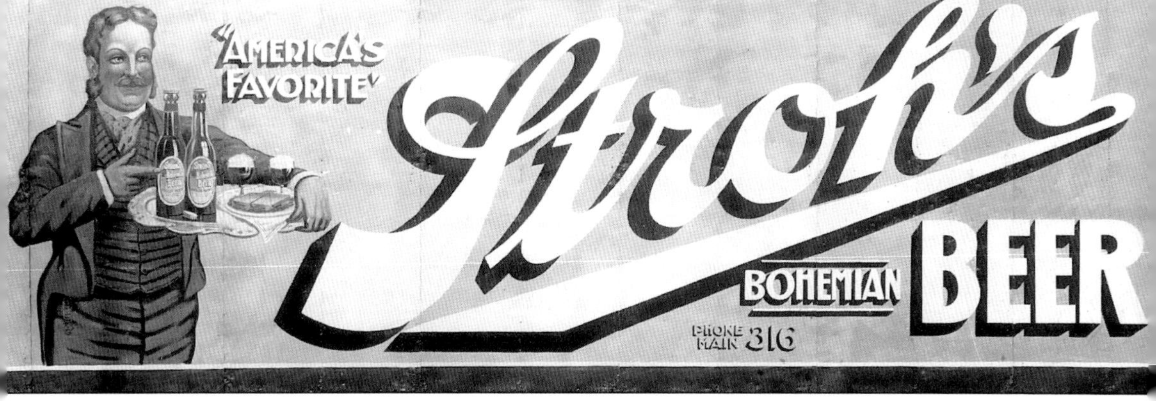

FIRE-BREWED ADVERTISING. In this early outdoor advertising venture with the the outdoor sign business Walker & Company, a handy butler is taking care of delivering the Stroh's to the table.

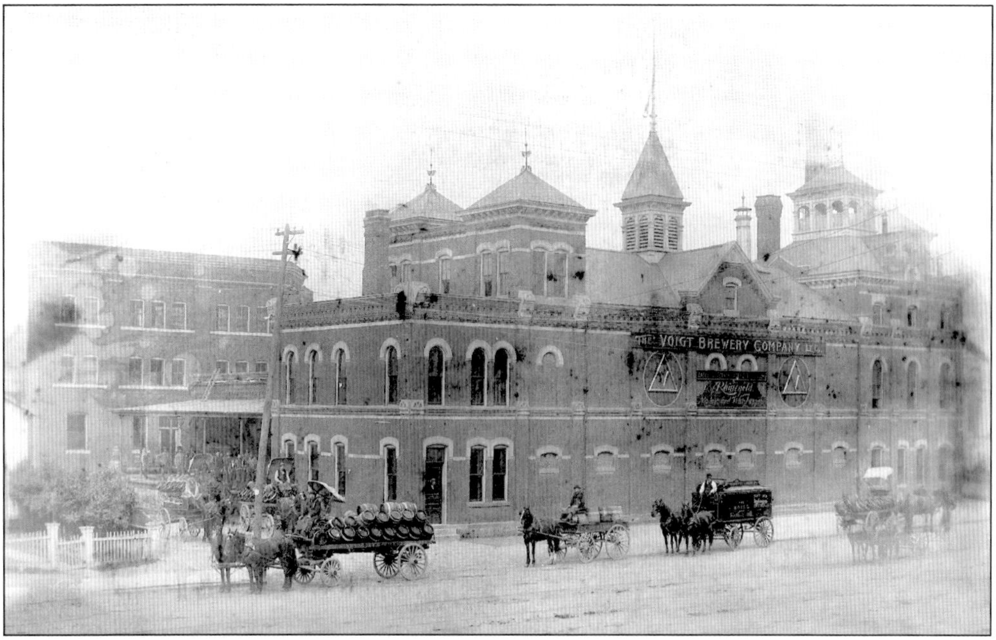

THE VOIGHT BREWING COMPANY. Carl William Voight established this 2,000 barrel lager brewery in 1866, and in 1871 he sold it to his son Edward for $30,000. By 1878, the brewery was the largest in Detroit, with sales of 17,500 barrels of a brand of lager named "Boss." In 1883, the Rheingold name was first adopted.

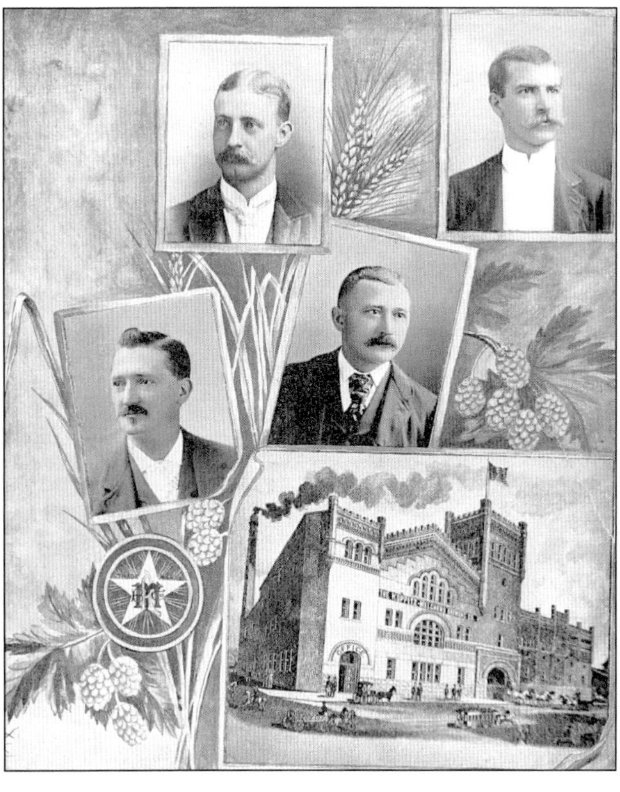

PALE SELECT LAGER. The Koppitz-Melchers brewery was established in late 1890 by Konrad Emil Koppitz, Arthur C. , and other partners. The partners financed a 60,000 barrel brewery on a block-long section of Gratiot Avenue. The four-story brew house, with its Romanesque arches and tower, resembled a castle. Their other brands included Silver Brew and Porter.

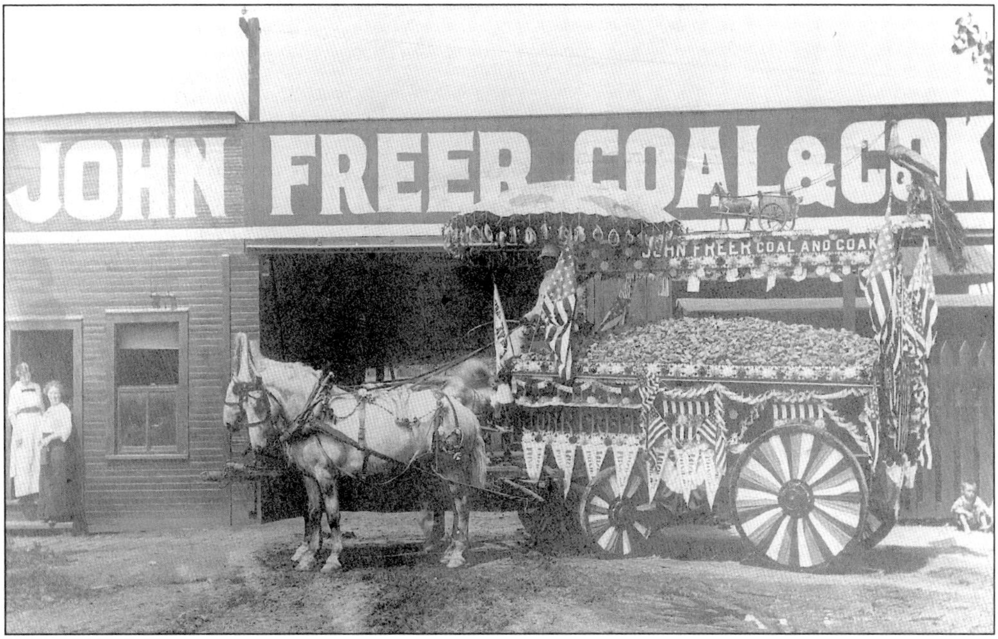

ALL DRESSED UP. One of the delivery wagons belonging to the John Freer Coal & Coke Company is festooned with red, white, and blue bunting in preparation for a parade. One can barely see Mr. Freer on the wagon underneath the large umbrella. He had his coal and coke yards at Atwater Street on the city's east side.

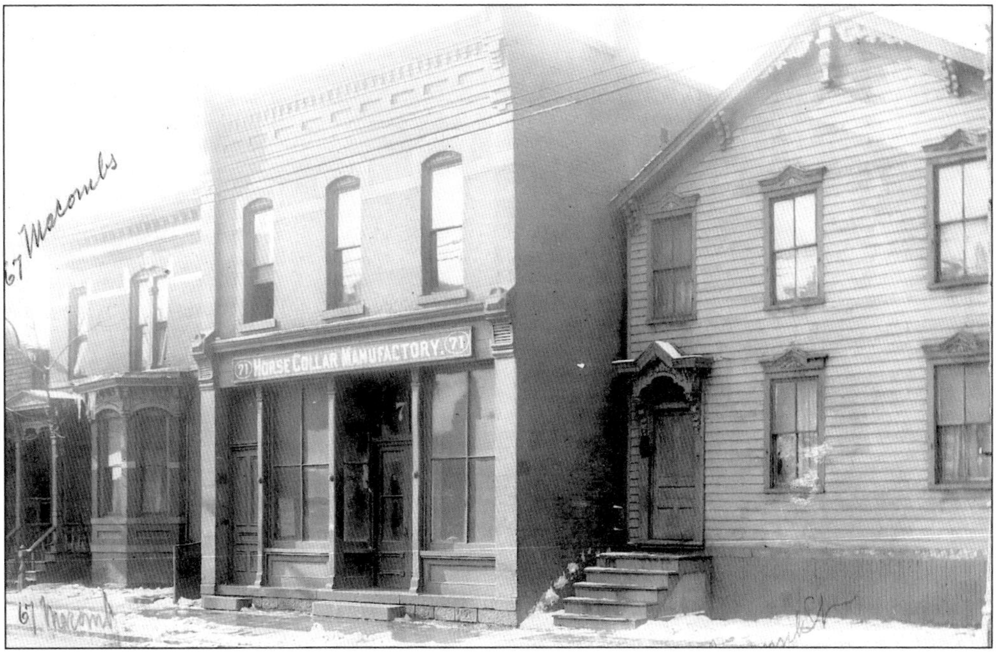

LEATHER GOODS FOR YOUR HORSE. This small horse collar manufactory was located at 71 Macomb Street and was run by Alfred, Arthur, and John Malcho. It probably did a lot of piece work for clients in the immediate area, including repair work to otherwise serviceable leather horse furniture.

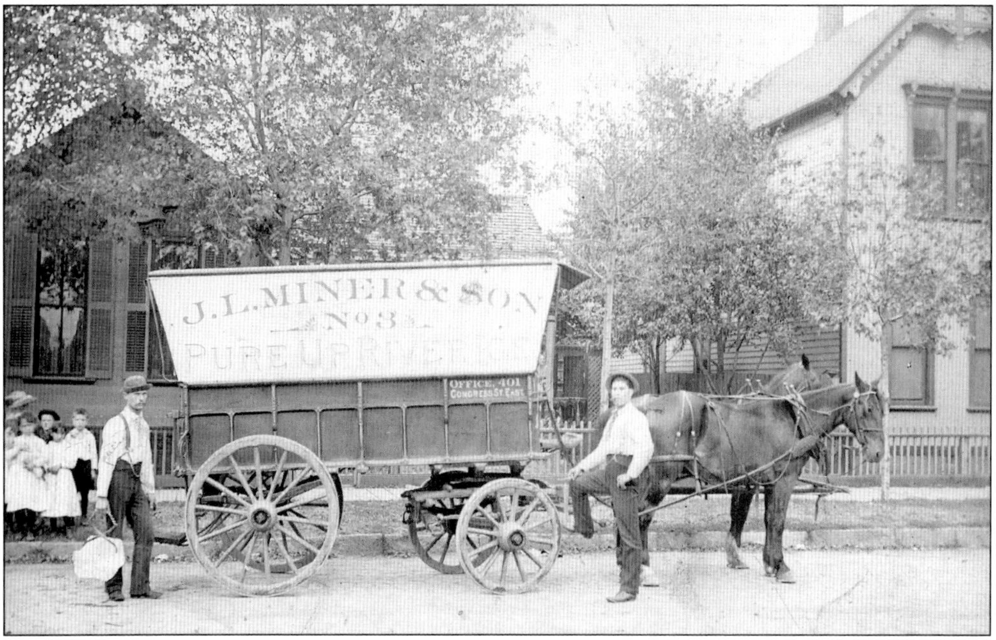

THE ICE MAN. The J.L. Miner (left) and Son (right) Ice Company delivered to residences on the east side of Detroit. This wagon is numbered "3" and may be a part of Miner's fleet of delivery wagons. The company offices were located at 401 Congress East. Advertising on the wagon declares that Miner delivered "Pure Up River Ice."

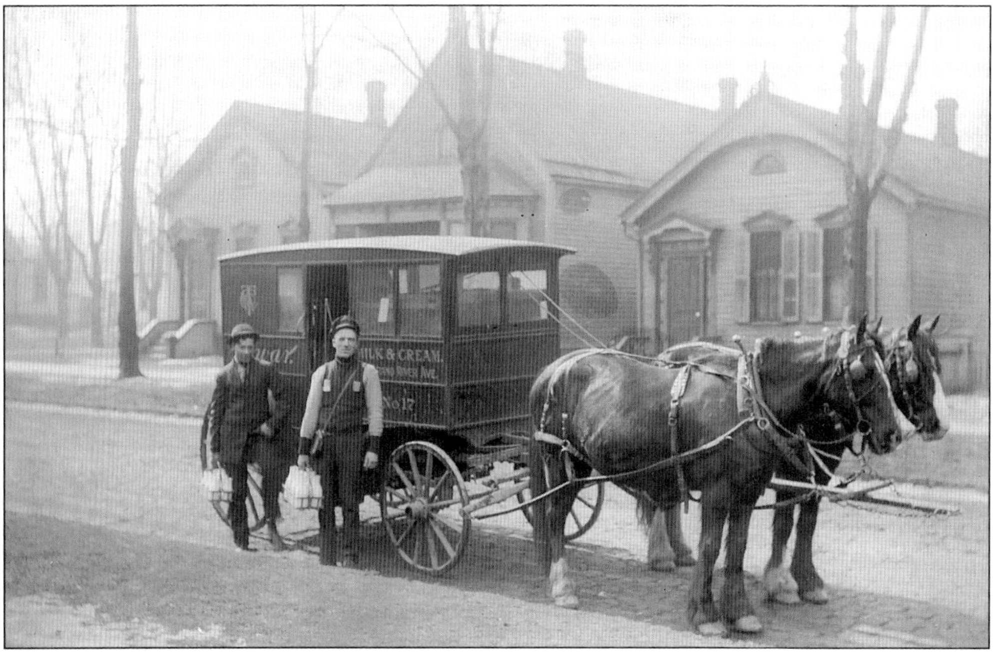

THE MILK MAN. Brothers Peter C. Peterson (left) and Anton R. Peterson (right) stand ready to go to work on their milk route for the Wayne County Cremery in this turn of the century photograph. Milk wagons such as these would continue to service Detroit neighborhoods until well into the 1920s.

STREET SIDE ADVERTISING. This city street scene somewhere in Detroit (possibly along Grand River Avenue), is a good illustration of the historic use of empty space in the city—advertising—most of which is for home-grown products. Lillian Russell was a popular star of the theater and stage and many products bore her name, including a man's cigar.

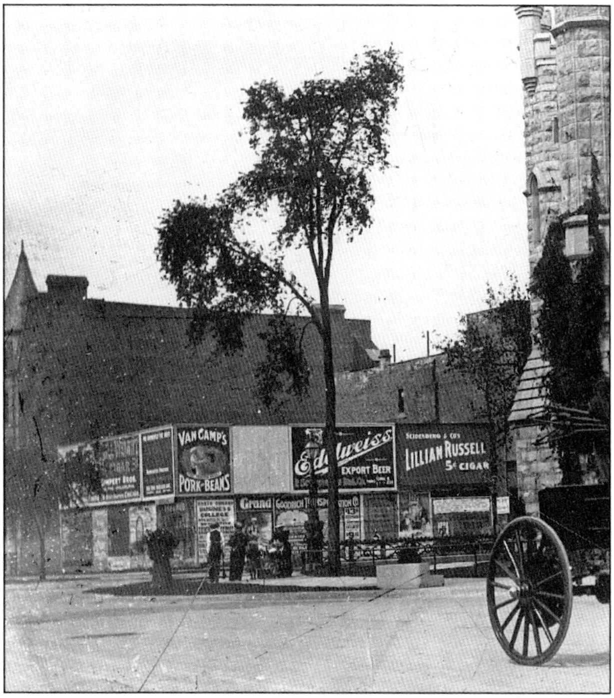

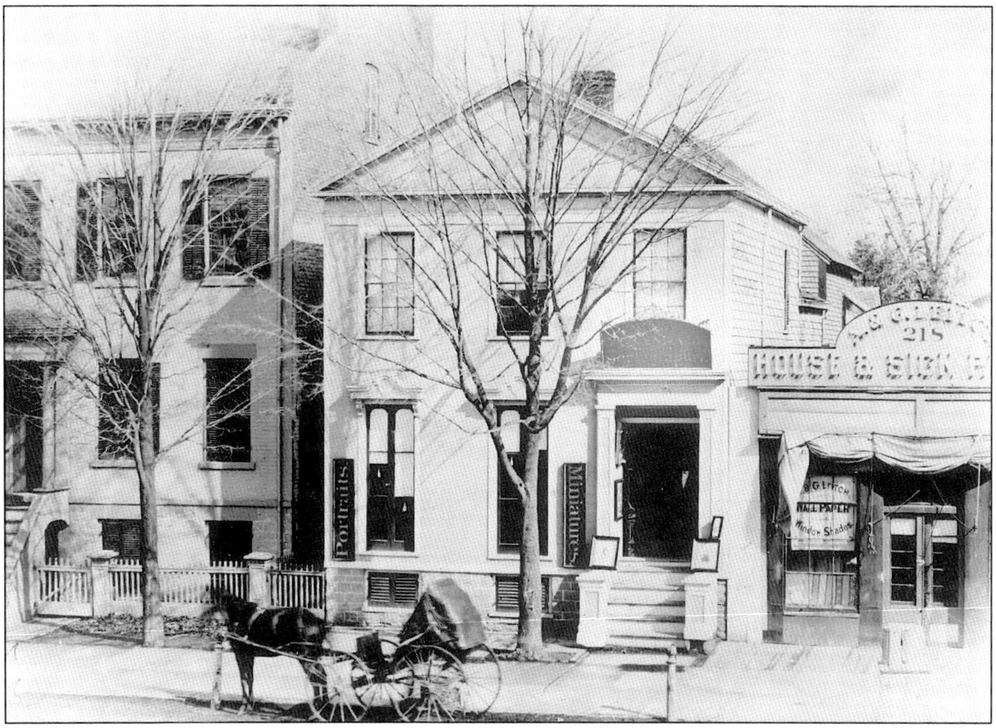

FEMALE PROPRIETORSHIP. Outside of a boarding house or two, not many 19th women were in the business world, let alone business owners. On the east side of Woodward Avenue between John R and Witherell stood Mrs. Richard W. Allen's portrait studio. However, convention dictated that she continue to use her husband's first name.

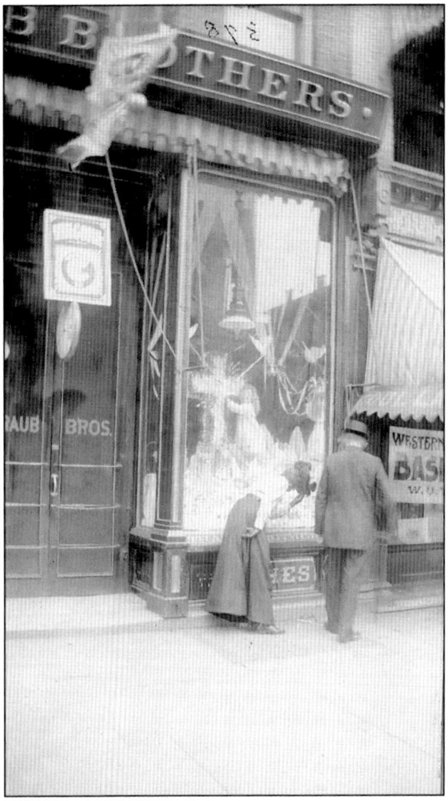

Window Shopper on Woodward Avenue. It must be a Sunday afternoon in Detroit, as these two are just window shopping at the Traub Brothers store on Woodward Avenue. The window display has a religious theme, featuring a crucifix and angelic child as the central piece, surrounded by an elegant silver service.

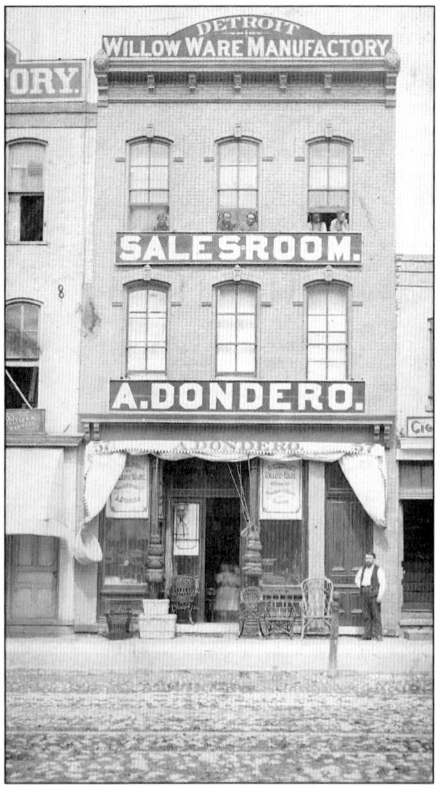

Detroit Willow Ware Manufactory. Mr. A. Dondero established his business in 1867 and it grew until it was lodged in this three-story building on Monroe Street near Randolph. He made and repaired reed and cane rockers, children's chairs, baskets, and similar items, as well as providing a large stock of dry flowers, holly, mistletoe, and reeding evergreens.

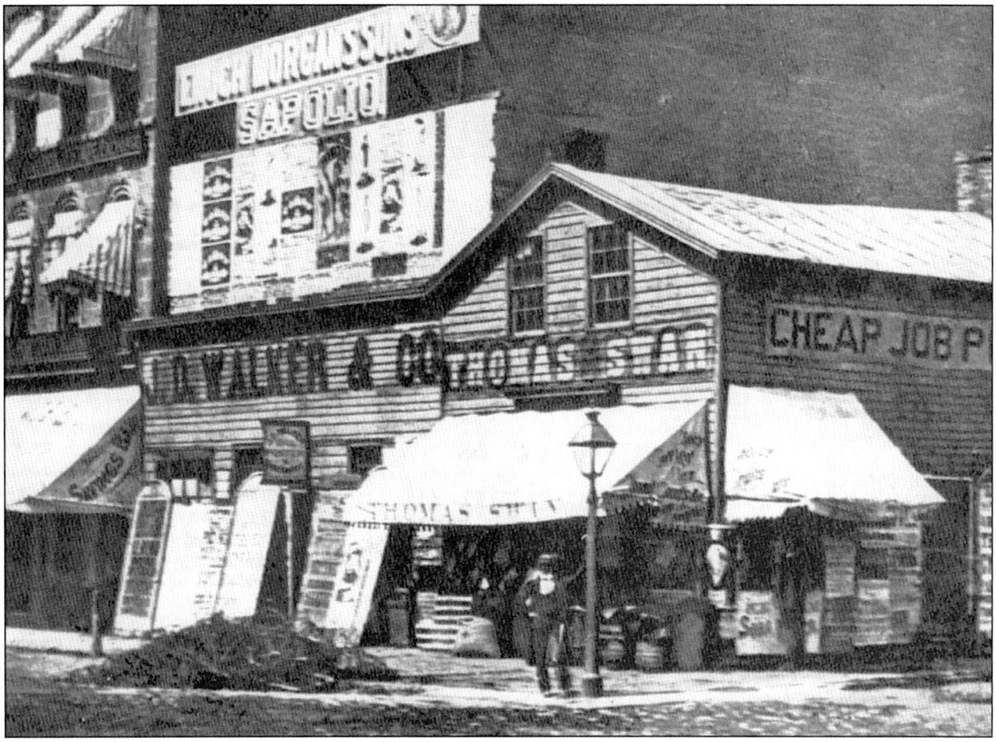

Job Printers. There were a multitude of small businesses located throughout the city of Detroit. One of the more or less well-known was Thomas Swan, who operated a small print shop in this older building on the corner of Griswold and Larned Streets. Swan ran his business from this location for over 20 years.

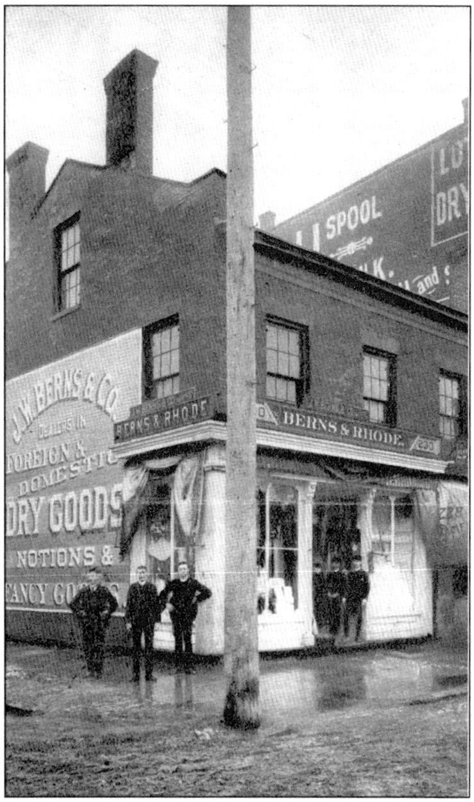

The Corner Store, 1887. The dry goods store of Berns and Rhode at Macomb and Randolph Streets on the east side carried foreign and domestic dry goods, notions, and fancy goods. The sales staff takes time out from this busy day to pose for this photograph some time in the late or early spring of 1887.

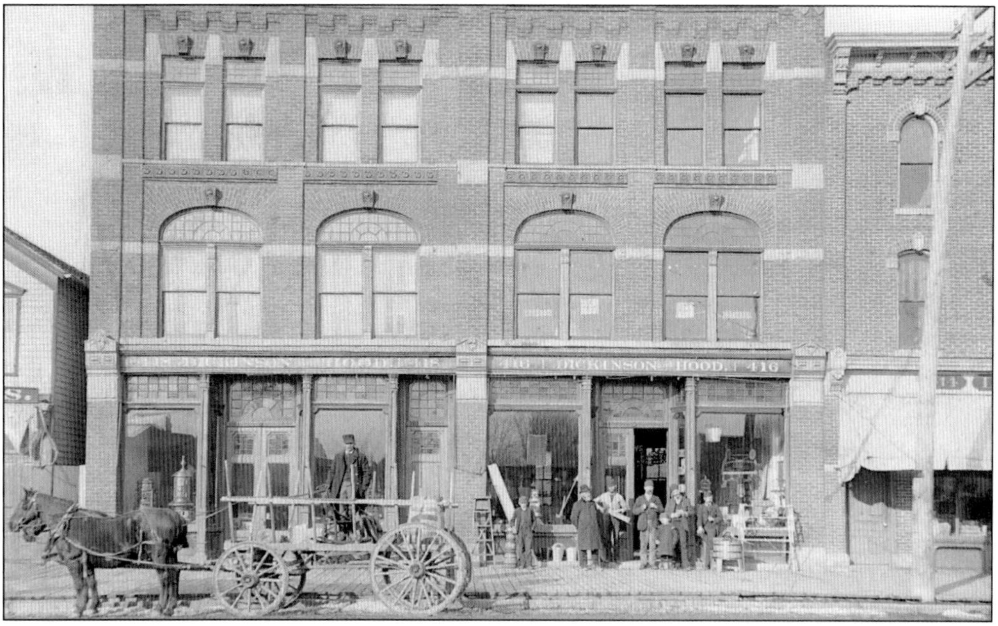

The Dickinson Block. The north side of Grand River Avenue between Sixth and South Streets was the location of the Dickinson and Hood hardware store, owned by Horace Hill, Dickinson, and James C. Hood. They carried a line of shelf and heavy hardware, stoves, ranges, and builders' supplies, as well as tin ware, paints, oils, and varnishes.

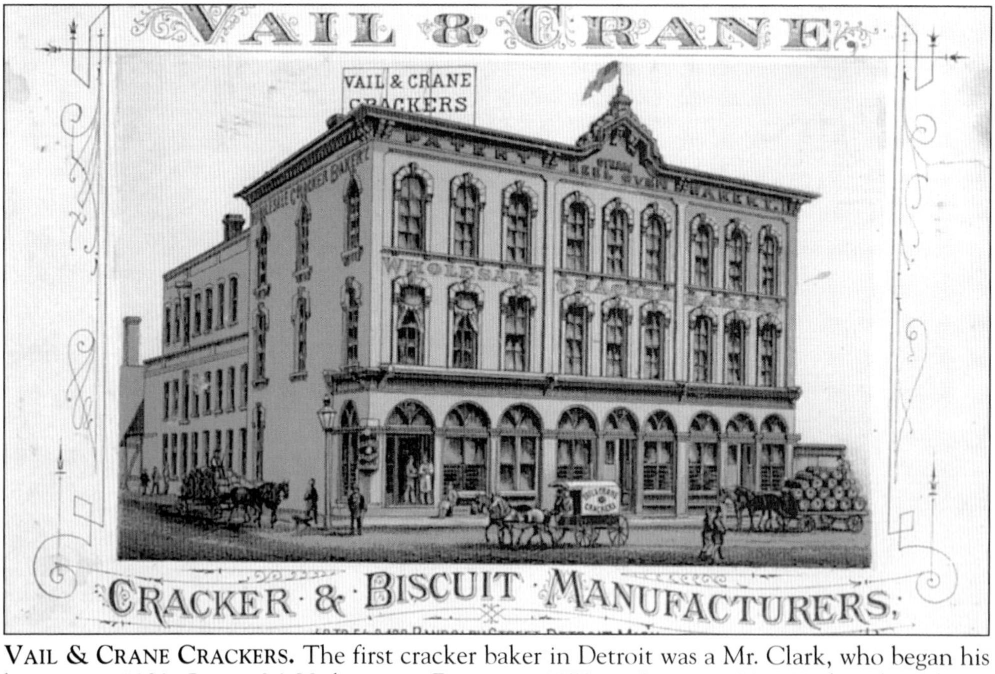

Vail & Crane Crackers. The first cracker baker in Detroit was a Mr. Clark, who began his business in 1830. George M. Vail came to Detroit in 1872 via Syracuse, New York and Ypsilanti, Michigan and started his business with Crane and a man named Curtis on Randolph Street. They moved to the corner of Randolph and Woodbridge in 1876. In May of 1890, the business became a branch of the United States Baking Company.

Good German Bakery. The Wagner Baking Company's first shop on Woodward Avenue near Montcalm Street was started by five Wagner brothers in 1869. John B., Edward, John, Christopher, and Henry, German emigrants, came to Detroit in 1861. They later built a retail store on the future site of the Fox Theater.

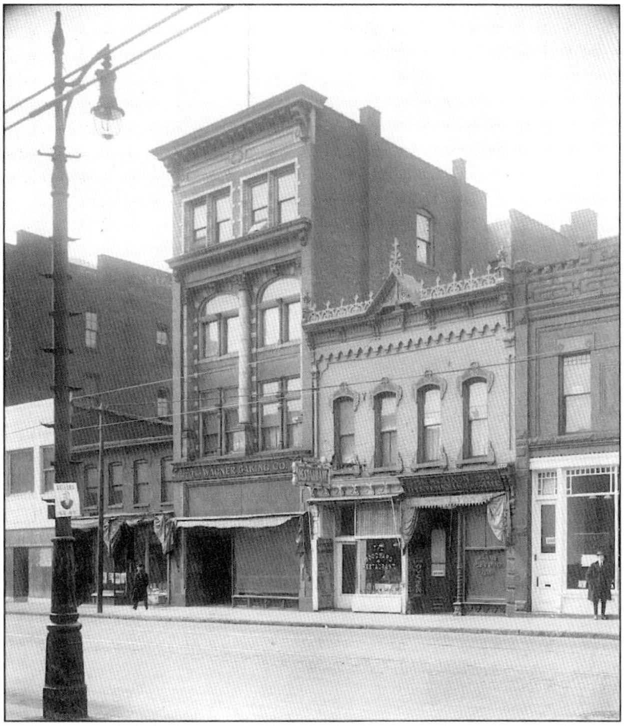

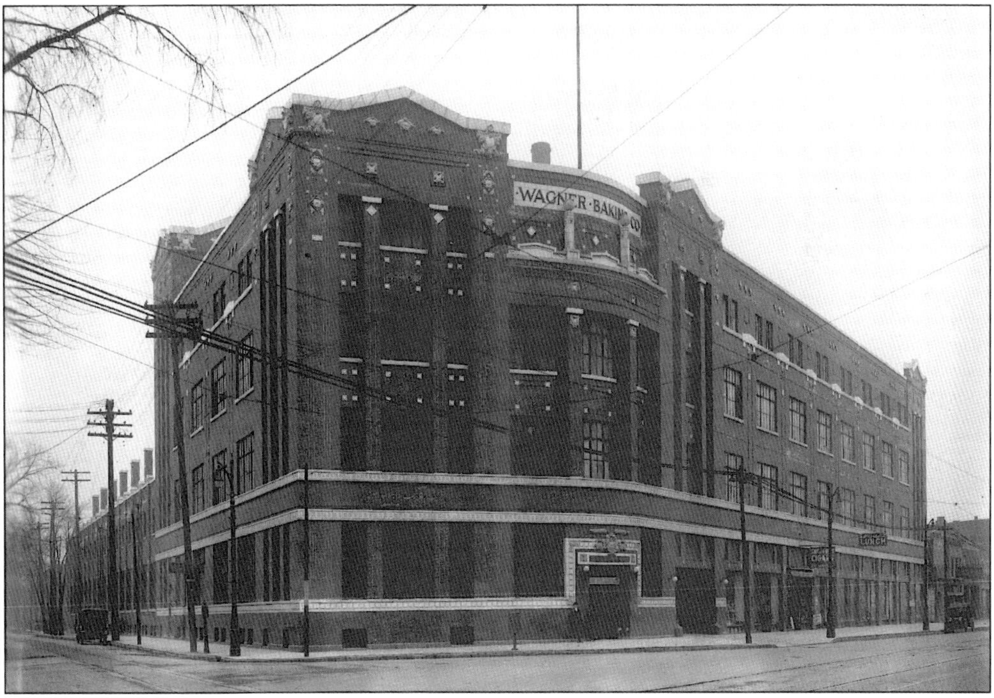

The New Bakery. The Wagner Brothers built a new plant on Grand River Avenue and Hamilton Street, and in 1915, they built what was at that time the largest bakery in the United States at Grand River and Sixth Street. They used a bluebird (for happiness), on their packages of "Eatmor", "Teddy Bear", "Quality", "German-American" and "Columbia Rye" breads.

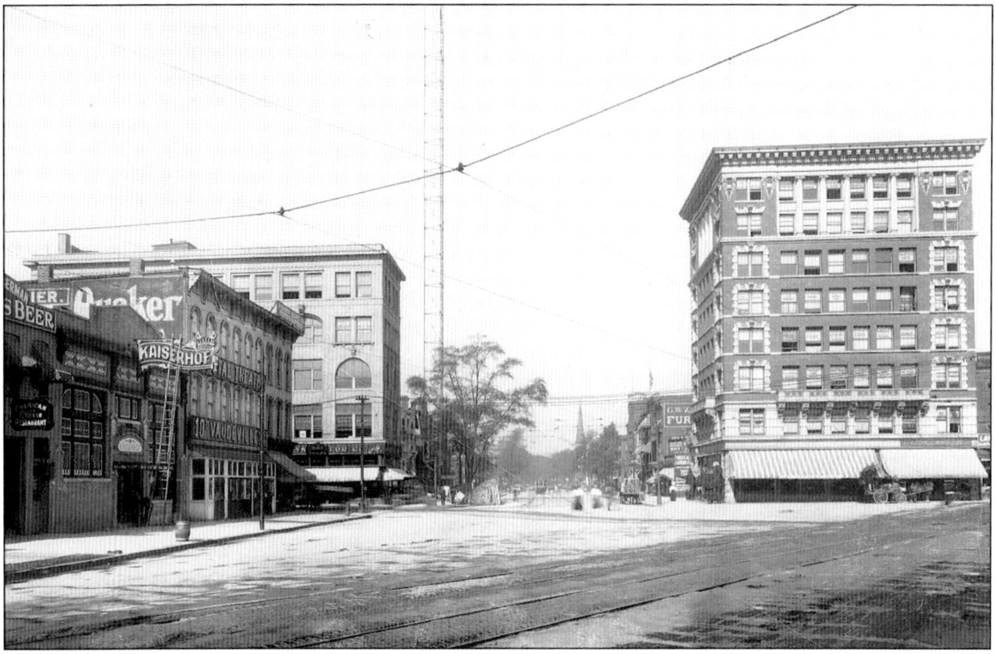

PINGREE SQUARE. The intersection of Broadway, Randolph, Gratiot, and Monroe Streets formed Pingree Square, named after the noted reform Mayor Hazen Pingree, who later on went on to be elected Governor of Michigan. The square held a lot of different businesses, including entertainment in the form of a restaurant and beer garden, and the famous Kaiserhof and the Capital Theater, which offered vaudeville shows.

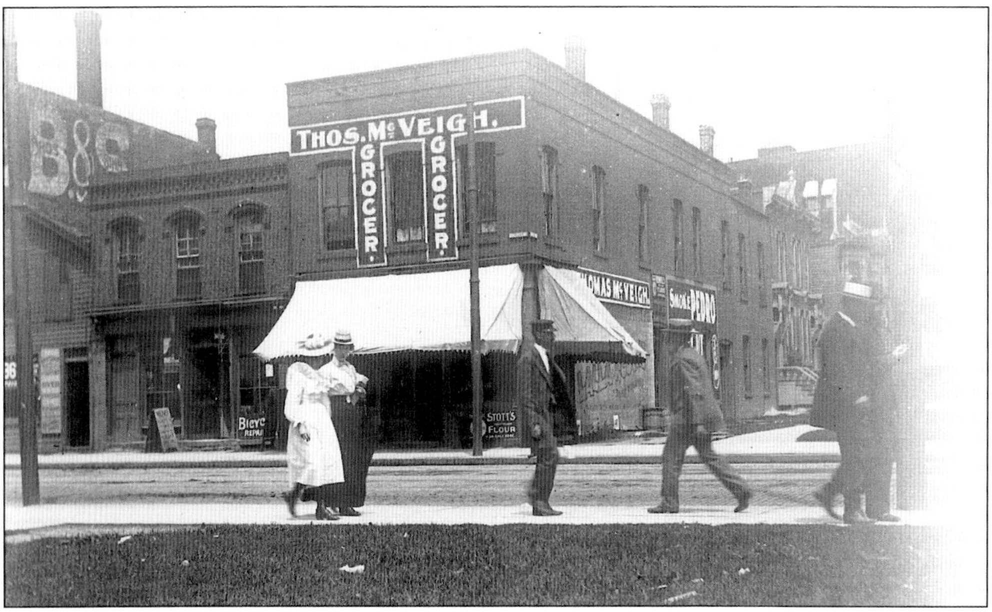

NEIGHBORHOOD GROCER. Detroiters stroll along Grand River Avenue, past the Thomas McVeigh grocery store, in the summer of 1882 . It was a style of corner store that is still very much in evidence today within the city. McVeigh handled just about everything you would find in a local store today.

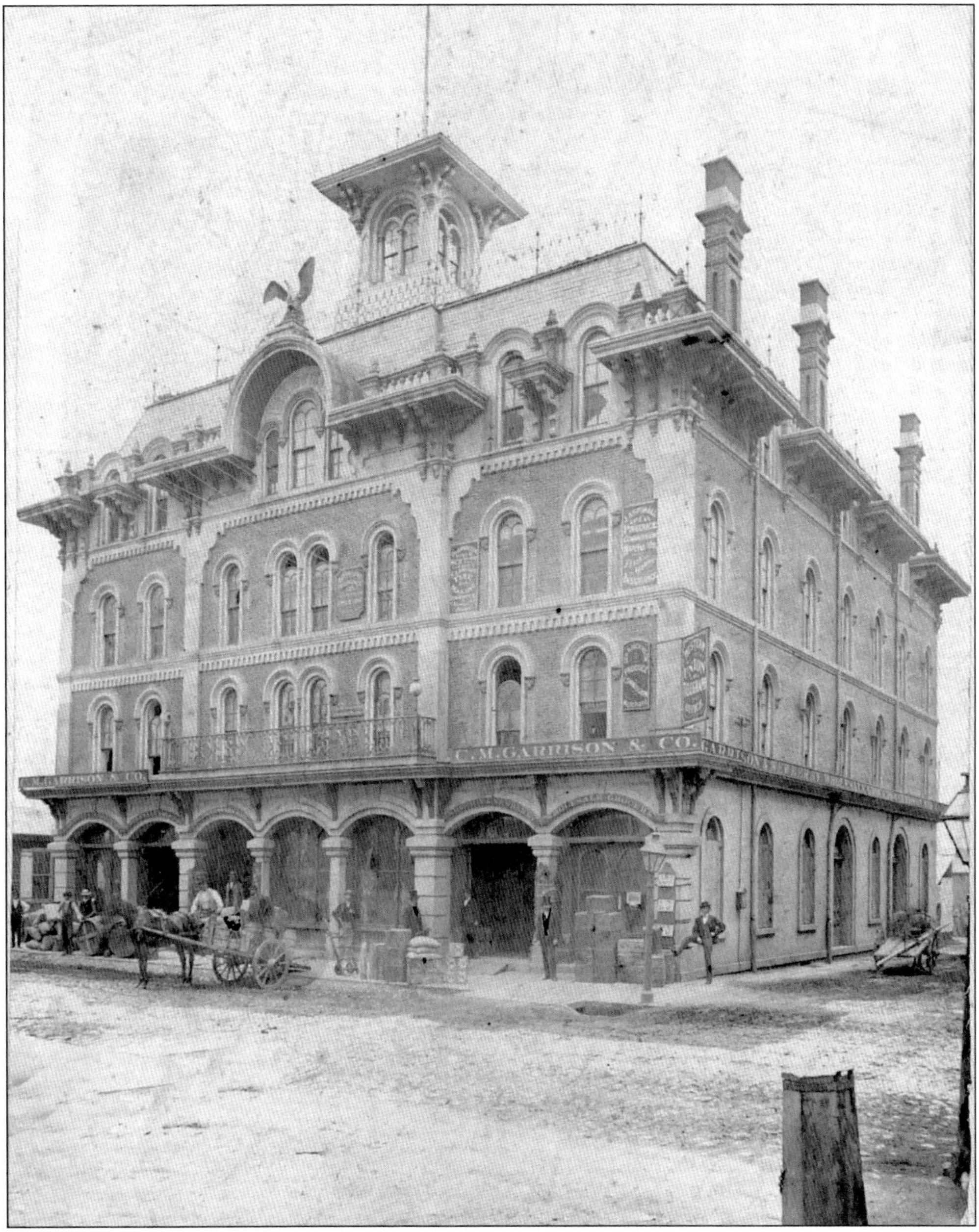

NOT YOUR MOM AND POP STORE. On three city lots on Woodbridge Street stood the C.M. Garrison and Company wholesale grocery store. This beautiful advertising piece from the 1880s-1890s, shows a magnificent four-story building with an observation tower complete with a flagpole on top. This building was also known as the Board of Trade Building. The Board of Trade was organized in 1856 and used this building until 1873, when they moved to separate quarters at Jefferson Avenue and Griswold Street. The Board of Trade promoted the interests of trade in Detroit and was empowered to settle business disputes between members, or others, by arbitration. Its decisions had the same power and effect as a judgement of the Circuit Court. The upper floors of this building were let out to various businesses as offices. A number of commission merchants and insurance companies maintained offices here.

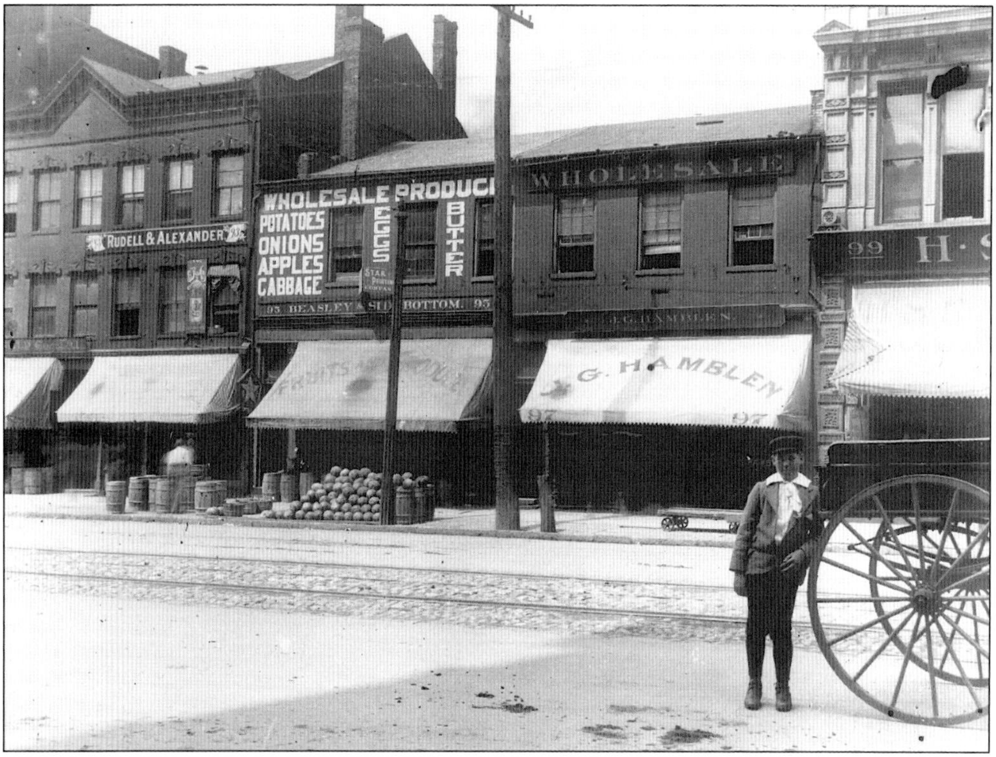

JEFFERSON AVENUE, CIRCA 1890S. A number of wholesale shops line the south side of Jefferson, while one of the neighborhood kids finds an opportunity to have his picture taken. The Beasley and Bottom wholesale produce sellers were located at 95 Jefferson Avenue and dealt in fruit as well as produce and dairy. What looks like a large assortment of pumpkins in front would date this photograph to the fall season.

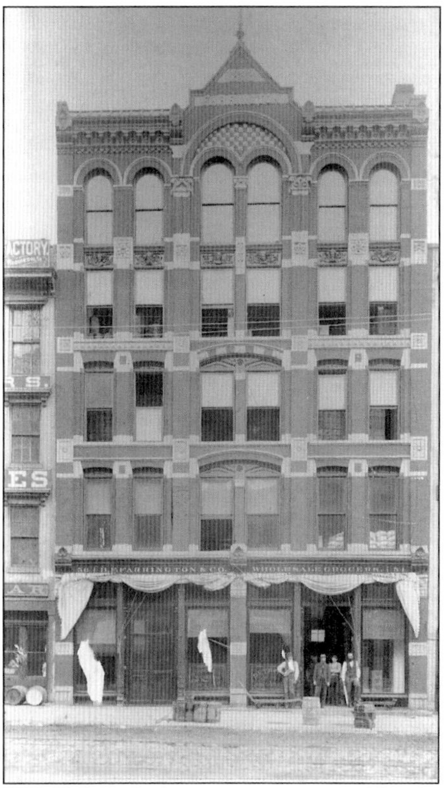

THE FARRINGTON BUILDING. Further down Jefferson Avenue, at 54 and 56, respectively, is another wholesale grocer, this one owned by B.F. Farrington, who also owned the building. This structure had open floors used to store goods in quantity, as opposed to rentable office space on the upper four floors.

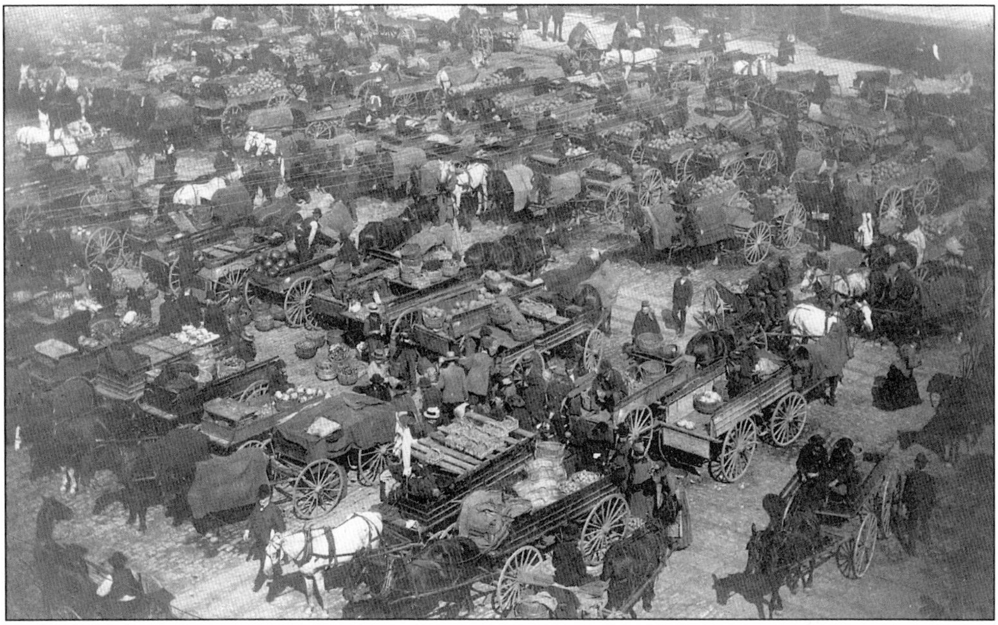

Open Air Market. Market day in Detroit brought farmers from practically everywhere in Michigan to a central location in the city to market their fresh produce. At the top of the photograph is a sidewalk with buildings, but it is almost impossible to locate this photograph. This may be on the west side of the city.

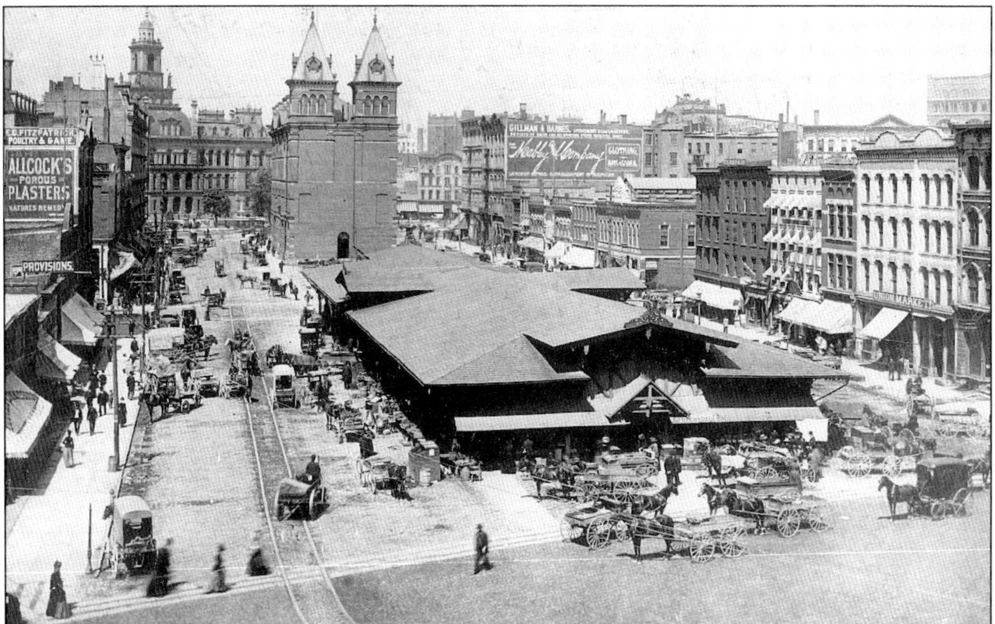

Central Market, 1885. More readily available for use and visited by a lot more potential customers, Central Market was a very busy place in Cadillac Square. This is a scene looking west from behind the open stall area toward the old City Hall. The twin-spired building in front of City Hall is the Central Market Building, where shopkeepers had permanent space on the ground floors.

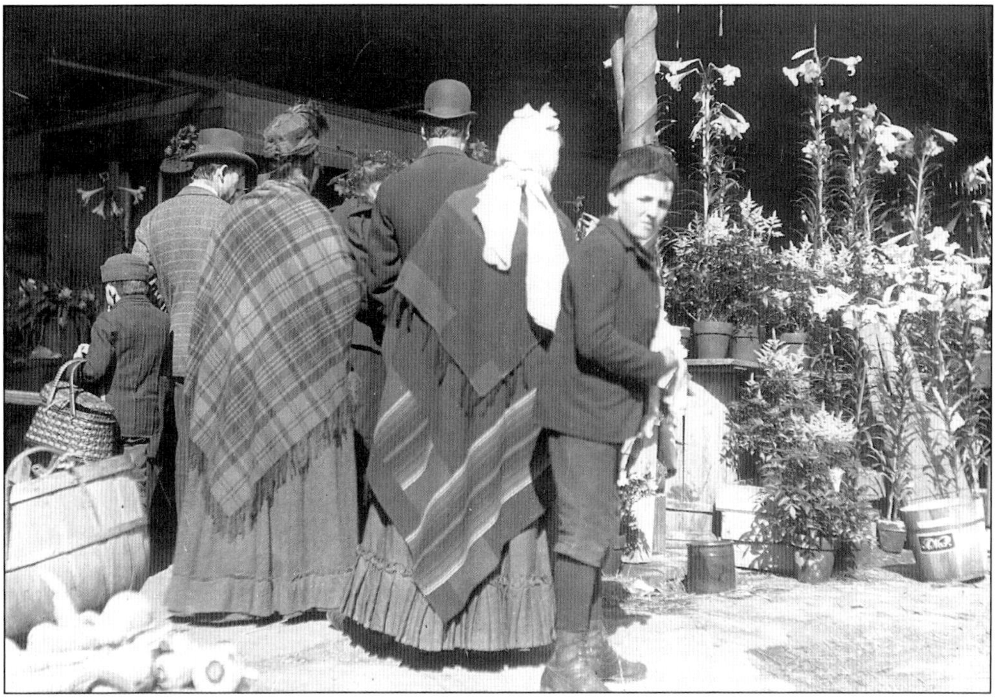

MARKET SHOPPERS, 1890. Detroit families are out in force visiting the flower stalls of Central Market. The market offered services for hire as well as perishables. One could hire the services of any of the more skilled trades, such as painters, plumbers, whitewashers, or builders. Judging from the Easter lilies and heavily dressed shoppers, this is an early Spring photograph.

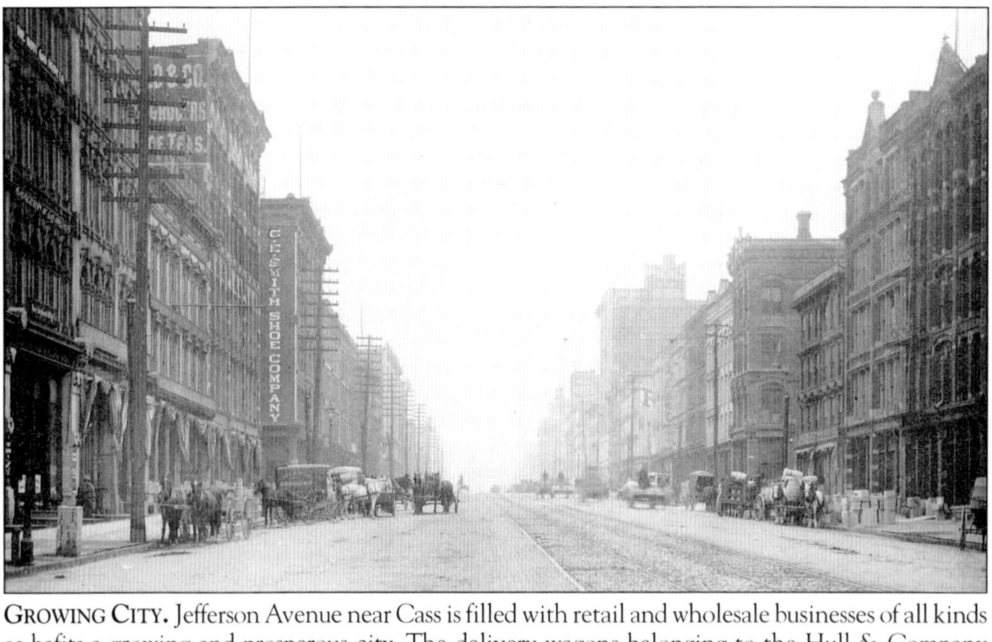

GROWING CITY. Jefferson Avenue near Cass is filled with retail and wholesale businesses of all kinds as befits a growing and prosperous city. The delivery wagons belonging to the Hull & Company grocers are in the street on the left. The C.E. Smith Shoe Company sits across the street from the Pingree & Smith Shoe Company, which was next to another boot and shoe manufacturer.

Four

COTTAGE INDUSTRIES

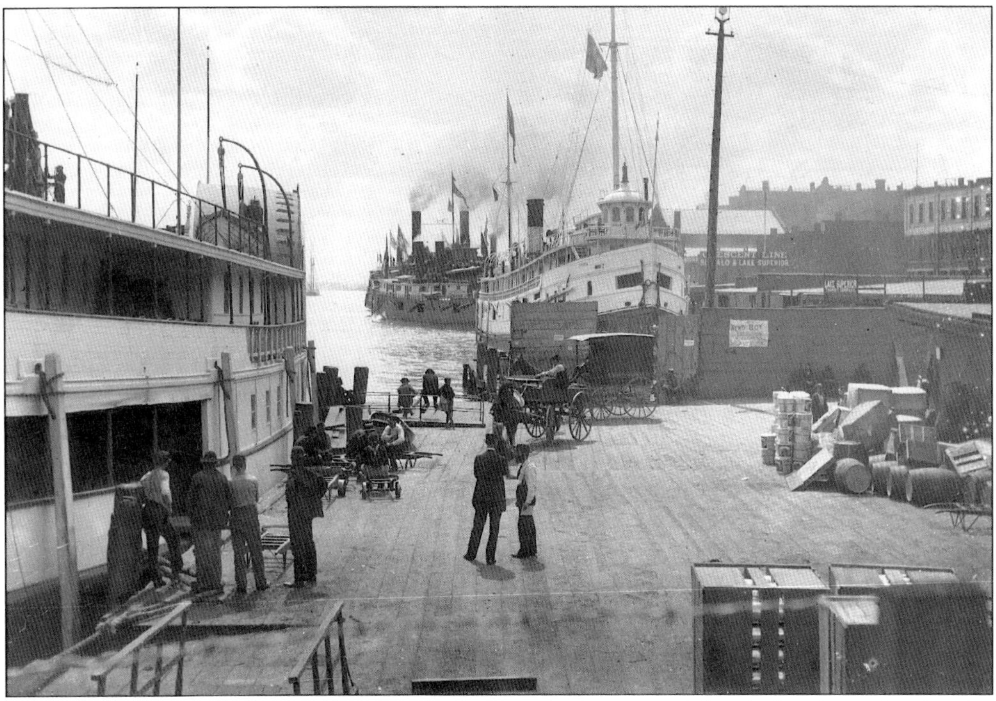

THE HEART OF THE GREAT LAKES. This scene of a portion of the docks along the Detroit River shows a gang of stevedores waiting to offload a steamer just arriving from the east. There are several other vessels tied up in the background; the first one is at the Lake Superior Transit Company dock.

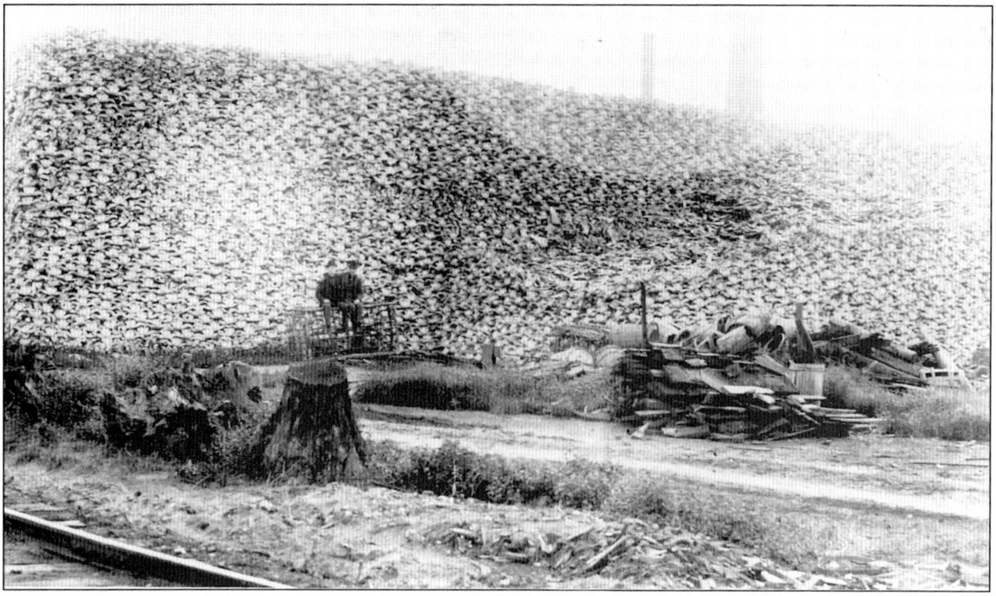

THE MICHIGAN CARBON WORKS. A pile of buffalo bones big enough to form a ridge line lays on the grounds of the Michigan Carbon Works located at the city limits near the Rouge River. Established by Deming Jarves in 1873, this company manufactured chemical manures, animal charcoal, ivory black, glue, gelatine, ammonia, lime, and various acids from the bones.

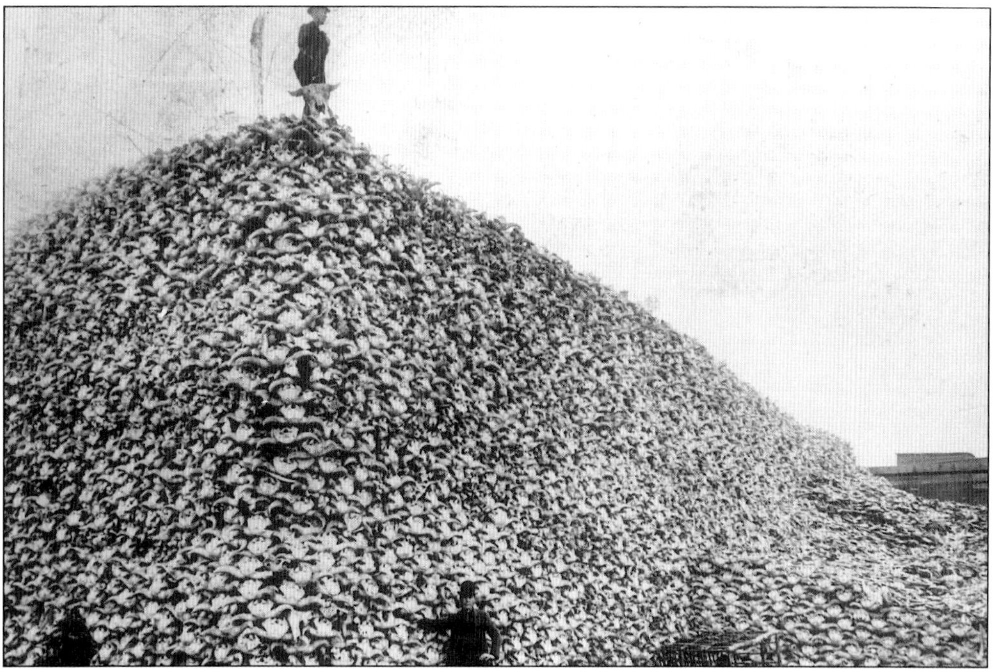

A MOUNTAIN OF BONES. The yard of the Michigan Carbon Works contains a mountain of buffalo bones. Seven hundred and fifty employees worked to convert the bones into useful products. The principle brand of fertilizer was "Homestead" and the company's output of it amounted to 20,000 tons a year. The company issued a newspaper, titled *Homestead*, which had a circulation of 100,000.

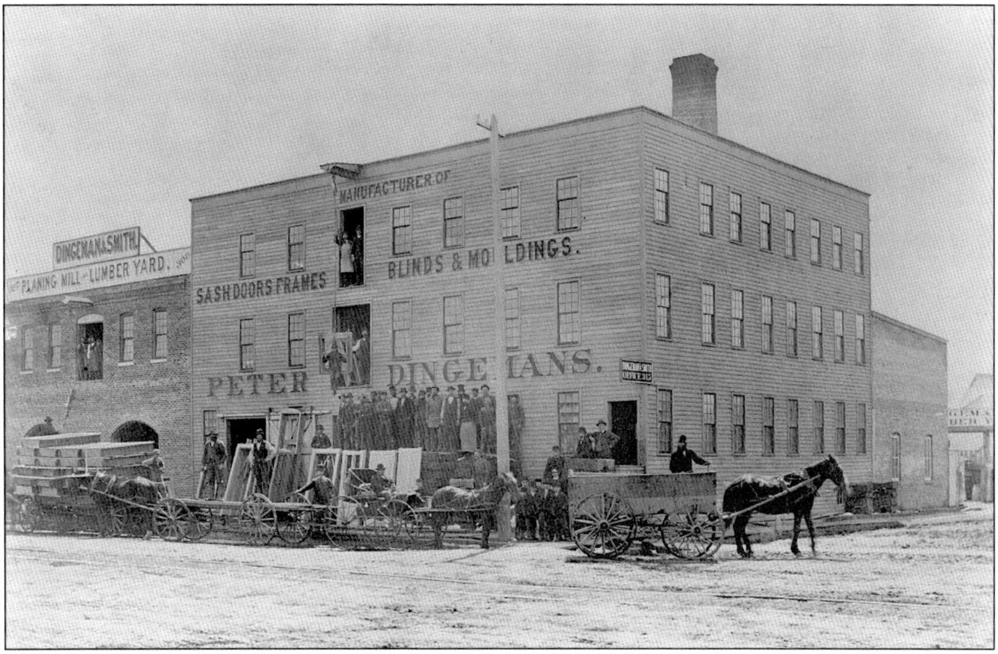

WOOD WORKERS. The entire work force of the Peter Dingeman Lumber Yard pose for a group photograph in front of their factory at Pine Street and Grand River Avenue. They manufactured blinds, mouldings, sash doors, and frames, while next door Dingemann had an interest with a partner named Smith in a planing mill.

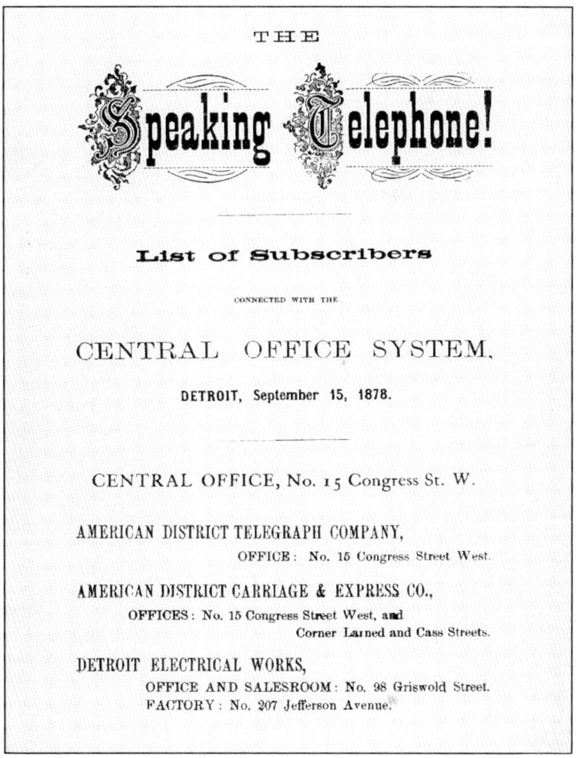

THE

Speaking Telephone!

List of Subscribers

CONNECTED WITH THE

CENTRAL OFFICE SYSTEM.

DETROIT, September 15, 1878.

CENTRAL OFFICE, No. 15 Congress St. W.

AMERICAN DISTRICT TELEGRAPH COMPANY,
OFFICE: No. 15 Congress Street West.

AMERICAN DISTRICT CARRIAGE & EXPRESS CO.,
OFFICES: No. 15 Congress Street West, and
Corner Larned and Cass Streets.

DETROIT ELECTRICAL WORKS,
OFFICE AND SALESROOM: No. 98 Griswold Street.
FACTORY: No. 207 Jefferson Avenue.

SPEAKING TELEPHONES! An advertisement from the Detroit city directory lists the places that one can subscribe to the speaking telephone. Alexander Graham Bell invented the apparatus in 1876, and the first telephone in Detroit was installed in Frederick Stearns drug store. By 1878 there would be almost one hundred subscribers on the Central Office System.

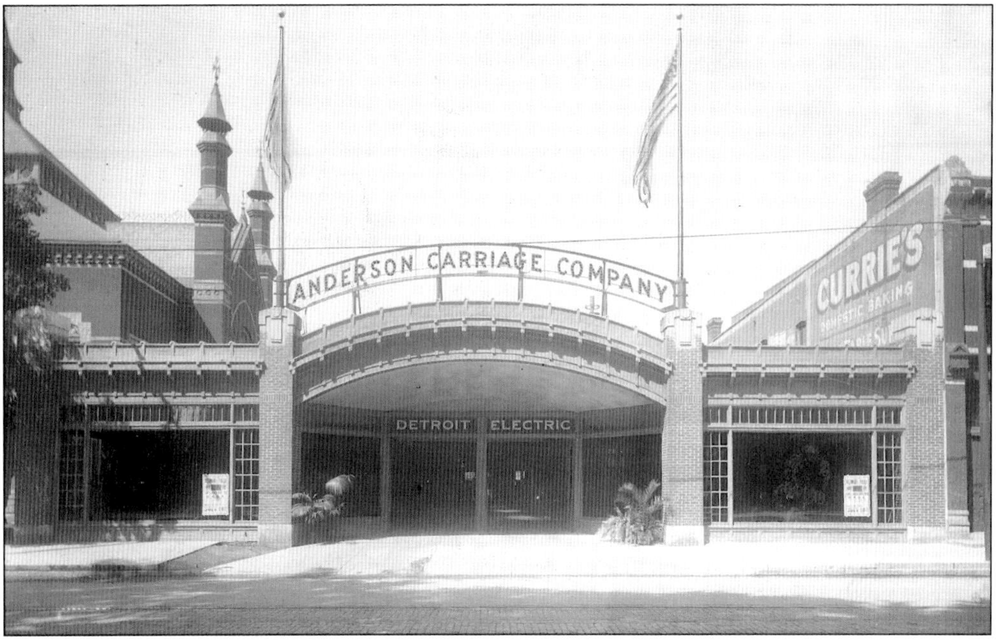

ANDERSON CARRIAGE COMPANY. Originally established in Port Huron, Michigan, the Anderson Carriage Company moved to Detroit in 1895 to this location at the corner of Clay and Riopelle Streets. Makers of fine carriages and ordinary work wagons, this turn of the century photograph shows the complex decorated with the sign "Detroit Electric," an easy transition to manufacturing an early electric car.

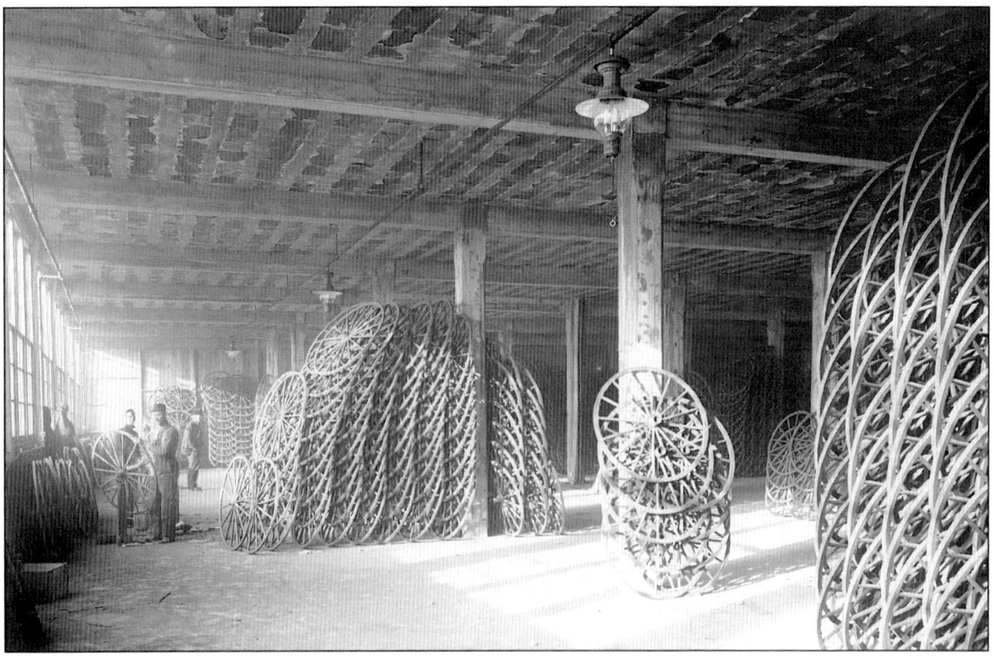

IN THE WHEEL HOUSE. The interior of this section of the Anderson Carriage Company houses the wheel-making component of the business. Thousands of carriage wheels are also stored here, very nicely stacked, waiting to be attached to the bodies of the vehicles.

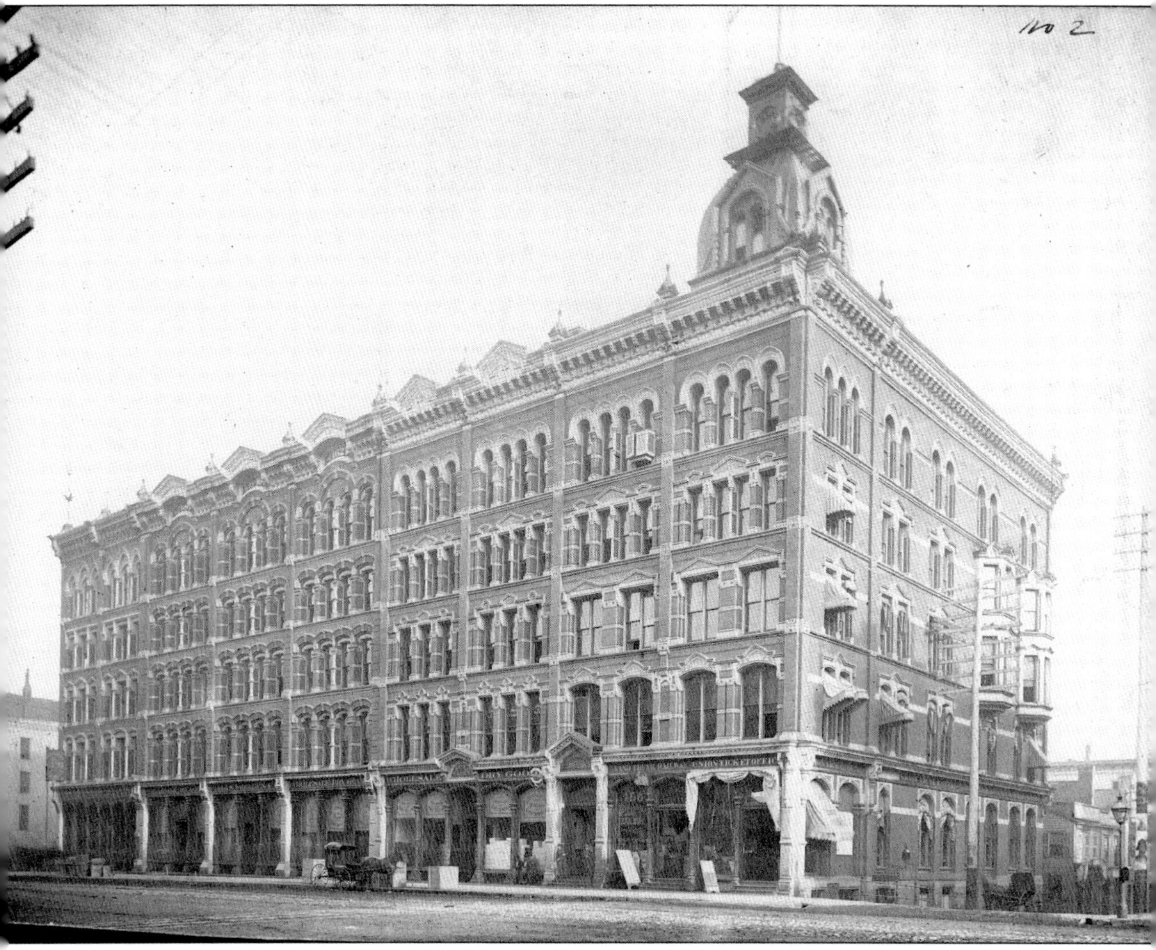

THE NEW BOARD OF TRADE BUILDING. The Board of Trade moved into the top floor of this new building from their old location on Woodbridge Street in about 1881. As Detroit was a grain-shipping and receiving port, it was through this Board that sales and purchases were made. This building also housed the United States Weather Bureau Office, whose observation tower is shown on the roof. Observations and measurements of weather were taken from there. Ground floor stores and the upper floors of the building were leased by such companies as the wholesale dry goods houses of Allan Shelden and Company and the Henry A. Newland and Company, at least one wholesale hatter and others, who came and went depending on the success of their business. The five-story building was located on the southeast corner of Jefferson Avenue and Griswold Street.

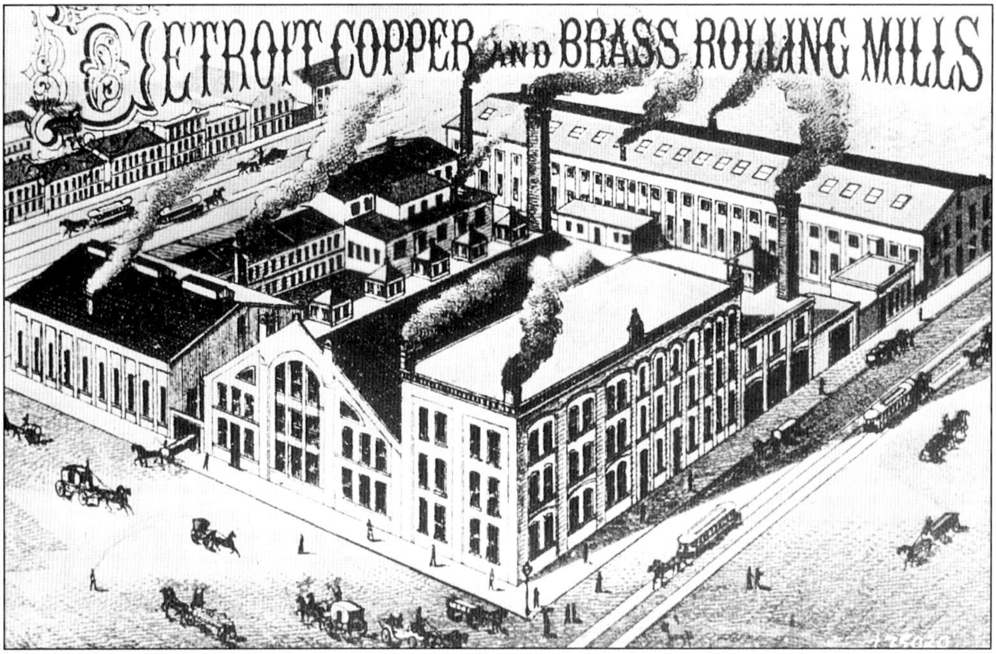

THE ROLLING MILLS OF THE DETROIT COPPER AND BRASS COMPANY Detroit Copper and Brass Company occupied the entire block of Fourth and Larned. Organized in 1880, Detroit Copper began business in June of 1881, with a capital of $100,000. The sum was found to be too small and was raised to $200,000, and then to $300,000, within one year, due to the demands of the business.

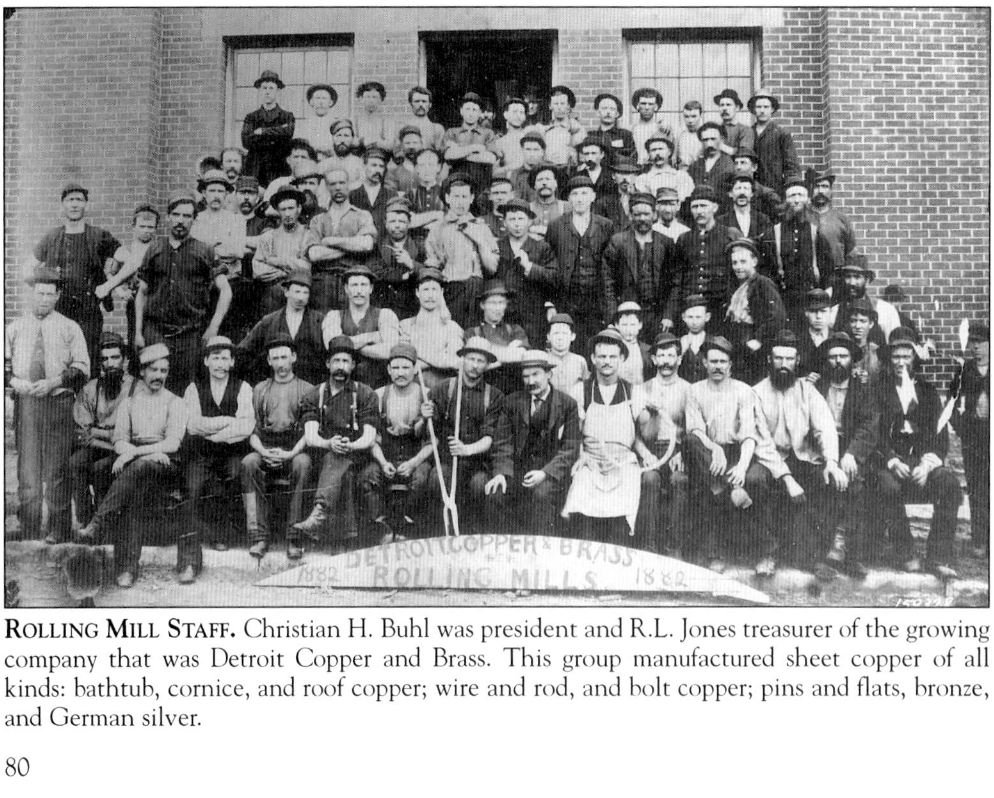

ROLLING MILL STAFF. Christian H. Buhl was president and R.L. Jones treasurer of the growing company that was Detroit Copper and Brass. This group manufactured sheet copper of all kinds: bathtub, cornice, and roof copper; wire and rod, and bolt copper; pins and flats, bronze, and German silver.

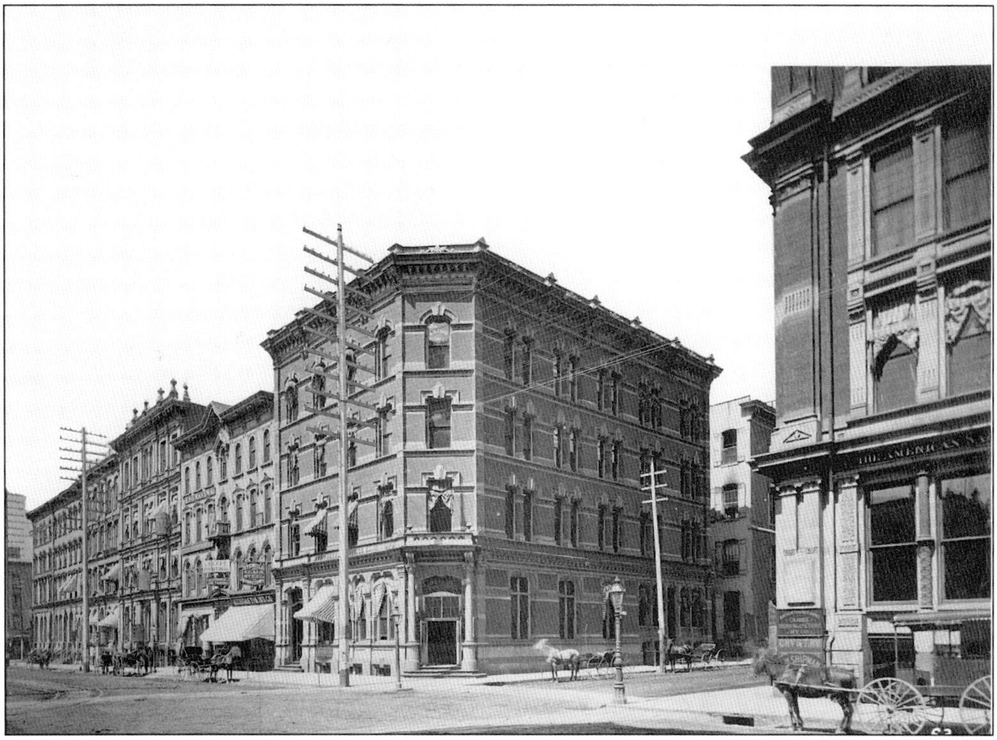

GRISWOLD AND LARNED STREETS, 1881. Among the eight national banks, ten State banks and nine substantial private banking firms in Detroit was the Detroit Savings Bank, one of the State firms located on this corner. It was gratifying that during this period of economic success, all of Detroit's banks prospered.

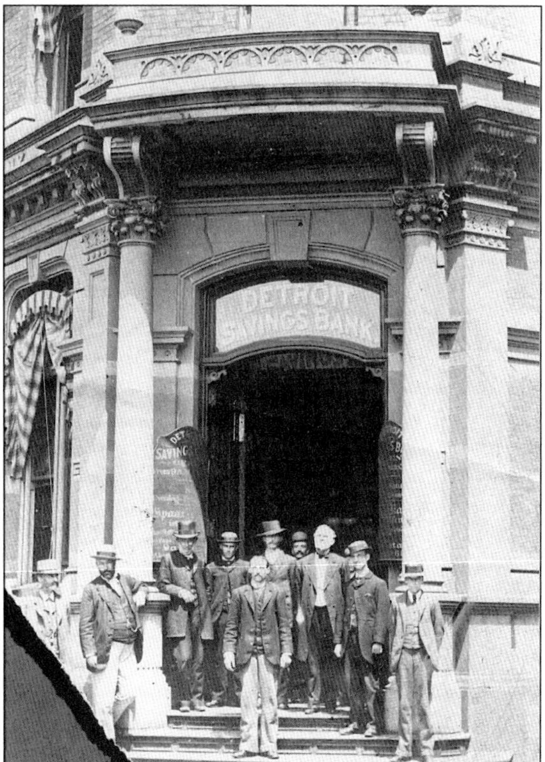

DETROIT SAVINGS BANK STAFF. One of the most prominent and successful of the city's banks, the Detroit Savings Bank was originally organized in 1849 as the Detroit Savings Fund Institute. At the expiration of its original charter in 1871, the name was changed. Its Board of Directors featured some of the city's most successful businessmen.

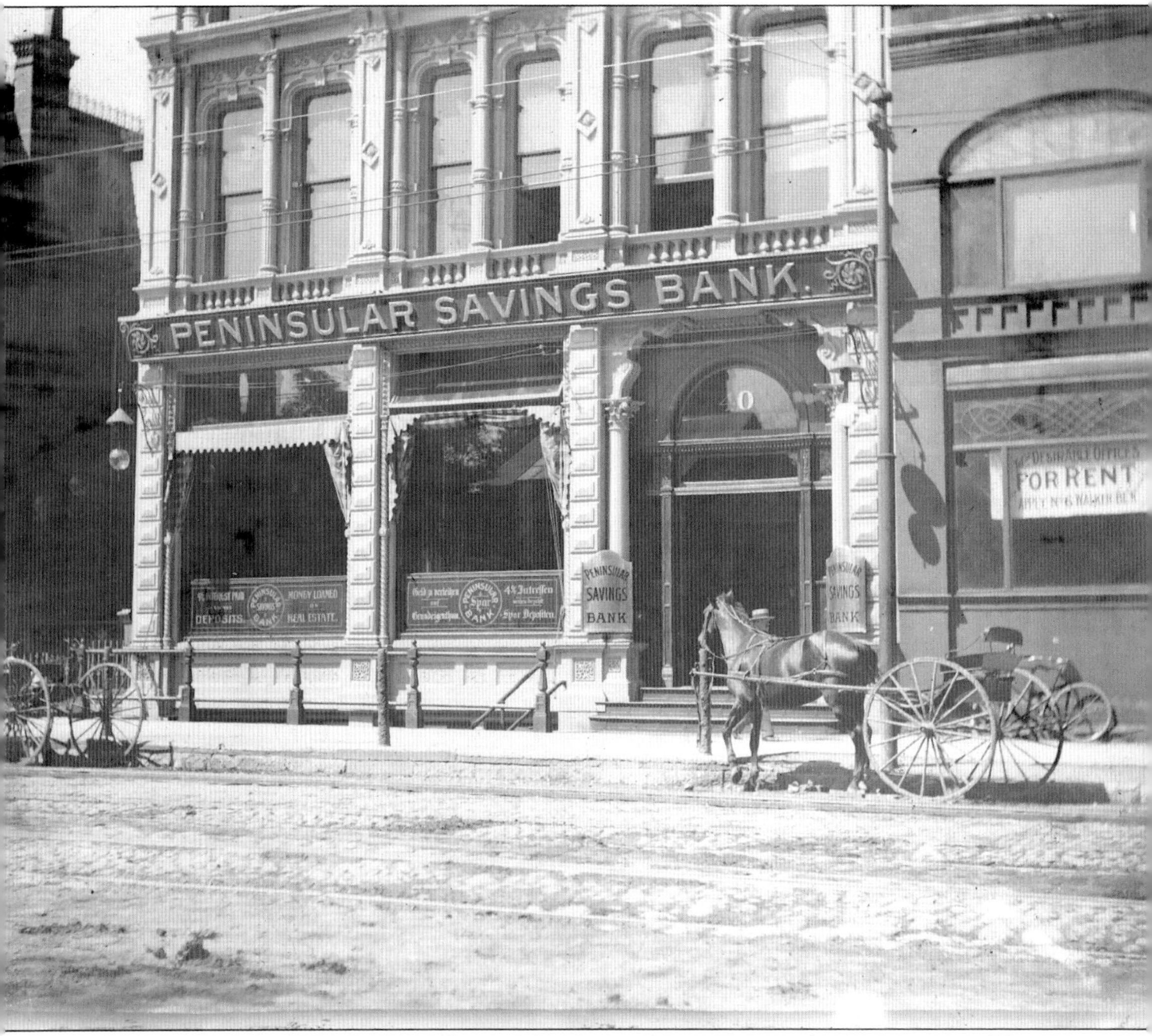

FOLLOW THE MONEY. The first offices of the Peninsular Savings Bank were on Griswold Street, which first opened for business on September 15, 1887, the same year that it was organized. Peninsular Savings transacted a commercial and savings business, paying four percent interest on savings deposits. By 1891, the firm was so successful that they bought the C.J. Whitney and Company's Building on West Fort Street for $100,000. After being entirely remodeled and refitted, the building would be known as the Peninsular Bank Building. Part of it was reserved for professional offices. It then had a capital of $350,000, with deposits of $1,250,000 and undivided profits and surplus of $41,000, even though it paid 21 percent in cash dividends. Sound and progressive practices made Peninsular Savings a good bank to deposit in and a better bank to invest in.

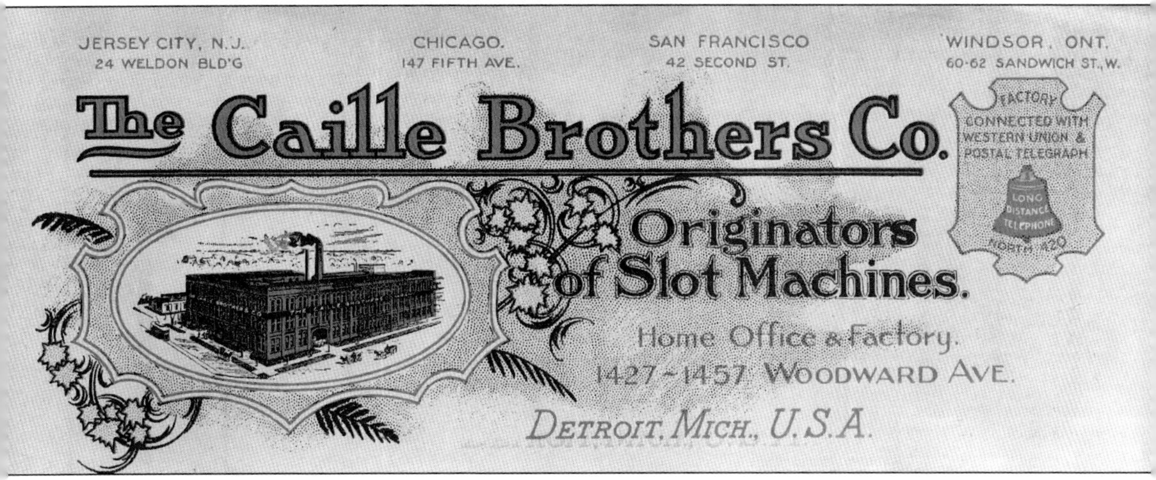

HOME OF THE SLOT MACHINE. Mr. Arthur Caille, the originator of the coin-operated machine, better known at the time as the slot machine, set up the only factory on Woodward Avenue in 1891. He ran the company with his brother, and it became the largest manufactory of its kind in the United States, employing 300 men and turning out over 100 machines per week. By 1901, the company had offices in New Jersey, Illinois, California, and Canada, and began to move into the European market through a distribution center in Paris. The machines were reported to be works of art; the music boxes were made in Switzerland and the cabinets for the machines were made in Saginaw, Michigan. If Mr. Caille was not the originator of these gambling devices, he is at least the creator of a more synchronized and intricate device.

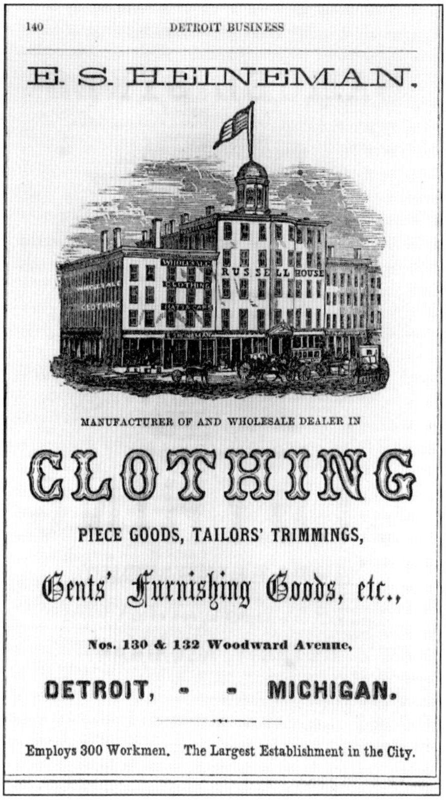

NEXT TO THE RUSSELL HOUSE. One of the city's oldest establishments as a clothing manufacturer and wholesale dealer was the E.S. Heineman Clothing Store, located at Woodward Avenue and the Campus Martius. Its location, right next door to one of the city's best hotels, was perfect, as a gentleman in need of a tailor did not have to go far. They claimed to be the largest in the city, employing 300 workmen.

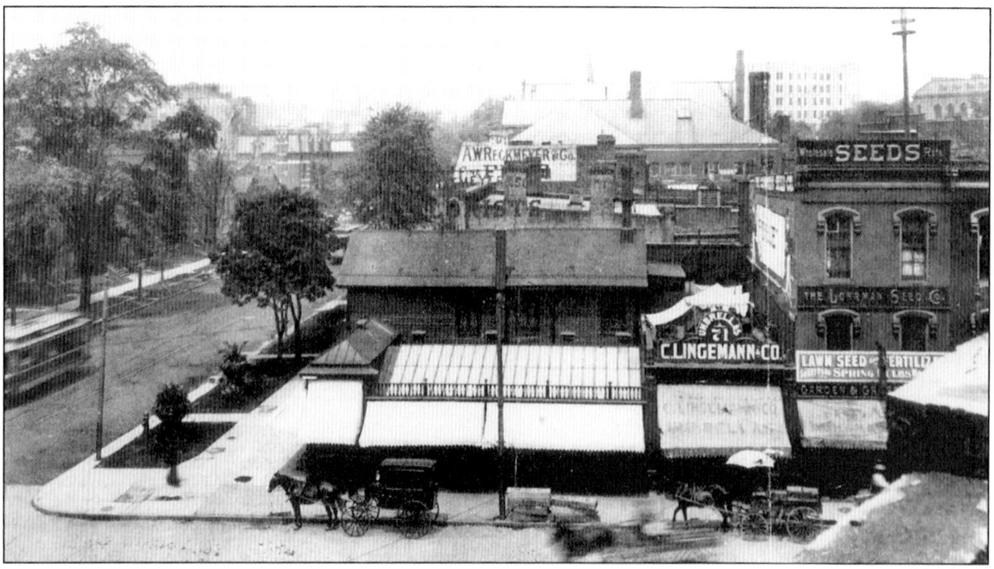

OLD BROADWAY AND GRATIOT. This photograph of a portion of Broadway and Gratiot reveals a mix of different businesses not necessarily related to one another. On the corner is a florist followed by an umbrella company followed by the Longman Seed Company. Perhaps the only thing they would have in common is rain.

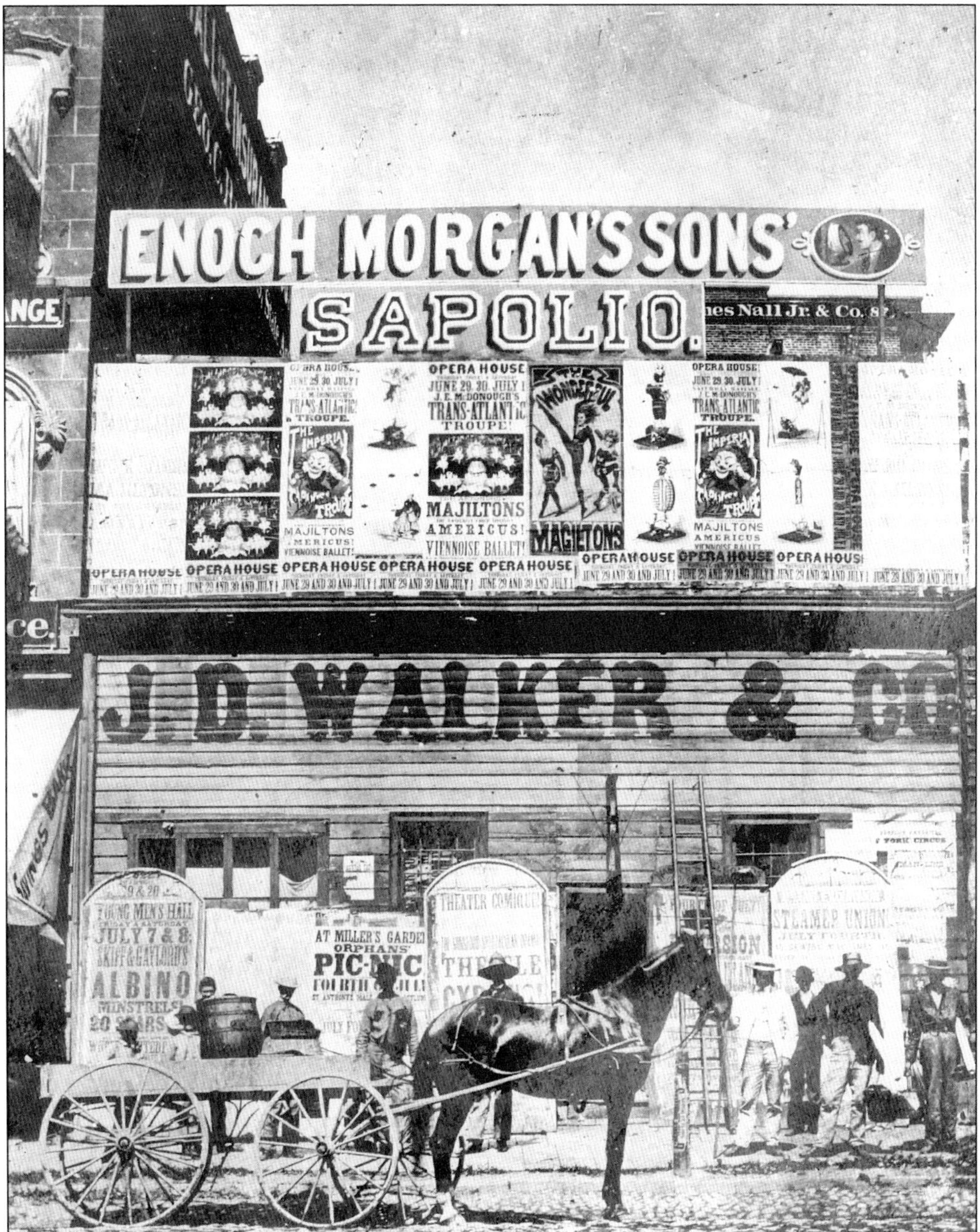

A Signal Beginning. The very first building of Walker and Company at Griswold and Larned Streets is covered with the firm's products: signs. Brothers Henry W. and John D. Walker operated the town's first outdoor advertising service. They started out as bill posters, gluing the circulars to wooden fences throughout the city. The circus, the theater, and patent medicine companies were the principle users of this advertising medium. Thus began the evolution of the billboard and other outdoor advertising mediums. Walker and Company quickly grew from a marginal two-man operation to a firmly established local enterprise. Henry Walker established the firm in 1885 and headed it for the next 26 years until his death in 1911. Growth was steady and the concern was incorporated in 1907.

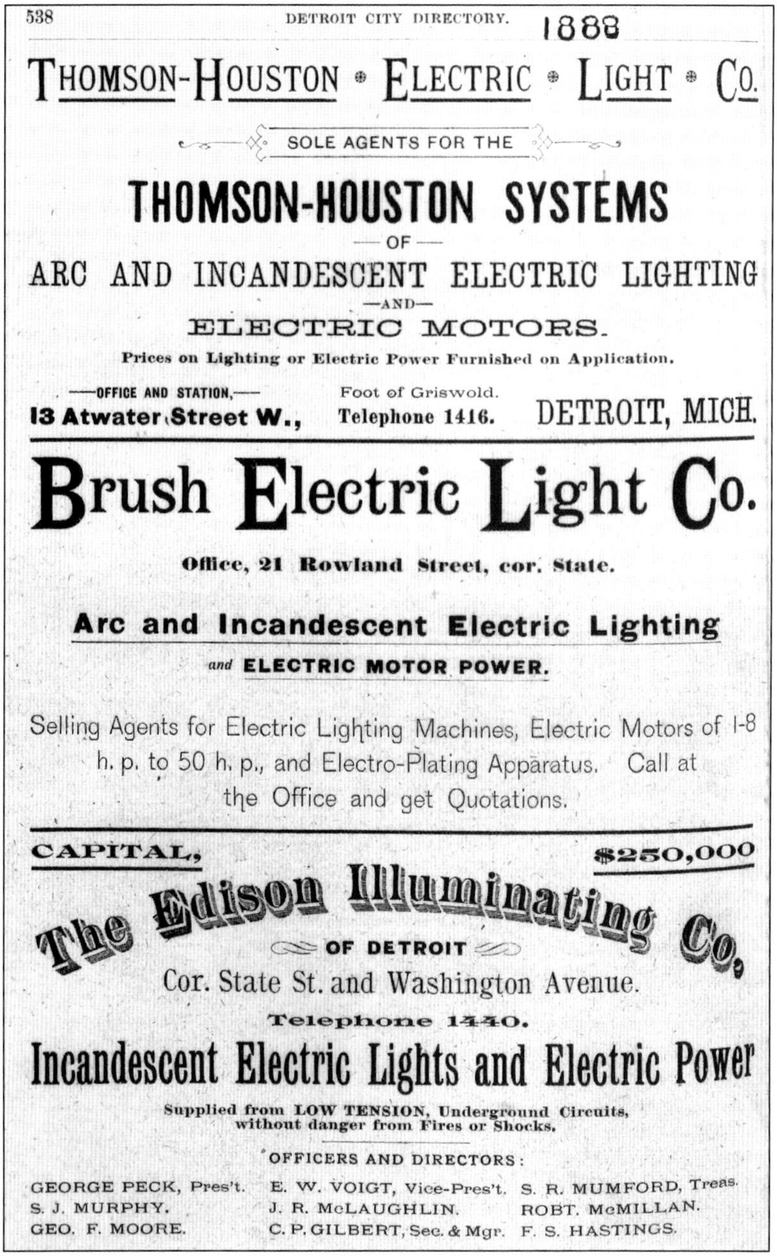

538 DETROIT CITY DIRECTORY. 1888

THOMSON-HOUSTON ELECTRIC LIGHT CO.

SOLE AGENTS FOR THE

THOMSON-HOUSTON SYSTEMS

— OF —

ARC AND INCANDESCENT ELECTRIC LIGHTING

—AND—

ELECTRIC MOTORS.

Prices on Lighting or Electric Power Furnished on Application.

—OFFICE AND STATION,—
13 Atwater Street W., Foot of Griswold. Telephone 1416. DETROIT, MICH.

Brush Electric Light Co.

Office, 21 Rowland Street, cor. State.

Arc and Incandescent Electric Lighting

and ELECTRIC MOTOR POWER.

Selling Agents for Electric Lighting Machines, Electric Motors of 1-8 h. p. to 50 h. p., and Electro-Plating Apparatus. Call at the Office and get Quotations.

CAPITAL, $250,000

The Edison Illuminating Co,

OF DETROIT

Cor. State St. and Washington Avenue.

Telephone 1440.

Incandescent Electric Lights and Electric Power

Supplied from LOW TENSION, Underground Circuits, without danger from Fires or Shocks.

OFFICERS AND DIRECTORS:

GEORGE PECK, Pres't.	E. W. VOIGT, Vice-Pres't.	S. R. MUMFORD, Treas.
S. J. MURPHY.	J. R. McLAUGHLIN.	ROBT. McMILLAN.
GEO. F. MOORE.	C. P. GILBERT, Sec. & Mgr.	F. S. HASTINGS.

LET THERE BE LIGHT. A page out of the 1888 Detroit city directory shows advertising for three major electric light businesses in Detroit. The Thomson-Houston Electric Light Company was organized in March, 1886, with J.L. Hudson as president. Their power station was located on Atwater at the foot of Griswold Street, where they sold their light and power with the generating help of two engines and seven dynamos. Detroit was arguably the most prominent city in the country as an electrical works center and was touted by city fathers as the birthplace of the storage battery. Beginning in 1883, electric companies were established continuously in Detroit. One of the oldest was the Brush Electric Light Company, which was a prominent player in the power game. Of course, another successful electric company was the Edison Illuminating Company, whose descendent is the Detroit Edison Company.

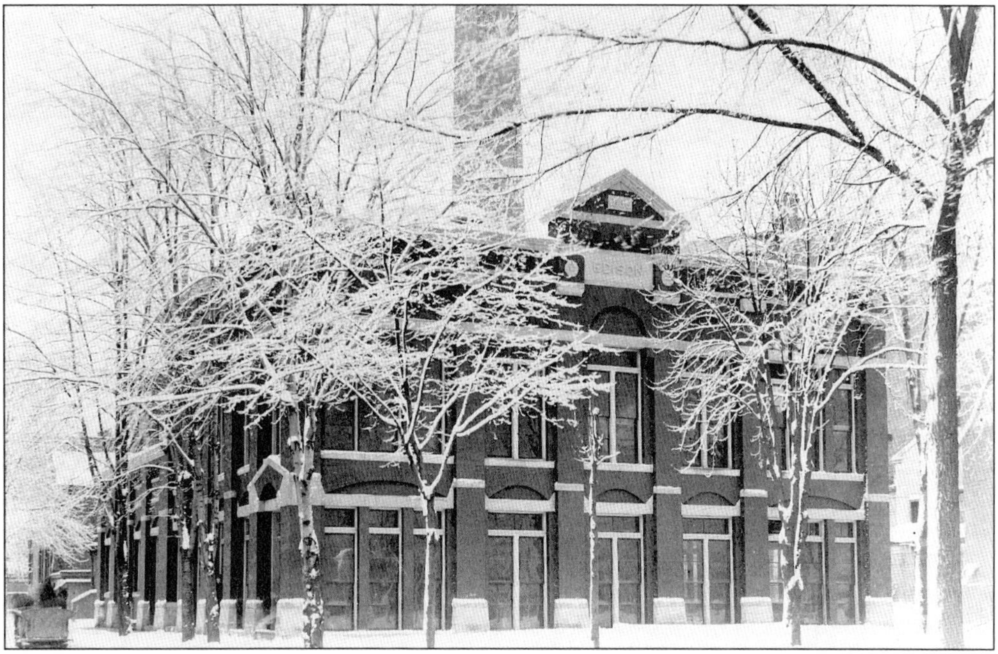

EDISON ILLUMINATING. "Station A", the first power house of the Edison Illuminating Company was built at the corner of Washington Boulevard and State Street in 1886. This power station is where a young engineer named Henry Ford learned the trade. He would eventually be promoted to chief engineer.

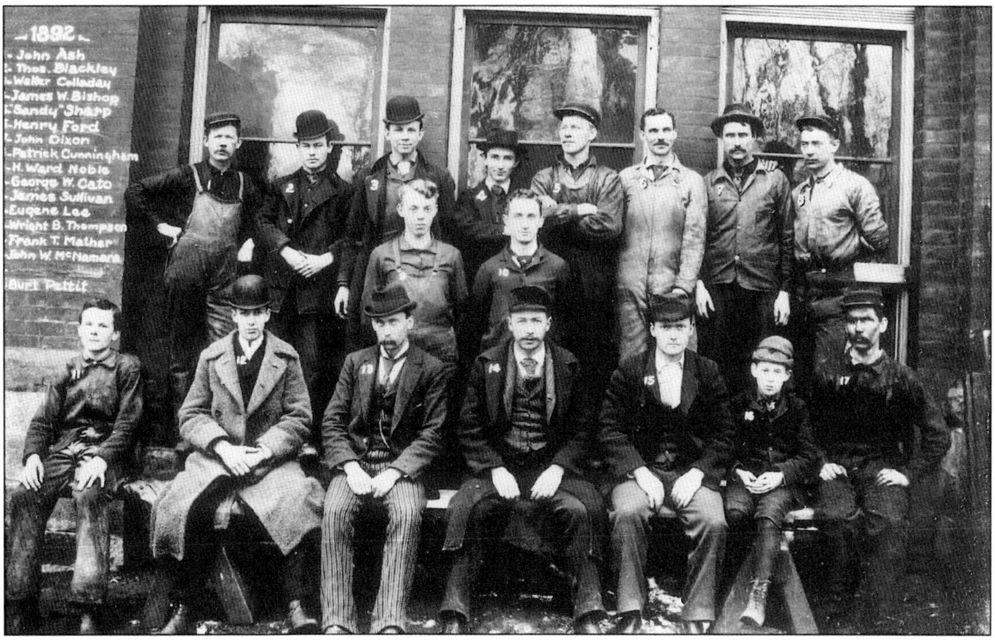

EDISON EMPLOYEES. The work crew of power Station A gathers for a group photograph. Across the top row, from left to right, are John Ash, Thomas Blackley, Walter Calladay, James W. Bishop, Sandy Sharp, Henry Ford, John Dixon, and Patrick Cunningham. This photograph is dated 1892.

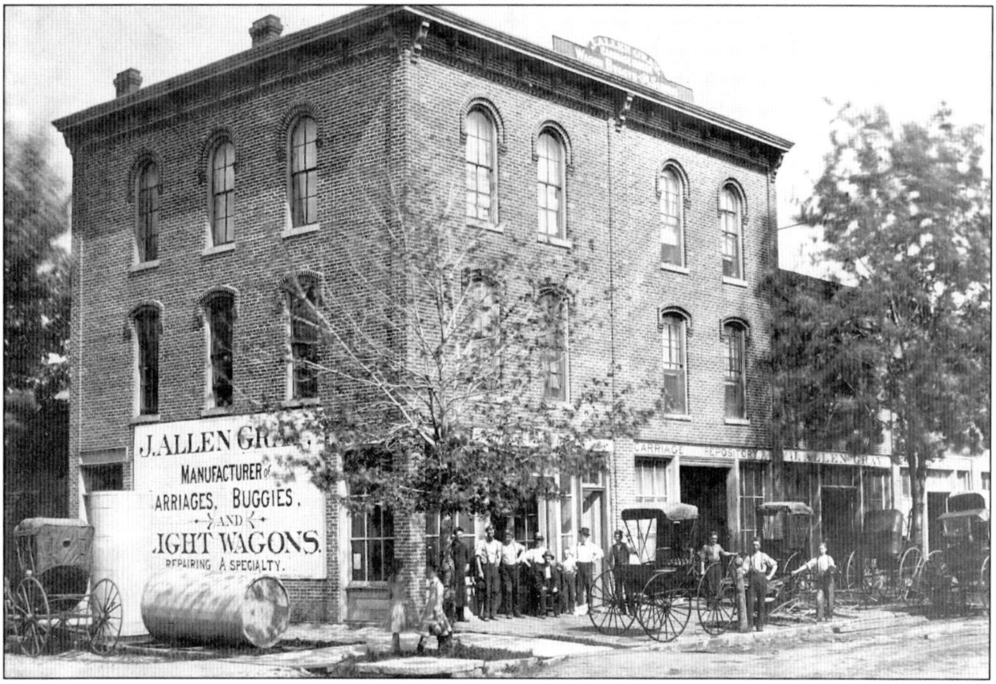

CASS AND ADAMS AVENUE. This impressive brick building houses the business of John Allan Gray, who established his carriage business in 1879. Gray made buggies, phaetons, and spring wagons of every description, such as laundry wagons, confectionary wagons, and patrol wagons. The quality of these products was such that Henry Ford made most of the parts for his first automobile here.

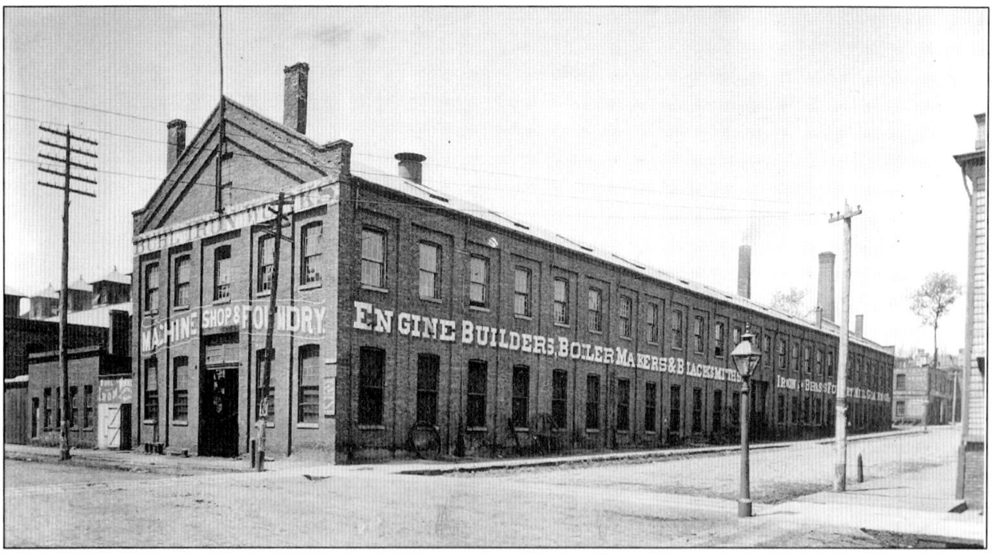

BUHL IRON WORKS. At the corner of Larned and Third Streets stood the Buhl Iron Works, owned by Christian H. Buhl and leased to O'Connor and Company. Under the Buhl logo engines, boilers and other foundry products were made. Buhl's company also had a blacksmith available to provide iron work of a smaller nature. Buhl owned the Detroit Copper and Brass Rolling Mill.

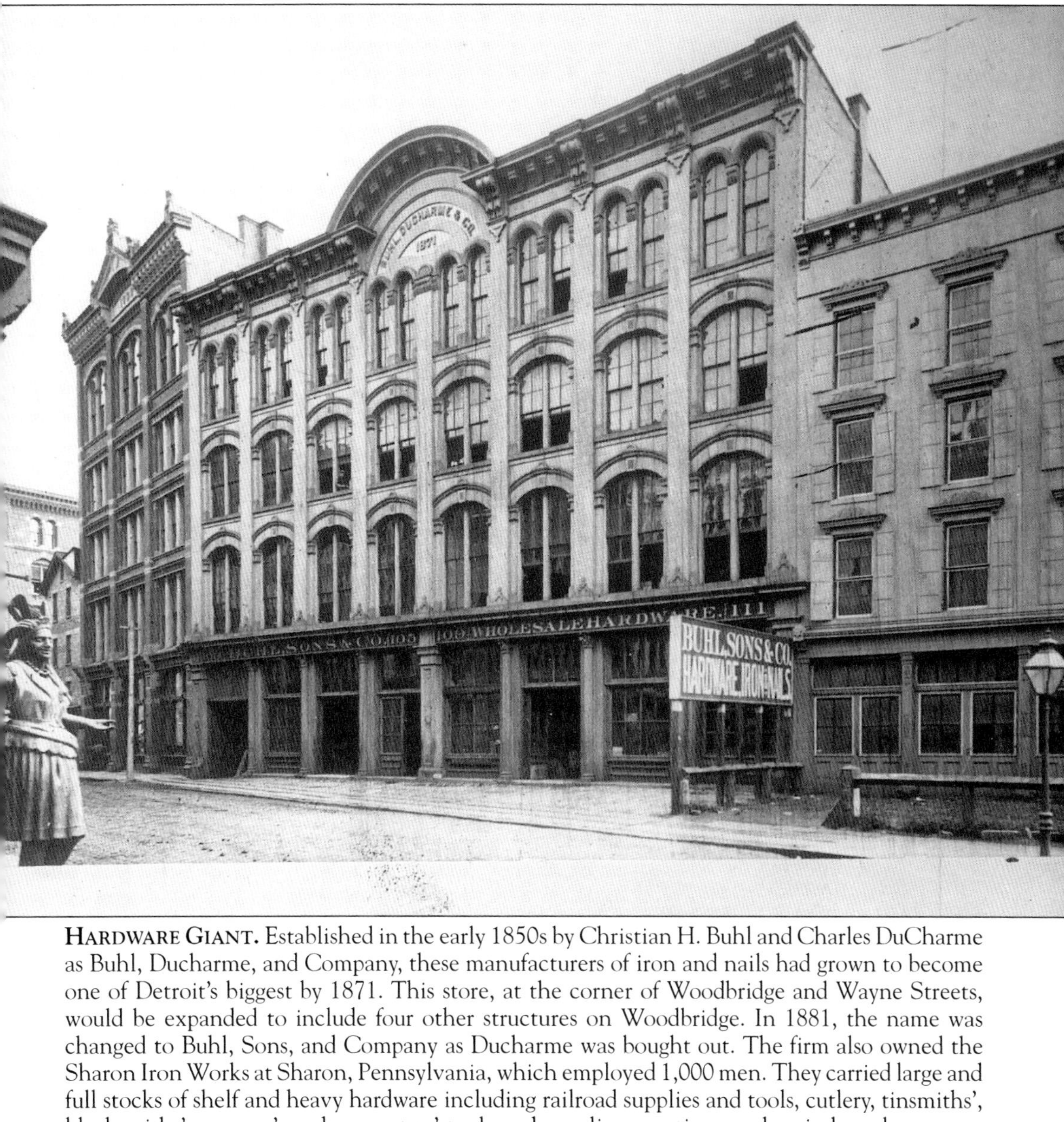

HARDWARE GIANT. Established in the early 1850s by Christian H. Buhl and Charles DuCharme as Buhl, Ducharme, and Company, these manufacturers of iron and nails had grown to become one of Detroit's biggest by 1871. This store, at the corner of Woodbridge and Wayne Streets, would be expanded to include four other structures on Woodbridge. In 1881, the name was changed to Buhl, Sons, and Company as Ducharme was bought out. The firm also owned the Sharon Iron Works at Sharon, Pennsylvania, which employed 1,000 men. They carried large and full stocks of shelf and heavy hardware including railroad supplies and tools, cutlery, tinsmiths', blacksmiths', coopers', and carpenters' tools and supplies, sporting goods, window glass, putty, and glaziers' supplies. The company employed seventy in the Detroit store and had, in 1886, nine traveling salesmen covering Michigan, Indiana, Ohio, Minnesota, and the Dakotas.

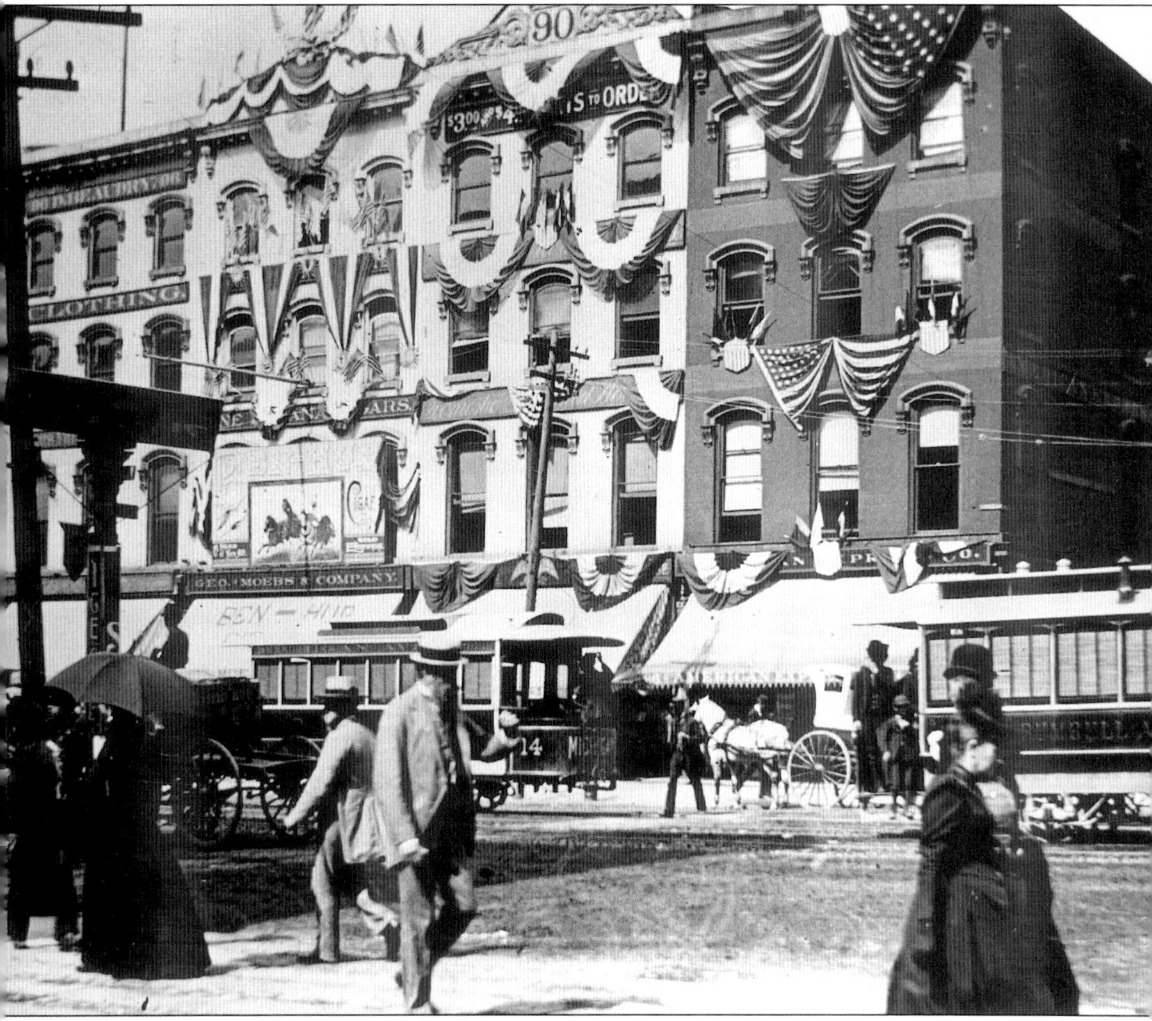

WOODWARD AT ATWATER STREET, 1888. Festooned in patriotic bunting, this block of Woodward Avenue features the George Moebs and Company store (third from the right), among others. Moebs established his company in 1870 with a partner named Burk, and after several name changes, became one of Detroit's leading importers and manufacturers of fine Havana cigars. He employed a force of skilled cigar makers, ranging from 150 to 175 in number, making brands such as "Flor de Moebs," "Ben-Hur," and "Detroit Slugger," among others. Moebs also imported Havana cigars, which made him exclusive to an extent. The output of his company amounted to 5,000,000 cigars annually and his trade covered the states of Michigan, Indiana, Ohio, Illinois, Missouri, Iowa, Nebraska, Minnesota, Wisconsin, New York, Massachusetts, Connecticut and Rhode Island. His retail store, on the ground floor of this building, was known to one and all as "The Grand."

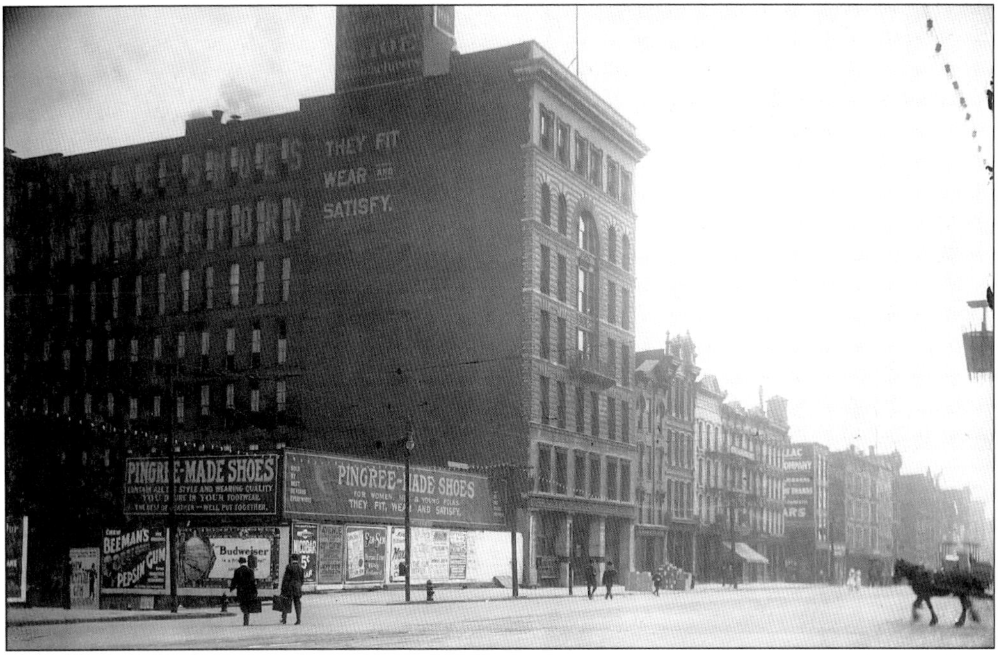

"THEY FIT, WEAR, AND SATISFY." The slogan of the Pingree Company adorns their building on East Jefferson Avenue in 1887. 700 employees were constantly engaged in the manufacture of boots, shoes, and slippers for men, women, and young folks. This work force turned out 2,000 pairs daily.

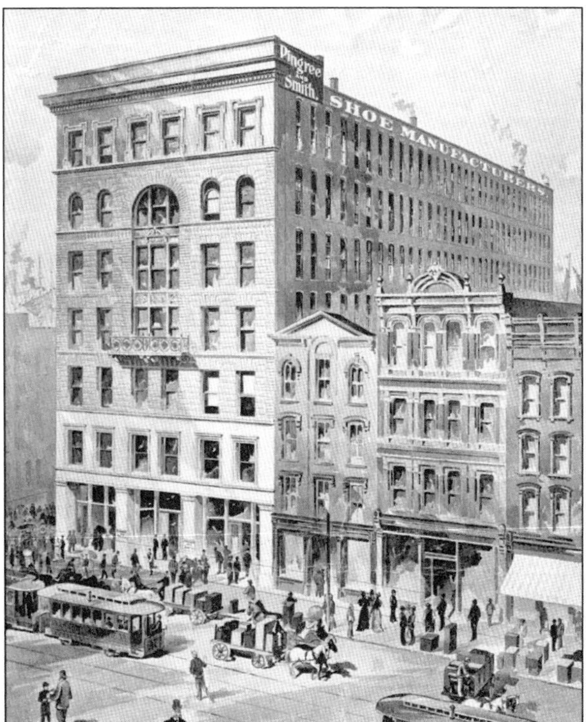

PINGREE AND SMITH. The earlier store belonging to partners Hazen Pingree and Charles H. Smith sat on Woodbridge Street. Pingree and Smith started their business in 1866 and later took in several partners. Mr. Smith retired from the firm in 1883 and Pingree later entered politics, becoming mayor of Detroit and governor of Michigan. He was noted for his reform platforms.

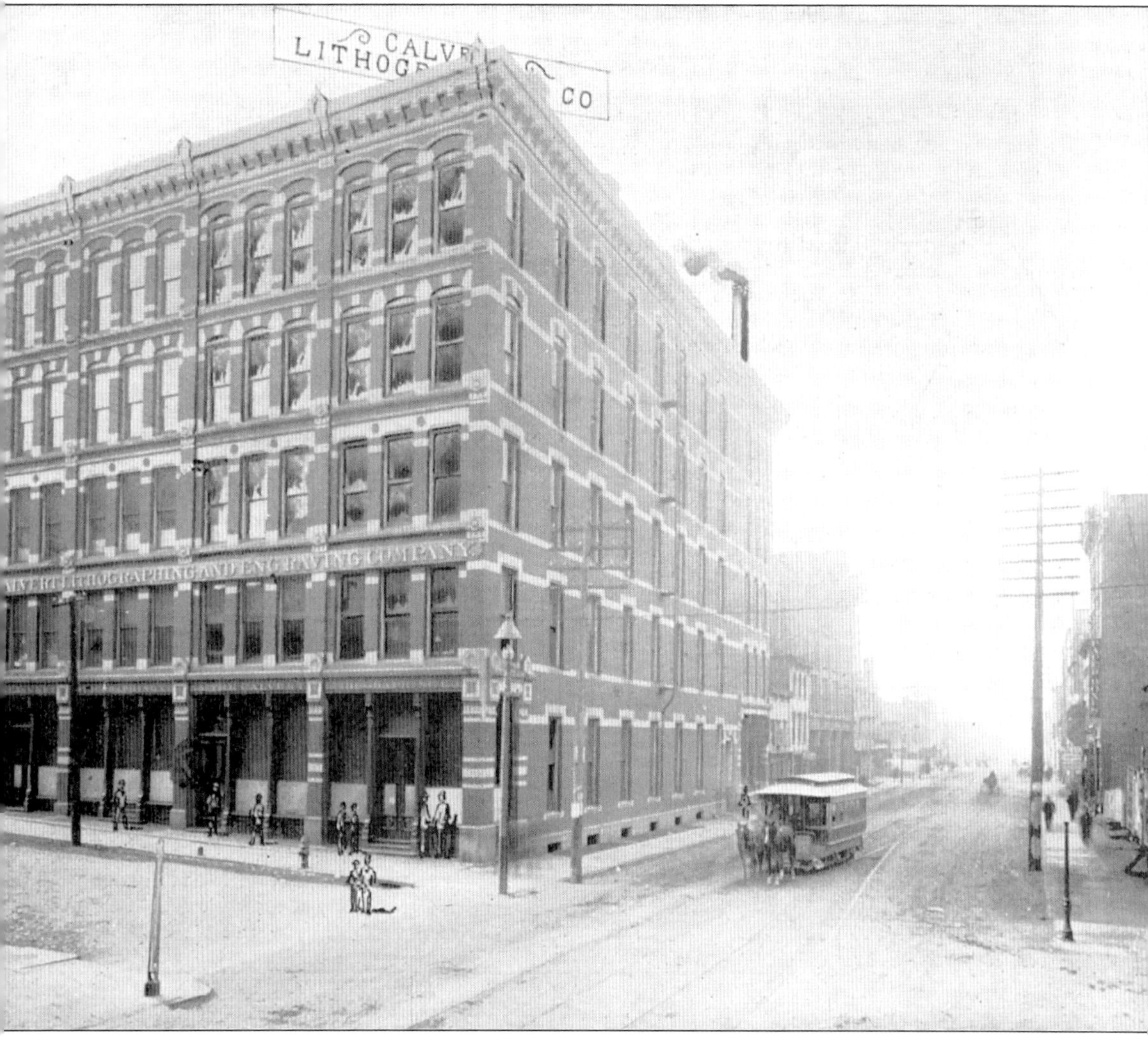

DETROIT ARTISTS. The Calvert Lithographing and Engraving Company was known nationwide for its beautiful designs of advertising pieces in full color. Established in Detroit in 1861 by Thomas Calvert as Calvert and Company, by 1885 they occupied this specially-designed building at the corner of Larned and Shelby Streets. Employing a force of 250 skilled workers, the company were strictly lithographers, engravers, and chromo publishers. Look through any Detroit city directory and you will find beautiful examples of their work in full color advertisements for any number of products and businesses. Calendars, note cards, trade cards, and full-sized illustrations depicting scenes from nature and history are among some of the most sought-after collectibles in the country today. Calvert maintained large offices in New York, Boston, Philadelphia, Baltimore, St. Louis, San Francisco, and two in Chicago. Their products had no superior and few equals.

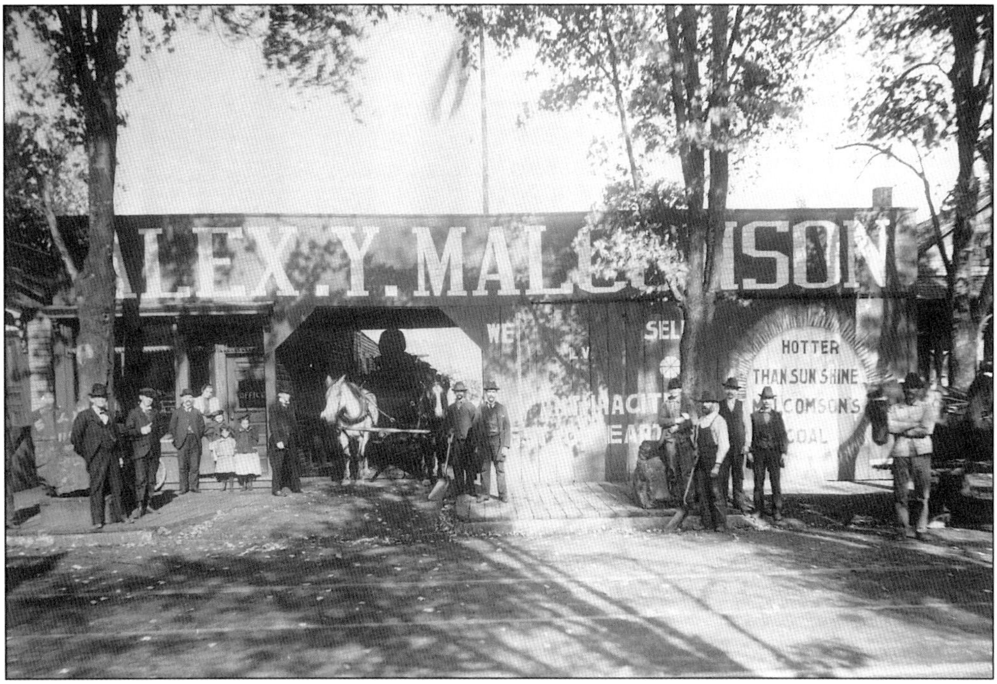

HOTTER THAN SUN SHINE. The slogan for Malcomson's coal adorns their coal yard at 250 Baker Street. Alex Malcomson, his wife, and their children stand to the left of this photograph, in front of the office, while the rest of the work force strikes a pose.

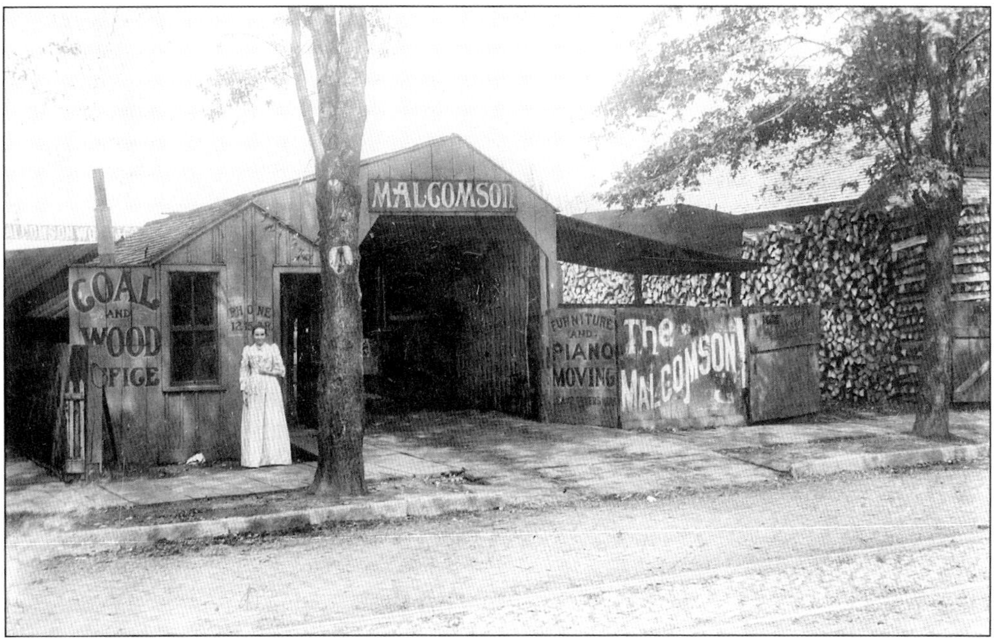

BAKER STREET COAL AND WOOD. Another photograph of the Malcomson Coal and Wood Company shows Mrs. Malcomson in front of the office. They have expanded the business to include wood and furniture and piano moving in this 1896 shot. The Malcomsons provided coal for the Edison Illuminating Company, where Henry Ford was Chief Engineer.

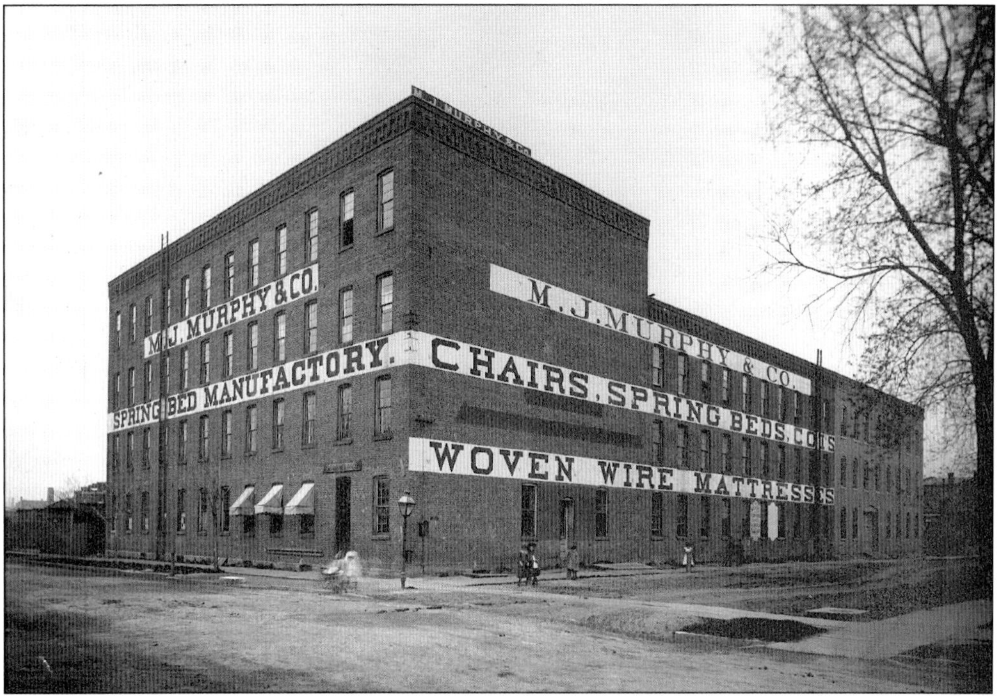

BEDS BY MURPHY. M.J. Murphy bought out a small spring bed establishment in 1872 and expanded his business to include beds, mattresses and all kinds of chairs: parlor, dining, easy, and rocking. By 1886, he was employing 325 workmen who made 1,200 chairs, 100 mattresses, and 100 spring beds daily.

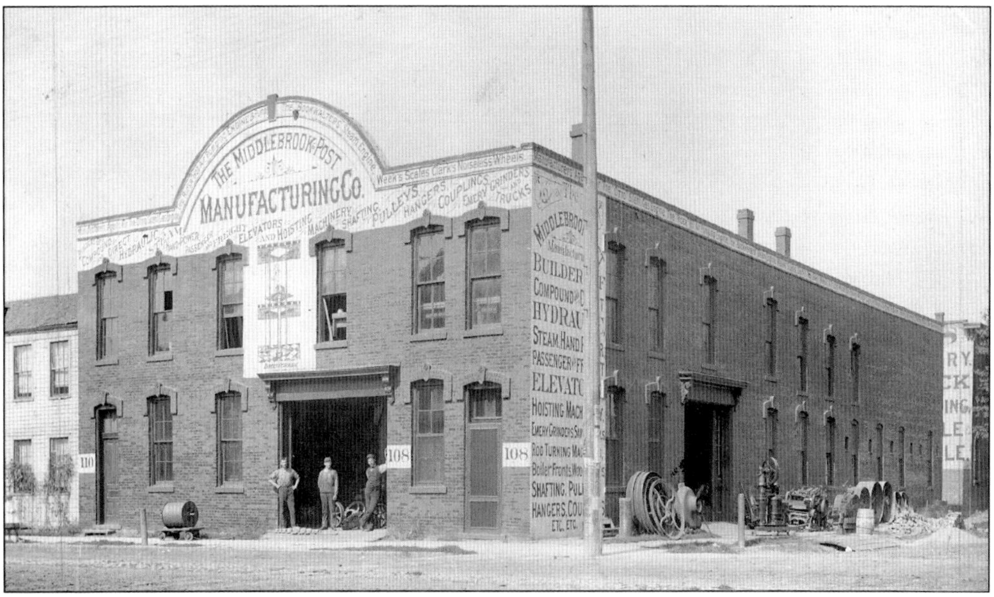

MIDDLEBROOK AND POST. At the corner of Larned and Cass Streets stood the Middlebrook and Post Manufacturing Company, who produced a variety of products. They made steam and hand-powered freight and passenger elevators, as well as hoisting machinery, pulleys, hangers, couplings, emery grinders, and rod turning machines.

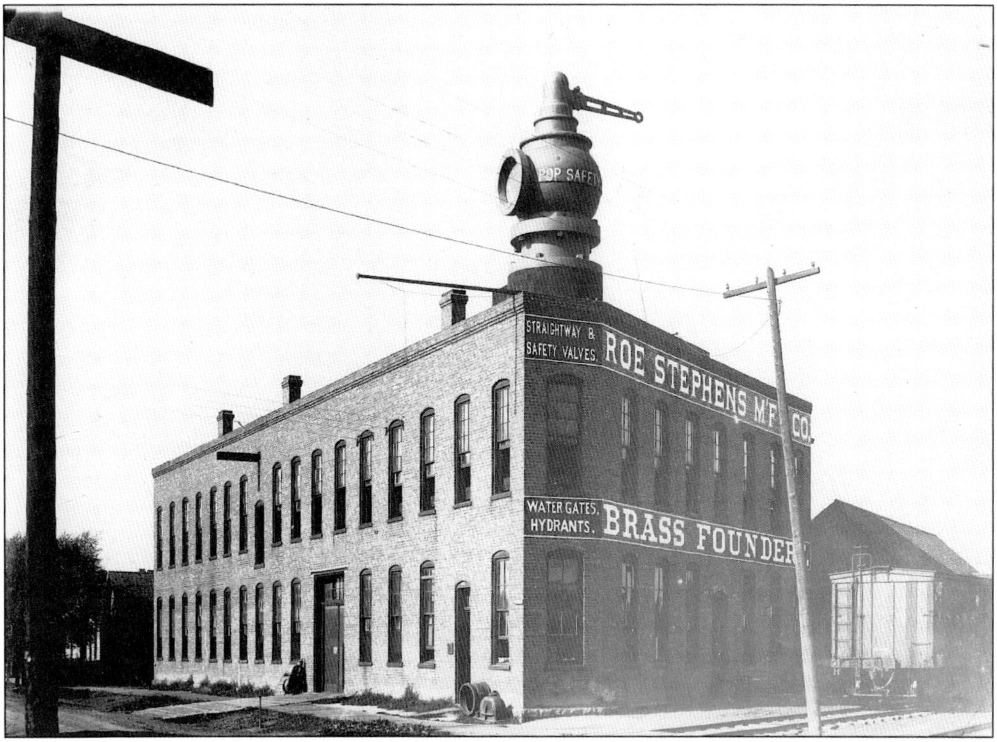

GIANT SAFETY VALVE. The Roe Stephens Manufacturing Company's Brass Foundry on 27th Street boasted what was most likely the world's largest safety valve on the roof. They produced a variety of products, including water gates and hydrants. Among their more well-known products were the McArthur Air Brake Valve and the Orme Pop Safety Valve.

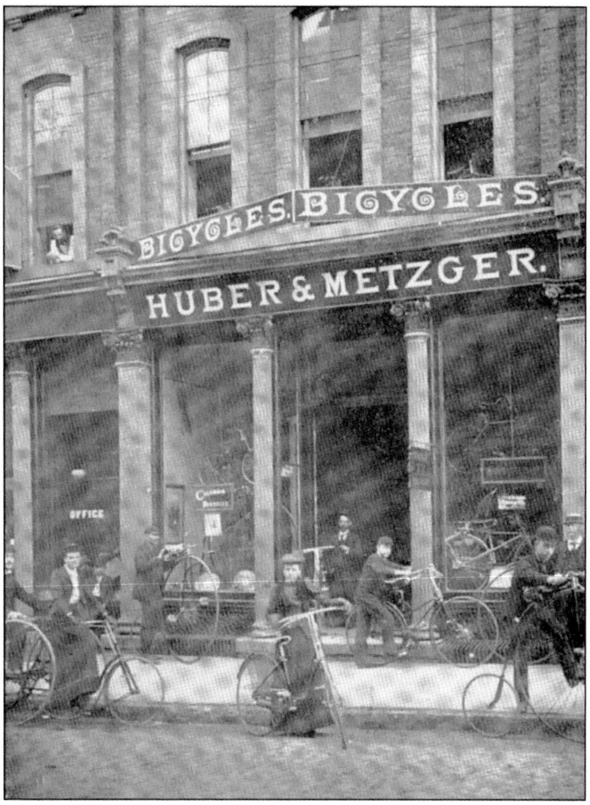

TWO-WHEELED FUN. The bicycle craze hit the United States in the 1880s, and Detroit was no exception. Here cyclists pose in front of Huber & Metzger's bicycle shop on Grand River Avenue in 1891. The business had just opened that year and sales in the first four months exceeded the total bicycle sales in the city for the previous two years.

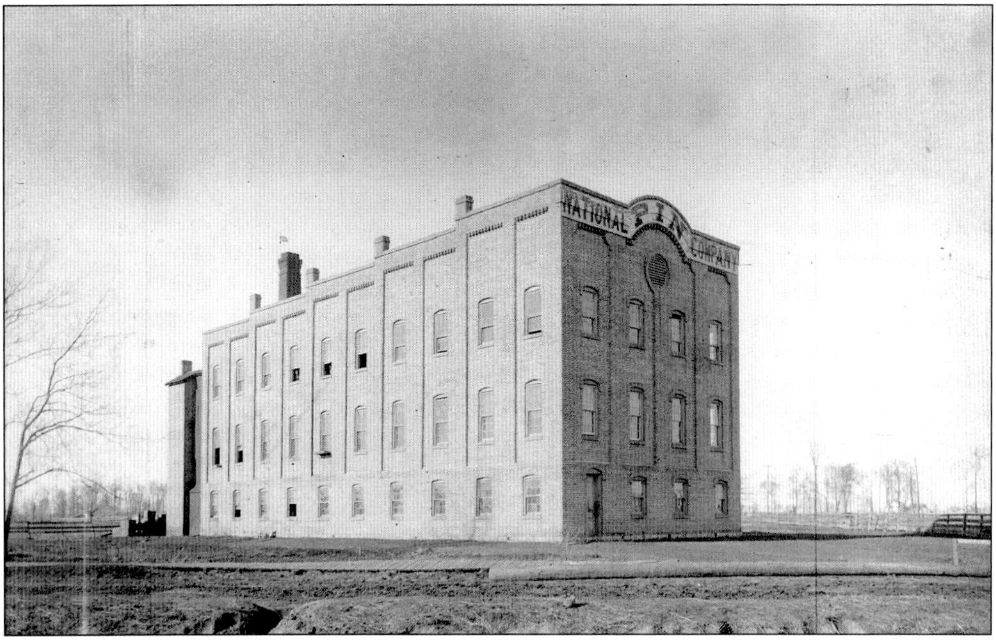

On Pins and Needles. There were fourteen pin companies in the United States in 1887, and one was located on Grand River Avenue between Sixteenth and Seventeenth Streets. Purchased by Detroit interests in 1873 and moved to Detroit from Indiana, National Pin consumed 2,000 pounds of wire to produce three million pins per day.

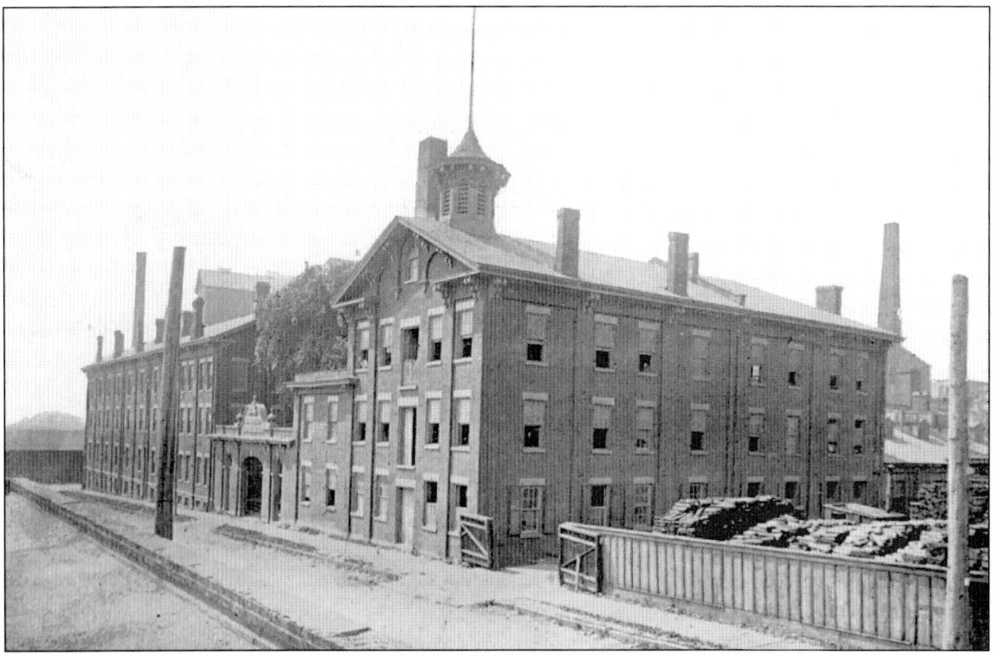

No Match For a Diamond. The Diamond Match Company was organized in 1880 and was considered the immediate successor of the Richardson Match Company, the first in Detroit in 1856. The largest works in the United States, it occupied nearly three acres at Fort and Woodbridge Streets, manufacturing over eighteen styles of matches.

Five

CAPITAL INDUSTRIES

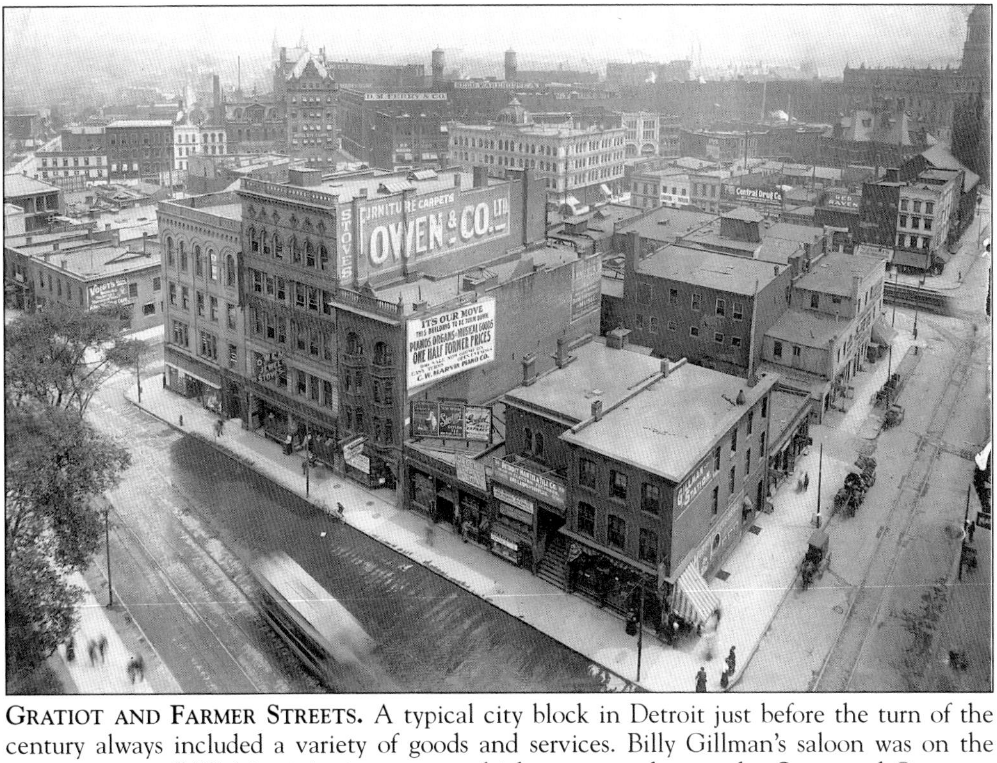

GRATIOT AND FARMER STREETS. A typical city block in Detroit just before the turn of the century always included a variety of goods and services. Billy Gillman's saloon was on the corner next to C.W. Marvin's piano store, which was next door to the Owen and Company furniture store. The last building was occupied by a number of firms.

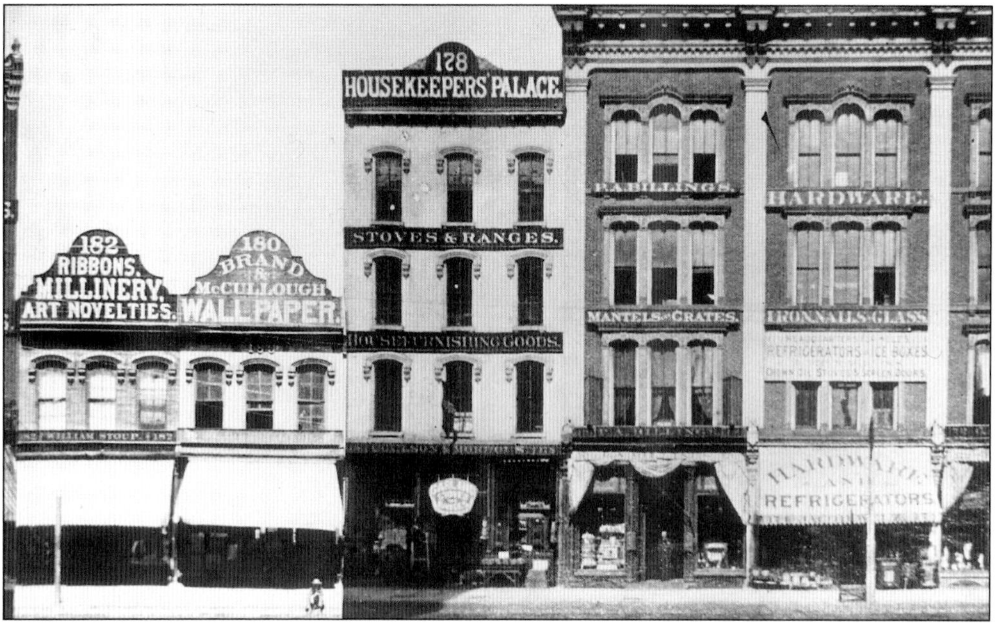

HOUSEWIFE'S DELIGHT. This block of Woodward Avenue between State and Grand River would have been heaven for the lady of the house. The Housekeeper's Palace, carrying Garland brand stoves and ranges, sat right next door to the headquarters for Welz's refrigerators and ice boxes. After selecting your favorite appliance, there was time for wallpaper and millinery items.

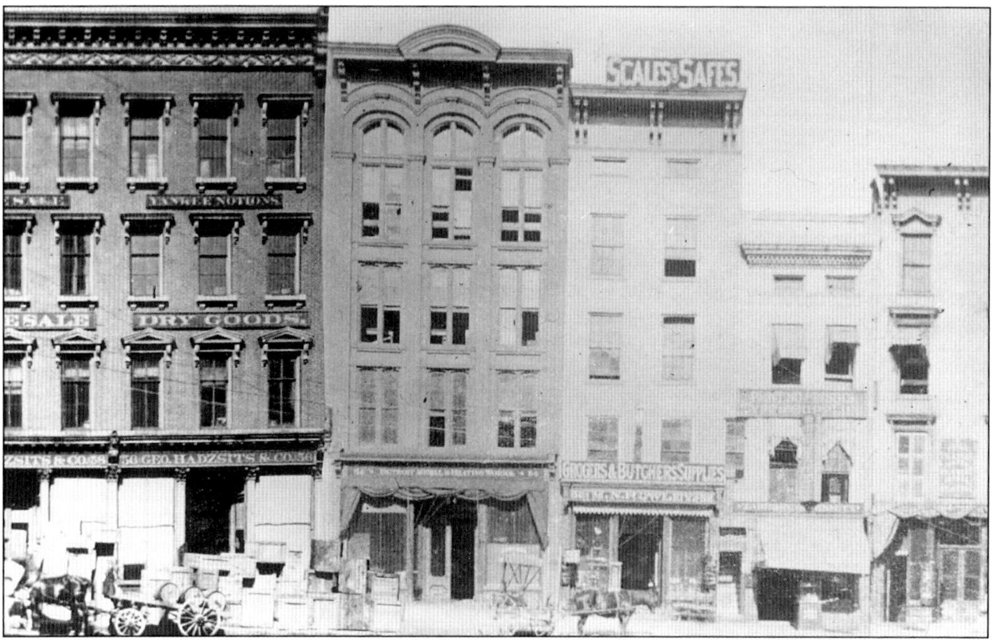

A HARD GOODS BLOCK. This portion of Woodward Avenue between Woodbridge Street and Jefferson Avenue features goods and services more attuned to the retail dealer. A typical dry goods outlet is run by George Hadzsit, the Detroit Metal and Heating Works is next, followed by M.N. Rowley's Grocers' and Butchers' Supply House. A printing press and printing supply house rounds out the photograph.

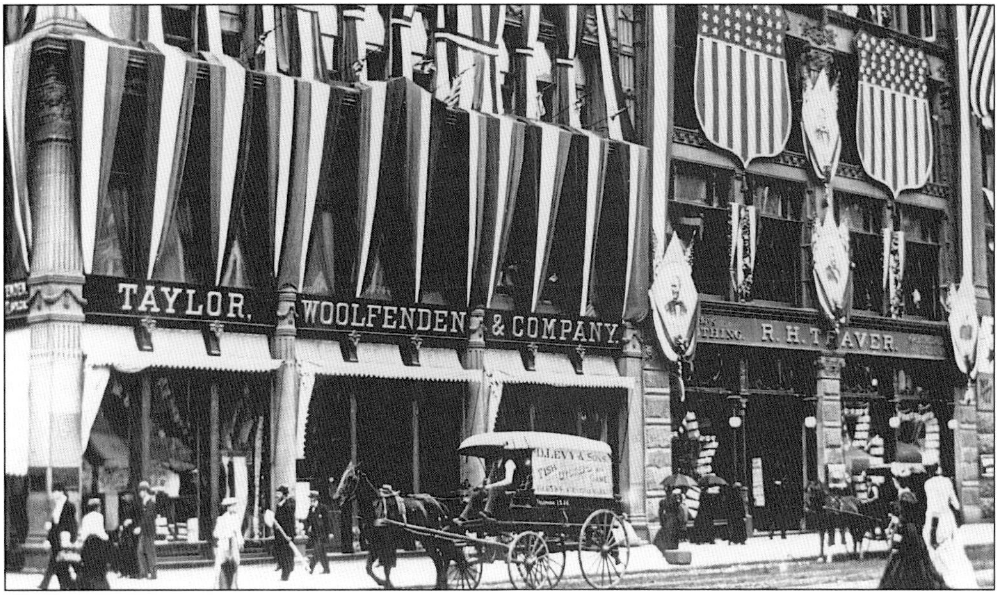

TAYLOR, WOOLFENDEN AND COMPANY. One dry goods emporium in Detroit to give Hudson's a run for his money was established by F.D. Taylor, J.B. Woolfenden, and George Morris in 1887. It was located in a five-story structure with a sandstone front on Woodward and State Street. All three men had extensive experience in the dry goods business. Taylor had been a junior member in the Newcomb, Endicott & Company firm.

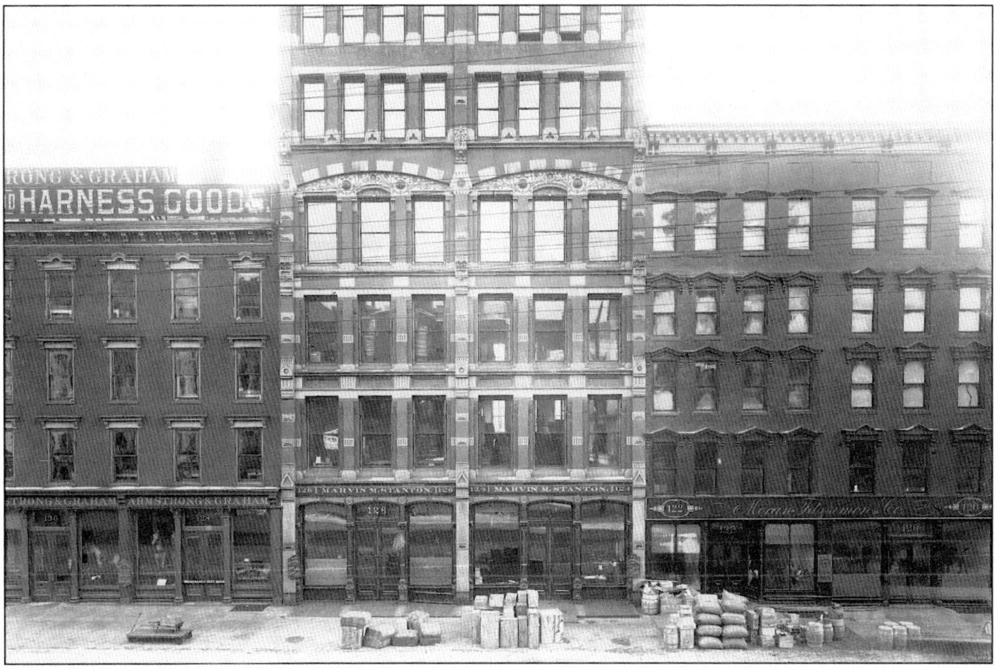

JEFFERSON AVENUE INDUSTRY. This stretch of Jefferson between Griswold and Shelby Streets looks ready for business. Armstrong and Graham sold saddles and harness goods, Marvin Stanton owned and operated a dry goods business, and Moran, Fitzsimmons, and Company imported teas, coffee, and other items in the line of fancy goods used by grocers.

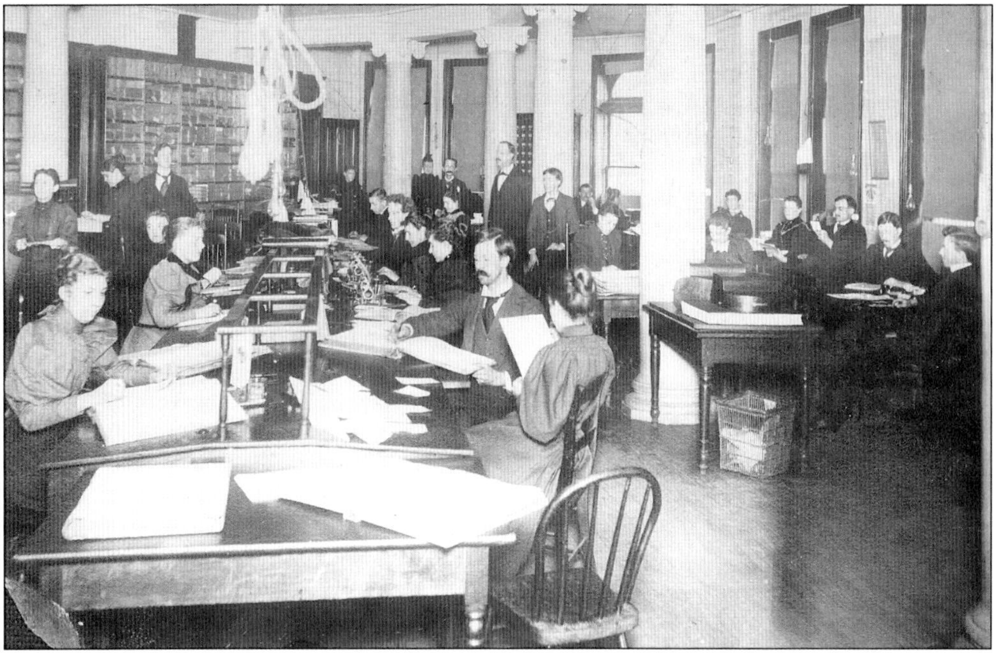

LAND TITLE OFFICE. The interior of the office of the Burton Title and Abstract Company shows both men and women working diligently to record the ownership history of lots in the city and county. Clarence Monroe Burton, a graduate of the University of Michigan, founded the business during the 1880s.

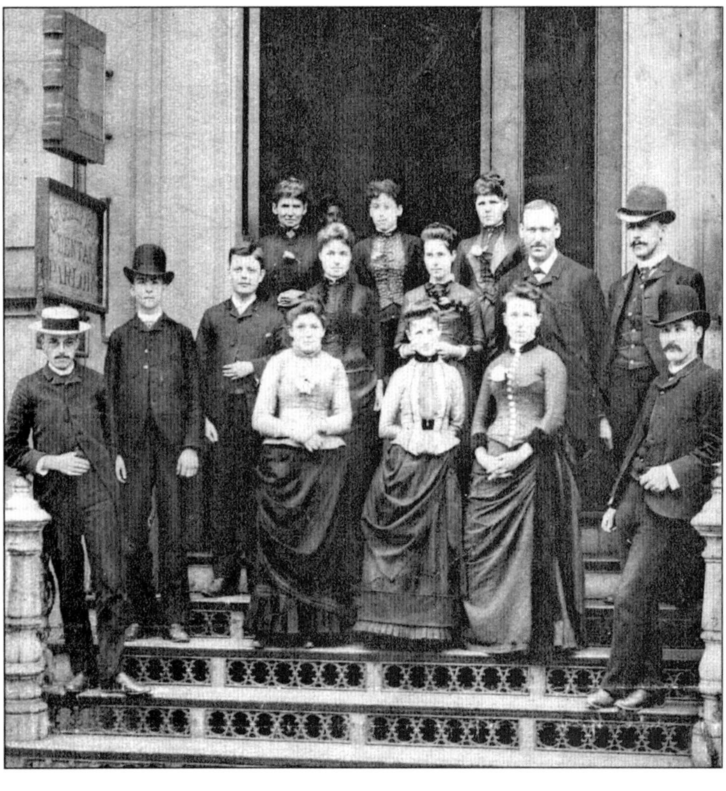

CLERKS AND SECRETARIES. The staff of the Burton Abstract and Title Company pose on the steps of the old Detroit Free Press building in 1887. One of the few businesses to employ women, it started out with offices in this building at Larned and Shelby Streets before moving into its own building. It employed a work force of 100. Mr. Burton is second from the right in the second row.

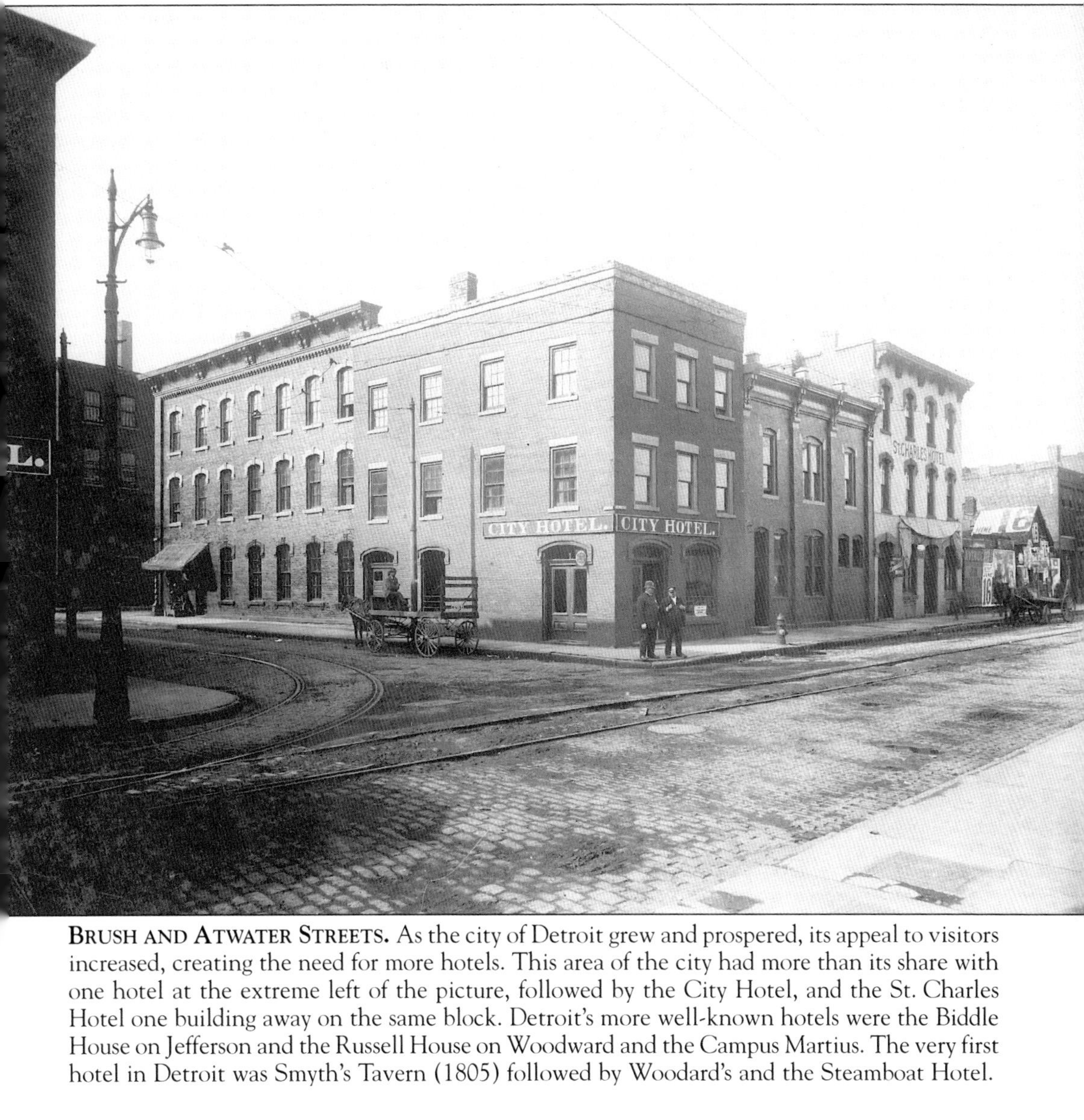

BRUSH AND ATWATER STREETS. As the city of Detroit grew and prospered, its appeal to visitors increased, creating the need for more hotels. This area of the city had more than its share with one hotel at the extreme left of the picture, followed by the City Hotel, and the St. Charles Hotel one building away on the same block. Detroit's more well-known hotels were the Biddle House on Jefferson and the Russell House on Woodward and the Campus Martius. The very first hotel in Detroit was Smyth's Tavern (1805) followed by Woodard's and the Steamboat Hotel.

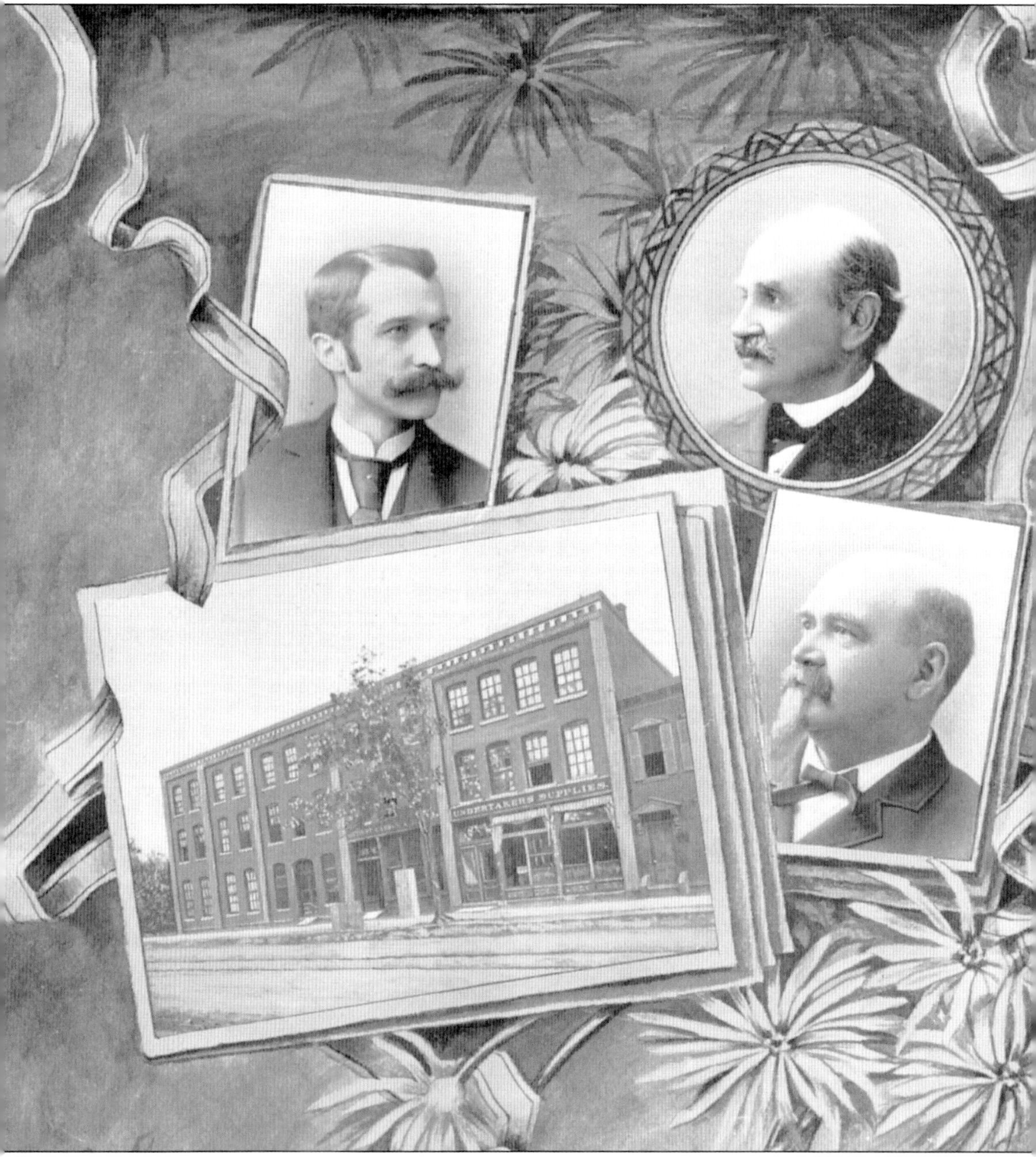

WHERE THEY'RE BURIED. The Detroit Casket Company occupied over thirty thousand feet of floor space in a building on West Congress Street in 1883. Their specialty, the "Shrine Casket," was in demand from coast to coast. The principal woods used were chestnut, walnut, and red cedar, with a huge quantity of Michigan pine used for the outside boxes. This company was among the first to introduce colors in the cloths for caskets and used broadcloth, velvets, and silk plushes of various somber hues. The Detroit Casket Company also "jobbed" everything demanded in the business, including hardware, robes, linings, and the cheaper kind of varnished coffins. At one point, they were able to make, ship, and deliver caskets to Albany, New York, and Kansas City, Missouri in a single day.

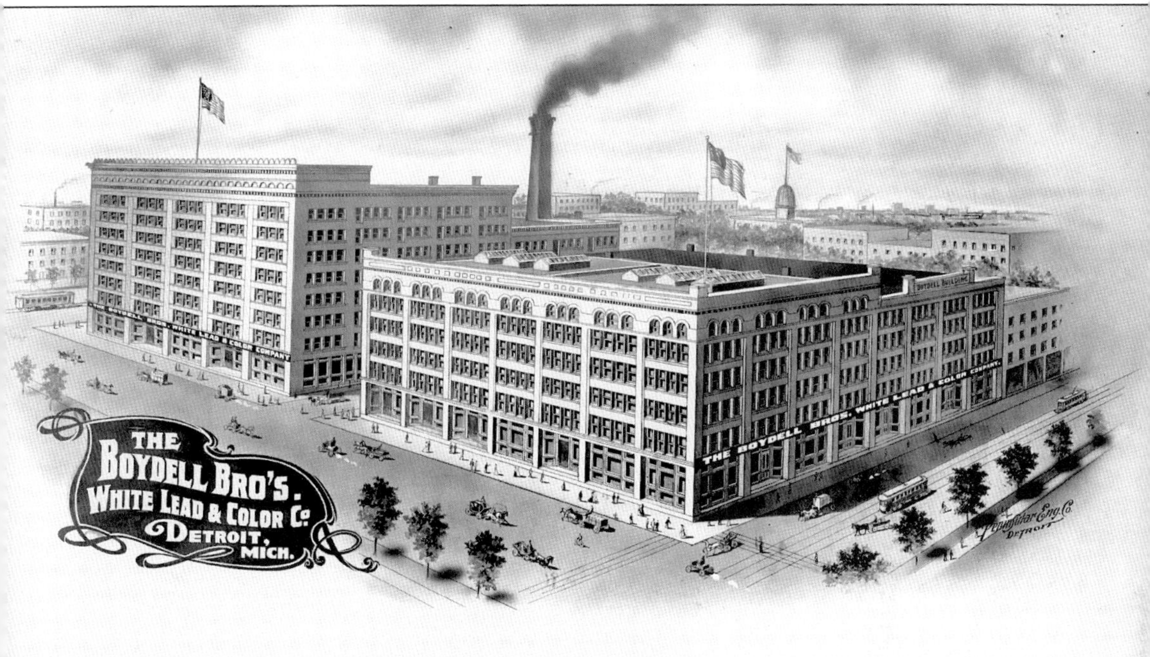

LEADING PAINT PRODUCER. The Boydell Brothers White Lead and Color Company's massive complex occupied nearly an entire block on East Fort Street in Detroit. John Boydell established the business in 1865 and was joined by his brother William in 1874. By the late 1880s, they numbered among the largest manufacturing concerns in the city. They manufactured white lead, zinc, putty, colors, and prepared paints, oils, varnishes, and dryers as well as brushes and painters' supplies of every description. The Boydell Brothers label enjoyed a solid reputation as producers of products unsurpassed in covering qualities, eveness, finish, and durability. They had a large clientele throughout Michigan.

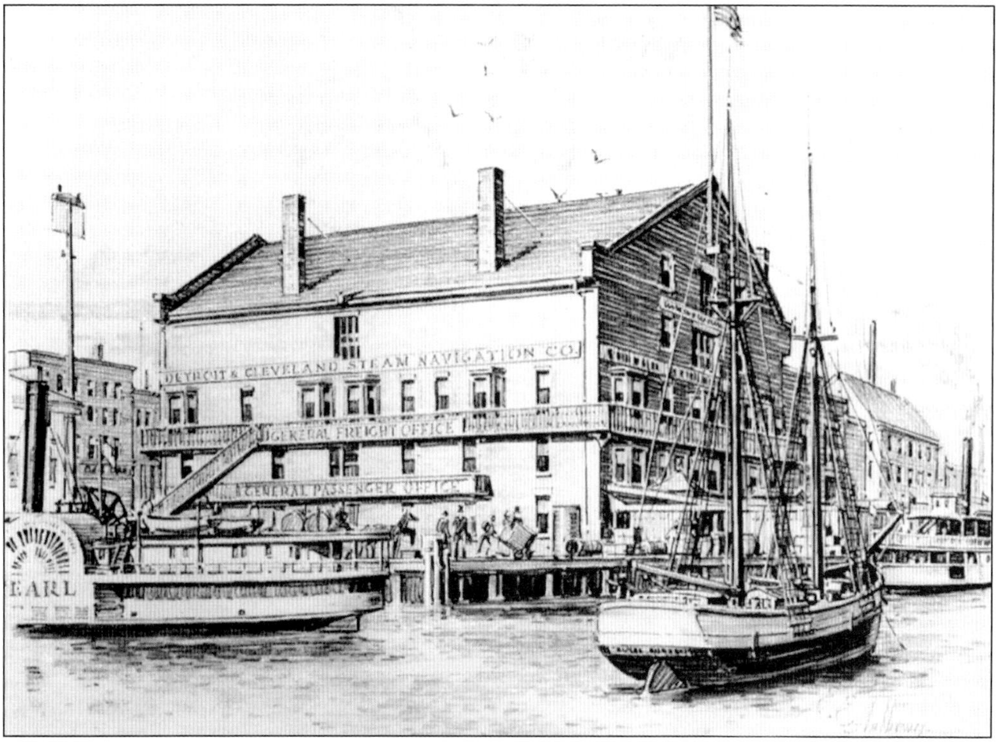

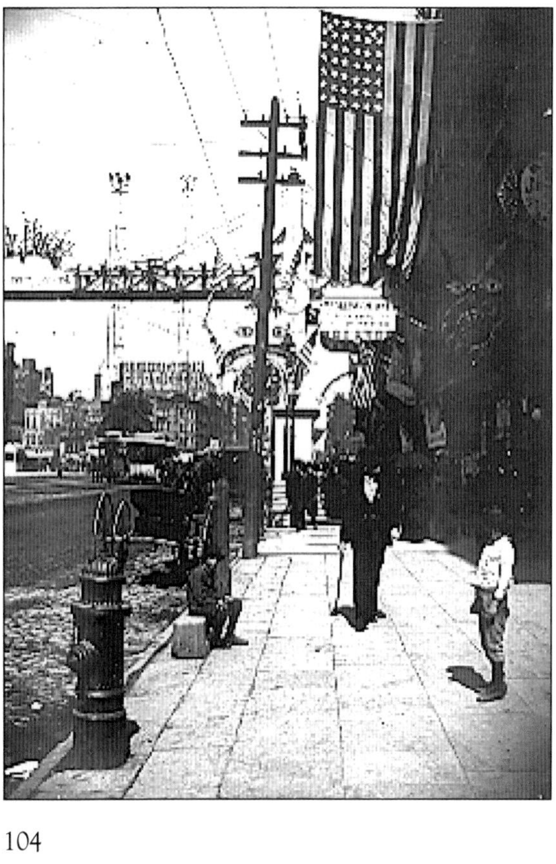

The Detroit & Cleveland Steam Navigation Company. Captain Arthur Edwards established this company in 1850 and operated it with two boats, the Southerner and the Baltimore. Until 1852, they ran between Detroit and Cleveland. By the 1890s, the D&C owned and operated the only iron and steel side-wheel steamers on the Lakes, which hauled both freight and passengers to various points along the system.

Department Store Competition. Woodward Avenue is decorated in celebration of the International Fair and Exposition in 1889. This section of the grand avenue contains the Mabley and Company and J.L. Hudson Company department stores, just across and down the block from each other. Mabley was the older of the two, founded in 1870. Mabley's was J.L. Hudson's first job.

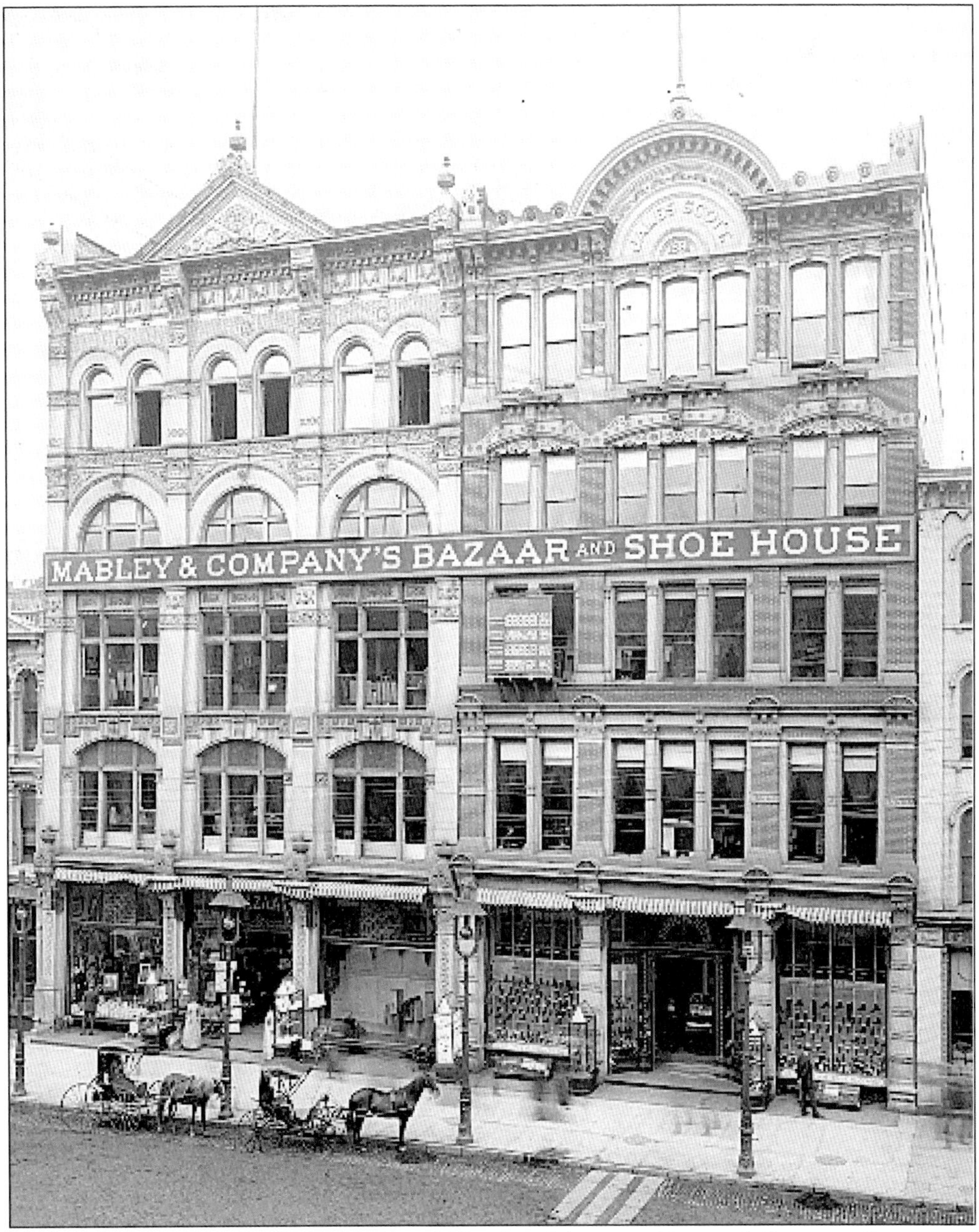

MABLEY'S BAZAAR. On the west side of Woodward between Fort and Congress Streets was the Mabley & Company Bazaar and Shoe House. Founded by Christopher Richards Mabley in 1870, less than 20 years later it was the largest retail business in Michigan. Mabley died in 1884 and the company was incorporated with a capital stock of $250,000. In addition to the boot and shoe store, other departments sold mantles, shawls, suits, jackets, millinery, ladies furnishings, crockery, glassware, toys, games, fancy goods, books, and jewelry. The floor space covered two and a half acres and was divided into twelve stores with 62 departments. The building was electrified and had "swift and elegant" passenger elevators to move shoppers from floor to floor. Three hundred clerks and assistants were on hand to help with the one and a quarter million dollars in annual sales.

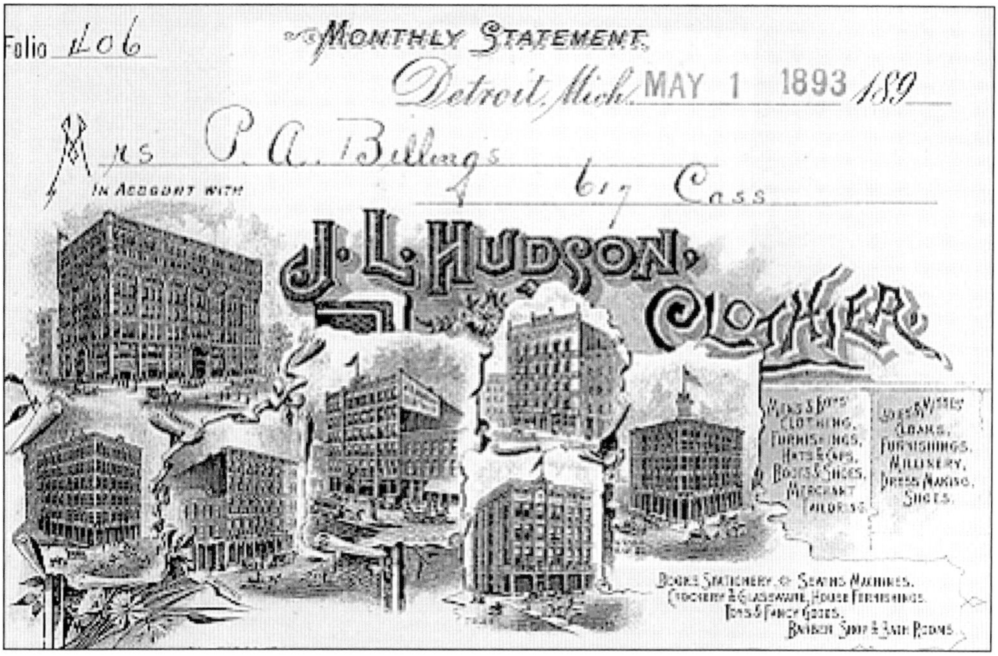

EXPANDING CHAIN OF STORES. No book on Detroit industry would be complete without J.L. Hudson's. The top half of a monthly statement illustrates the various Hudson's stores in Detroit and other cities in 1893. Starting with the Detroit store on the upper left and continuing counterclockwise are as follows: St. Paul, Buffalo, Cleveland, Toledo, St. Louis, and Grand Rapids stores.

PERSONAL CHECK. An earlier illustration of the Hudson's store adorns this personal check for $40.50, made out to J.L. Hudson by Mr. George Duffield in 1885. This is Hudson's first store, on the ground floor of the Detroit Opera House building, and the check is for Mrs. Duffield's clothing bill.

HENRY NEWLAND FURS. Covering four lots on Jefferson Avenue, Newland's was an important manufacturer, wholesale and retail jobber of furs, hats, gloves, and caps. In January of 1880, Henry Newland opened his own emporium with three partners, after 25 years in the same line of business with the Buhls.

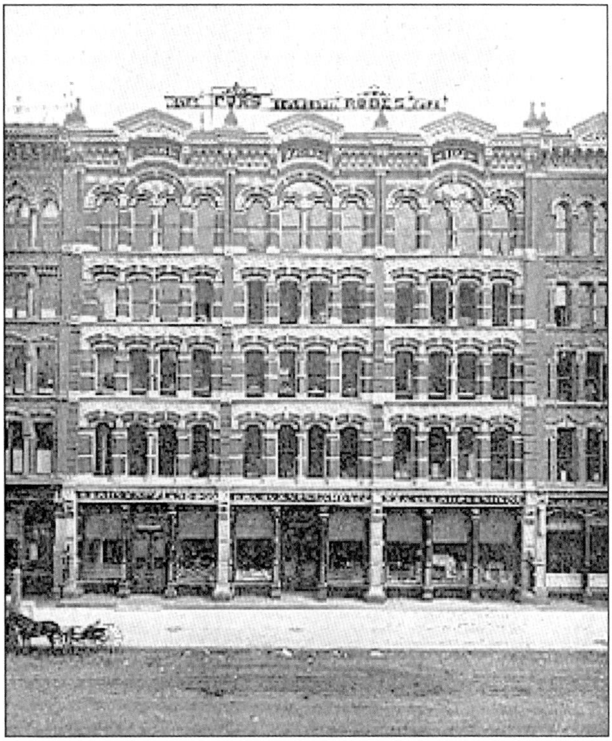

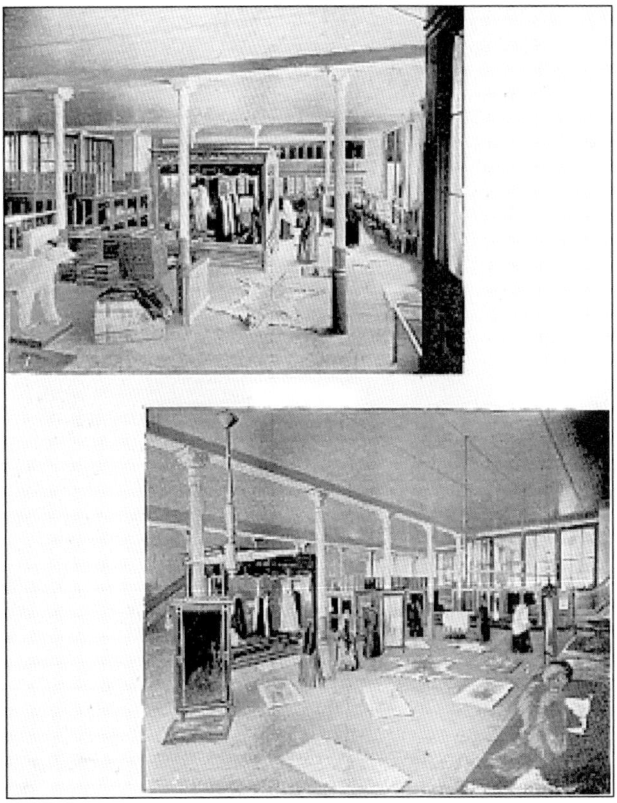

STORE INTERIOR, 1891. The fur department was the only direct importer of Alaska seal, Russian sable, and other foreign furs west of New York. Sealskin garments were the firm's specialty, winning medals in Paris, France for elegance of design and superiority of work. The firm employed over 150 men to manufacture their products.

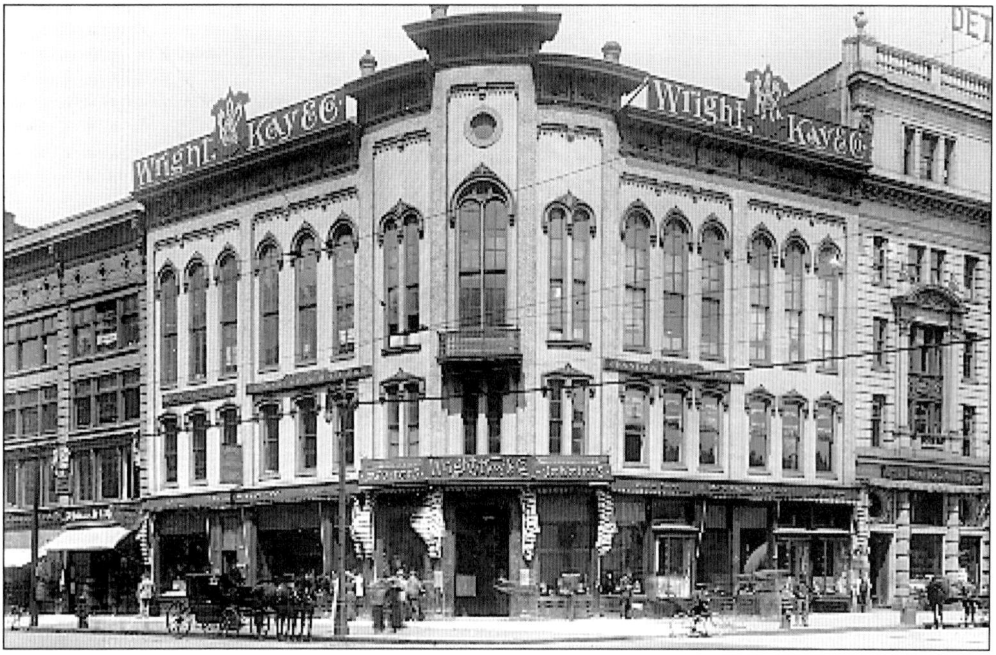

THE CAMPUS MARTIUS AT WOODWARD AVENUE. Detroit native Henry Wright established his business in 1872 with partner R.J.F. Roehm and, in 1886, after Roehm sold his shares, he opened this store with John Kay. A Detroit landmark through the Gay Nineties, Wright, Kay was one of only three U.S. firms importing from Europe.

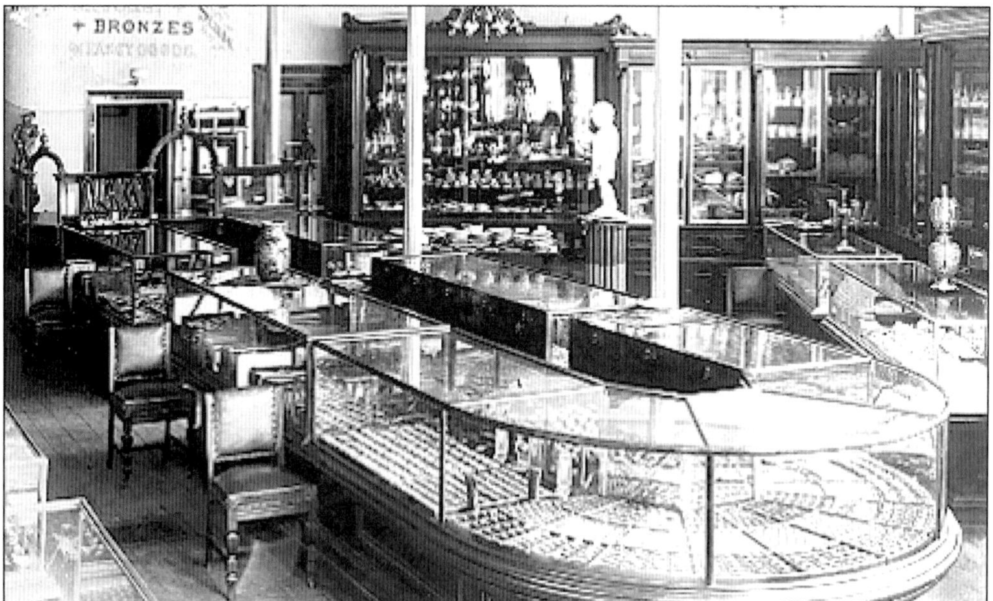

THE GLITTERING INTERIOR. The interior of the Wright, Kay jewelry store glitters with a fantastic assortment of items in all price ranges. Henry Wright's slogan "buy with confidence from a firm you can trust" led to the success of the firm. In alternate years, Wright and Kay traveled to foreign markets to buy jewels, enameled silver, and China.

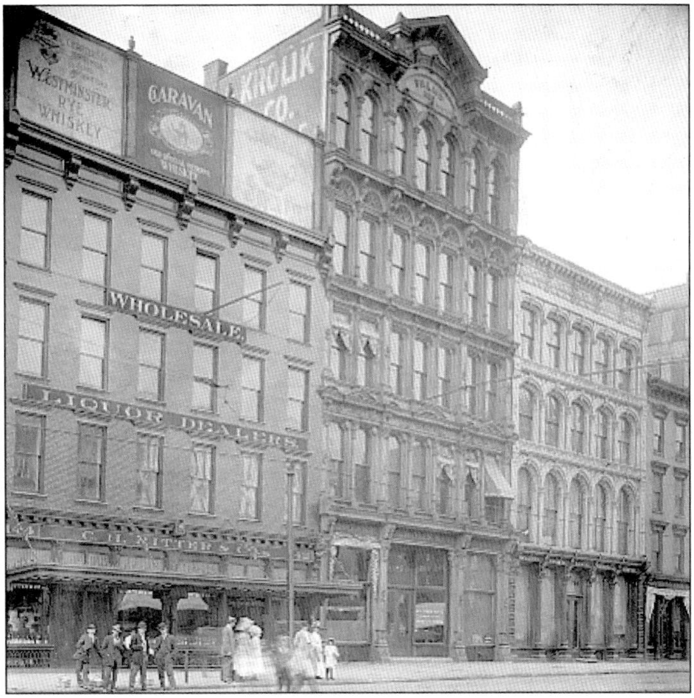

EAST JEFFERSON BUSINESS. The A. Krolik and Company Dry Goods store occupies the tall building in the middle flanked by C.J. Ritters' wholesale liquor (left) and Beecher, Peck and Lewis (right), manufacturers and dealers in paper, paper bags, twine and stationery. Adolph, Henry, and Herman Krolik moved their business here from Rochester, Michigan in 1872.

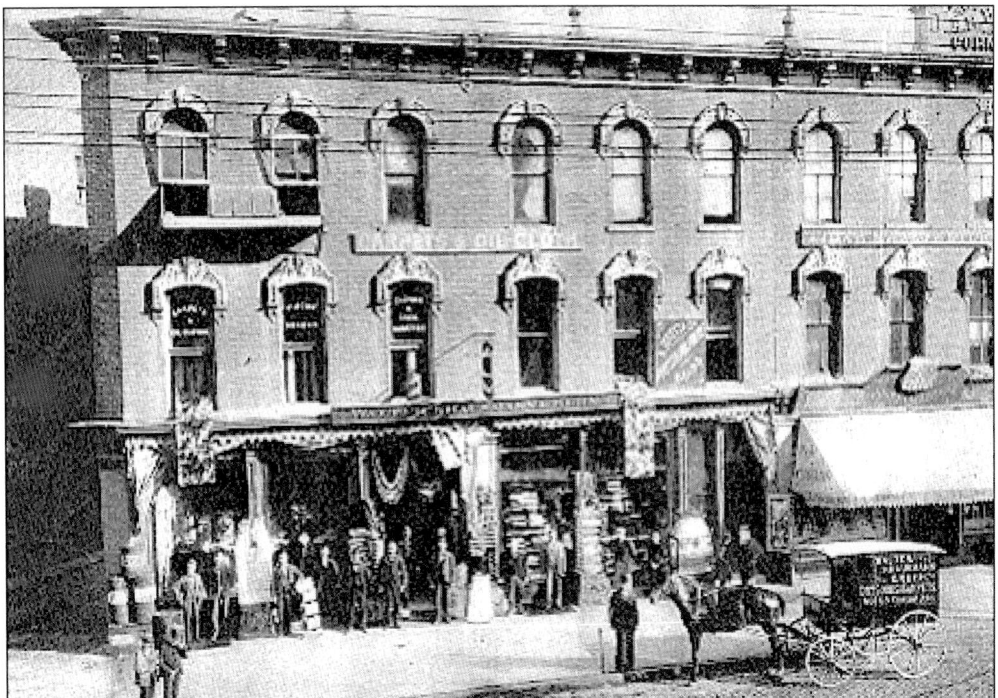

KRAUSEMANER AND KUHN. On Gratiot near Woodward Avenue was the dry goods emporium of Walter Krausemaner and Jacob Kuhn. One day in 1890 the entire staff and delivery wagon posed for this photograph. They were considered the "big store" on the east side, carrying carpets, oil cloths, window shades, cloaks, and lace curtains in addition to the normal run of goods.

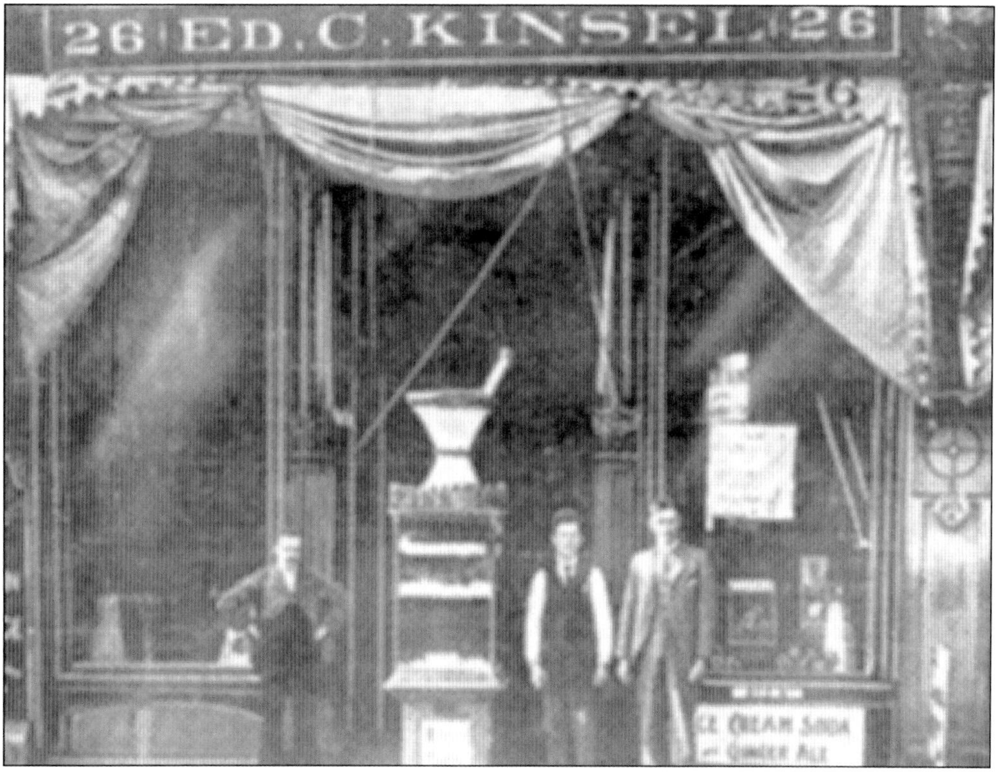

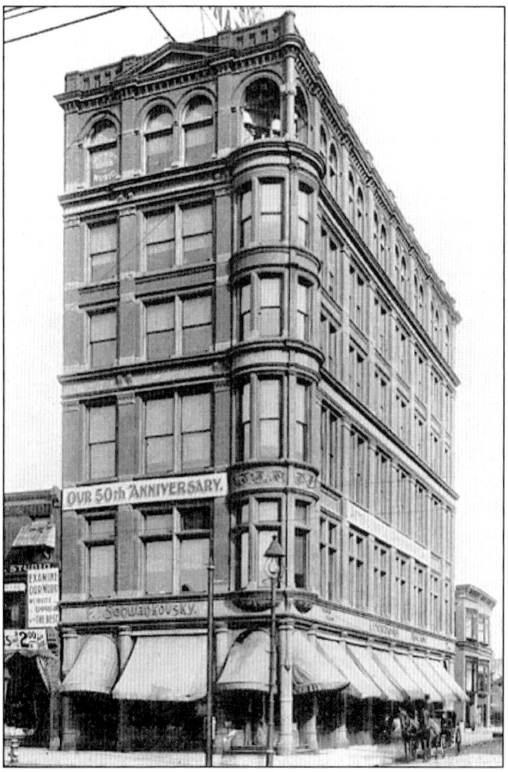

THE FIRST KINSEL'S.
Mr. Edward C. Kinsel stands first on the right in front of his first drug store on Michigan Avenue near Woodward. The huge mortar and pestle symbolized the pharmaceuticals for sale, while a smaller sign advertises ice cream and ginger ale.

SCHWANKOVSKY'S MUSIC STORE.
Frederick J. Schwankovsky was born in Wisconsin and educated in Maryland and Pennsylvania. He moved to Detroit in 1876 and took a position in a music store. He bought that business three years later, and in 1880, moved it into this grand building on Woodward Avenue and John R Street. Musicians performed outdoor concerts on the fifth floor balcony.

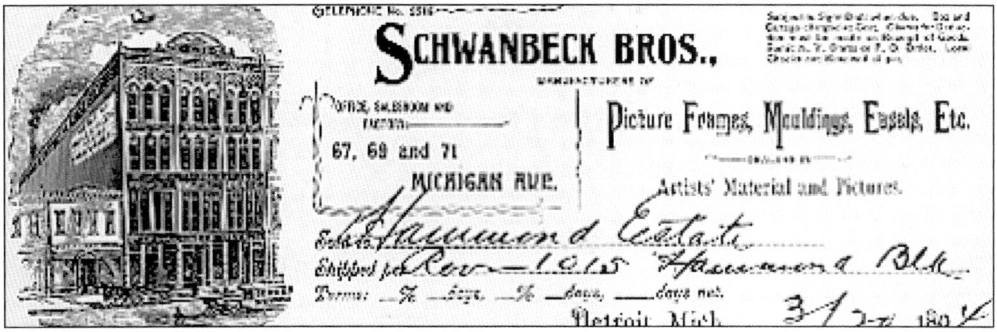

SCHWANBECK BROTHERS. This lovely four-story building on Michigan Avenue, not too far west from Woodward, was built in 1888 and served as the office, showroom, and factory of the Schwanbeck Brothers. They made picture frames, moldings, easels, and other artists' materials. There were at least seven big producers of picture frames in the city.

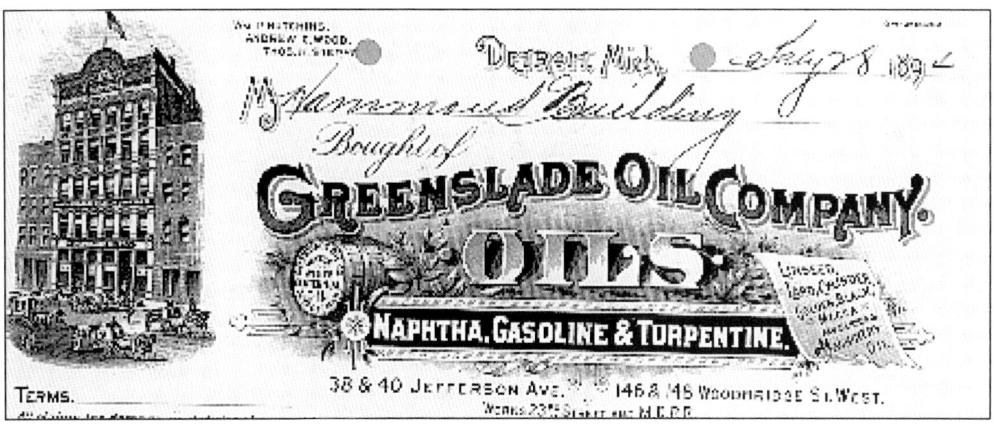

WELL OILED BUSINESS. John Greenslade had a long tenure in the oil and vinegar trade beginning in 1870. By 1885, he worked from this building and had expanded the business to include all kinds of lubricants. Greenslade carried seven different kinds of machine oil and employed ten clerks and assistants in their store.

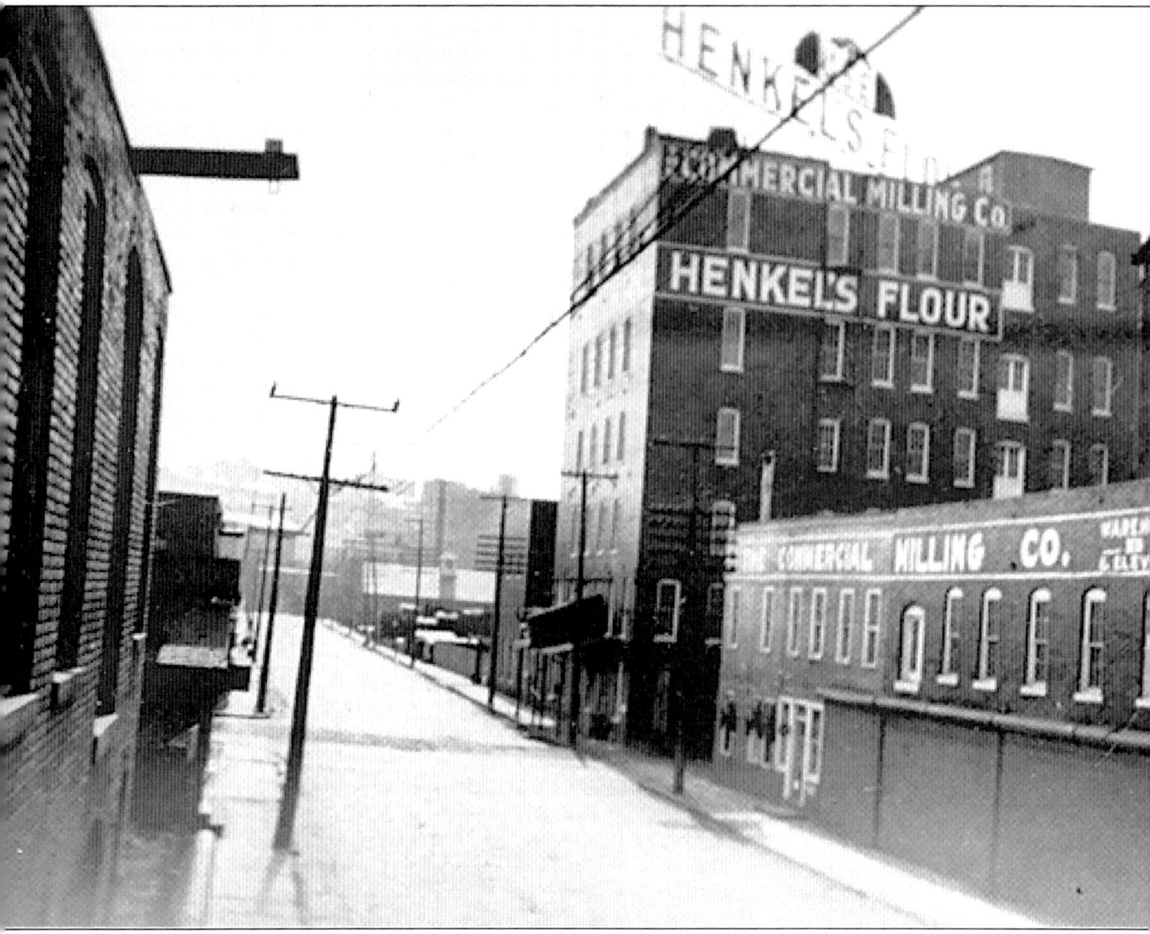

COMMERCIAL MILLING COMPANY. This panoramic photograph shows the Commercial Milling Company's complex as it looked in 1900. Peter Henkel emigrated to the United States in 1842, settled in Detroit and opened his flour mill at this site in 1855. His daily production at that time was 60,000 pounds of flour. In 1887, the name of the company was changed to the Detroit

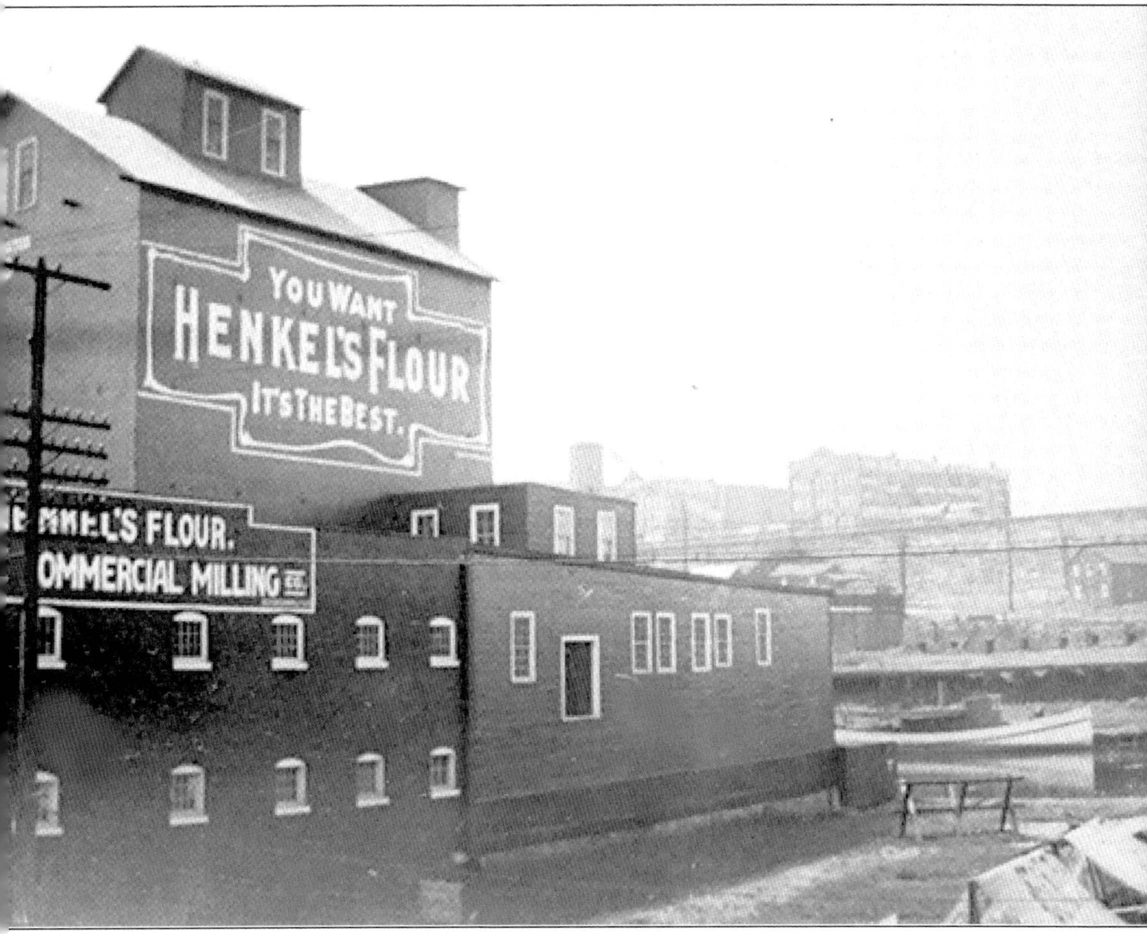

Commercial Mill and then to the Commercial Milling Company in 1900. They produced flour, meal, and feed, and sold chicken wheat, corn, oats, and a variety of other products. The company owned mills in Boston, Massachusetts and in Portland and Bangor, Maine.

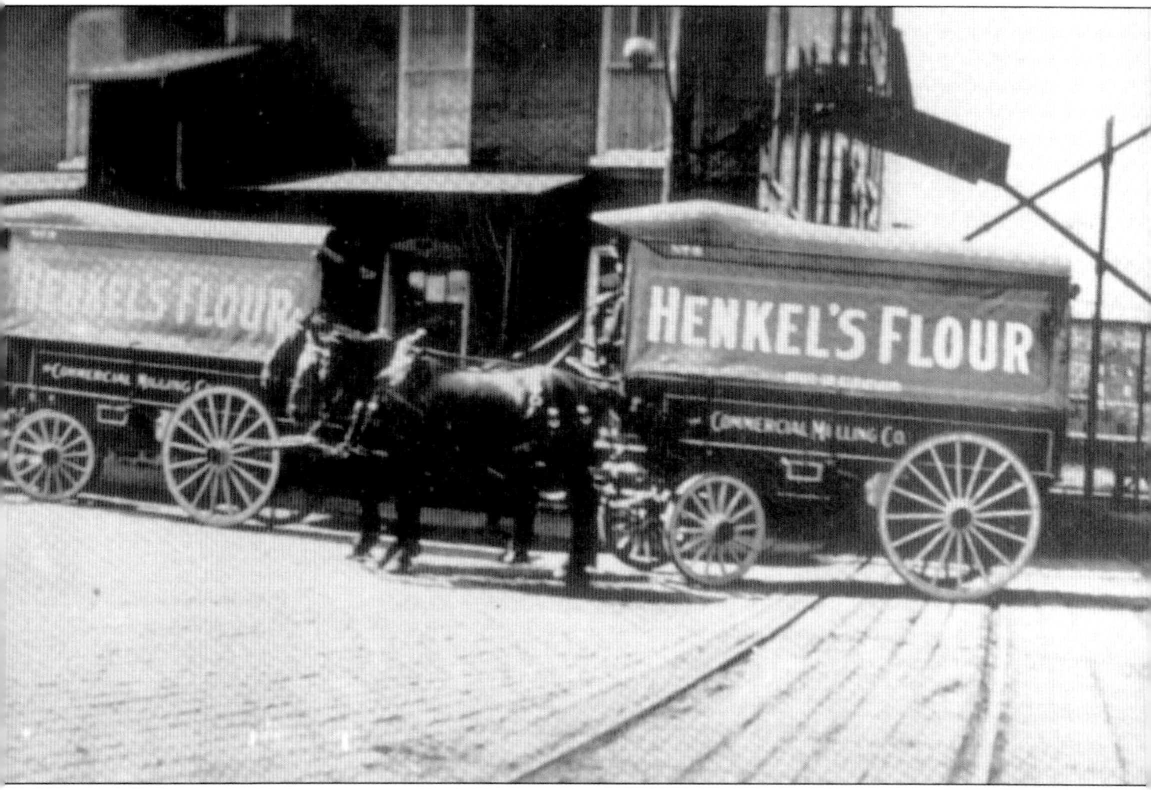

HENKEL'S DELIVERY WAGONS. The wagons are ready to roll, loaded with Henkel's Best, Royal Star, and Fancy Straight brand flour, among others. The mill had four brands of flour selling in 1900, for $4.25 per barrel: Henkel's Best, Royal Star Patent, First Patent, and Whole Wheat Flour. The average price for the other fourteen brands was right around $3.25 per barrel. The

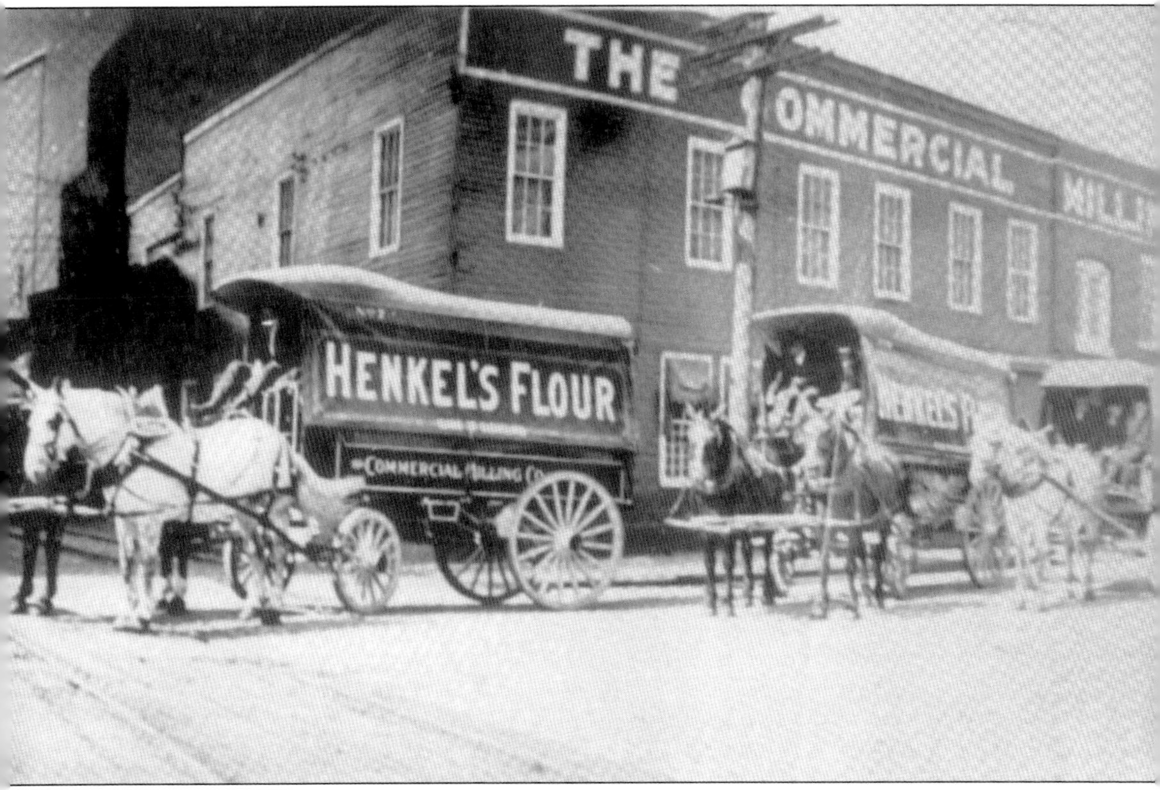

mill also sold corn meal, wheat meal, rye meal, rolled oats, and farina by the barrel or bag. There would be a flour mill on this riverfront site for a total of 117 years, until an urban renewal riverfront project called for the demolition of the Robin Hood Flour Mill in 1967.

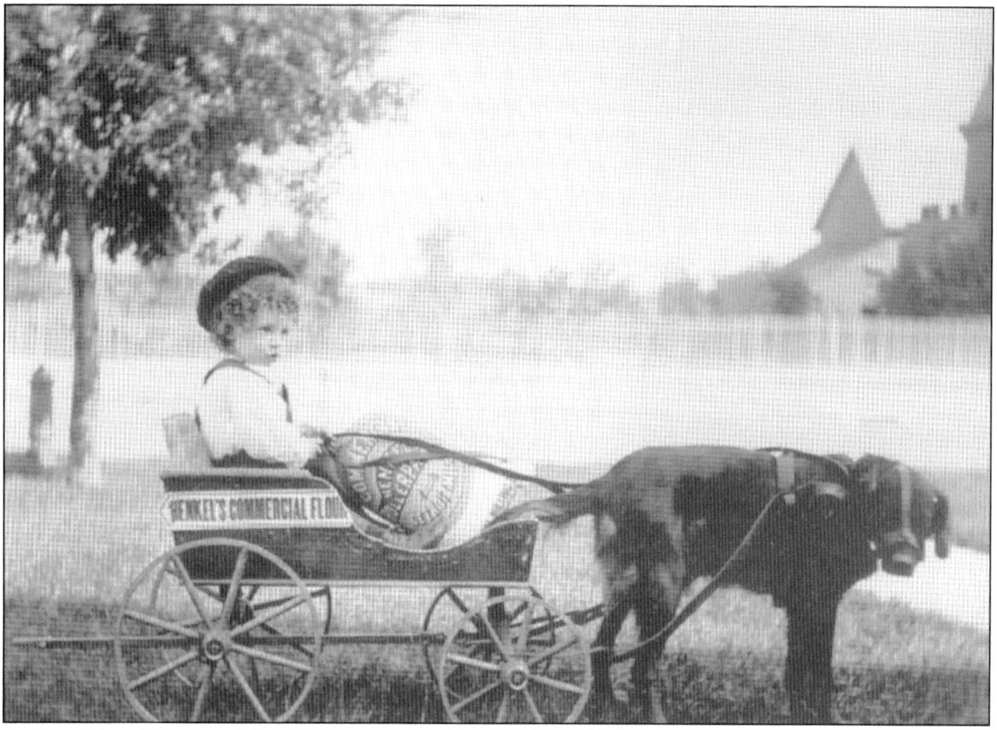

A One-Dog Team. Advertising is everything and Henkel's pulled out all of the stops on this one. A scaled-down version of Henkel's delivery wagon is driven by a very cute child and the family dog. This is evidently a one-day express delivery service.

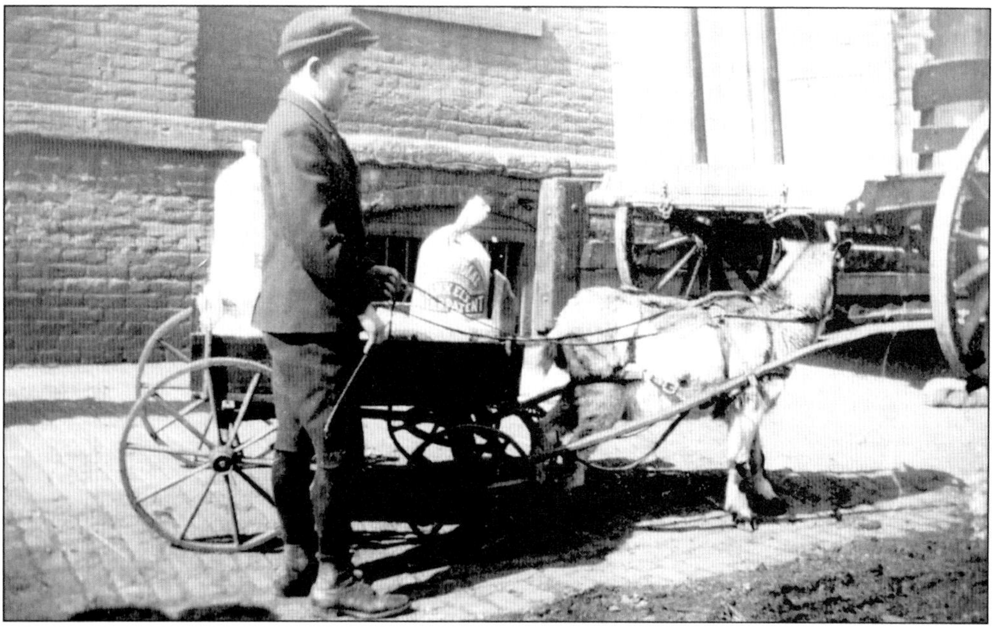

Boy, Don't Let Them Get Your Goat. Another excellent advertising piece has an older boy and a one-goat-powered wagon ready to make its rounds with a full load of Henkel's Flour products. This seems to work more effectively with the younger children.

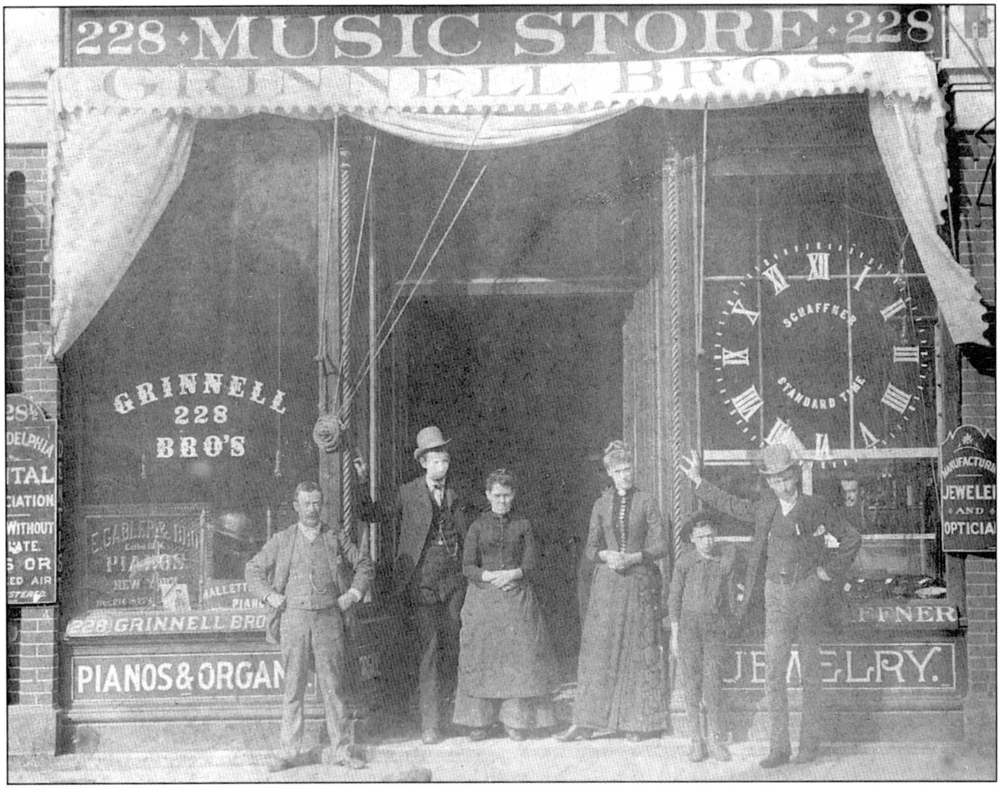

The Brothers Grinnel. Ira and Clayton Grinnel, the dudes in the hats, stand in front of their second store on Woodward Avenue, which they operated from 1884 to 1896. In addition to pianos and organs, they also carried jewelry, watches, and clocks, and provided optical services as well.

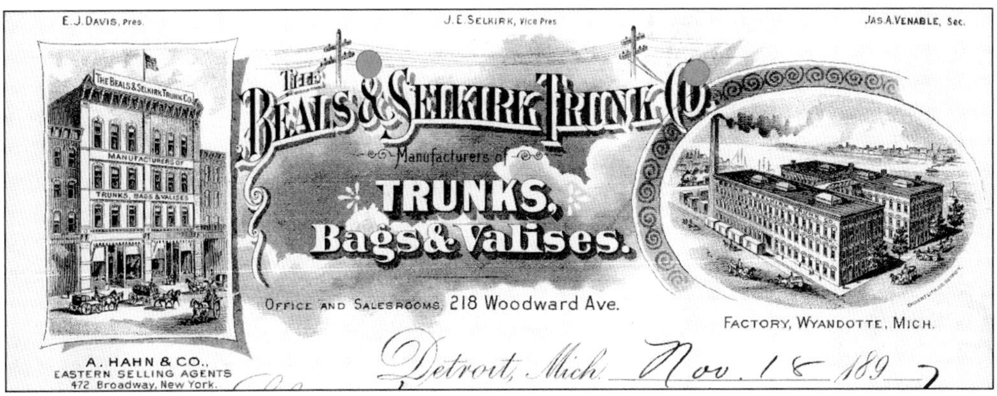

Baggage Needs. The Beals and Selkirk Trunk Company, makers of trunks, bags, and valises had their offices and salesrooms on Woodward Avenue and their factory in Wyandotte, Michigan. By 1897, the company also had an eastern sales agent on Broadway in New York City.

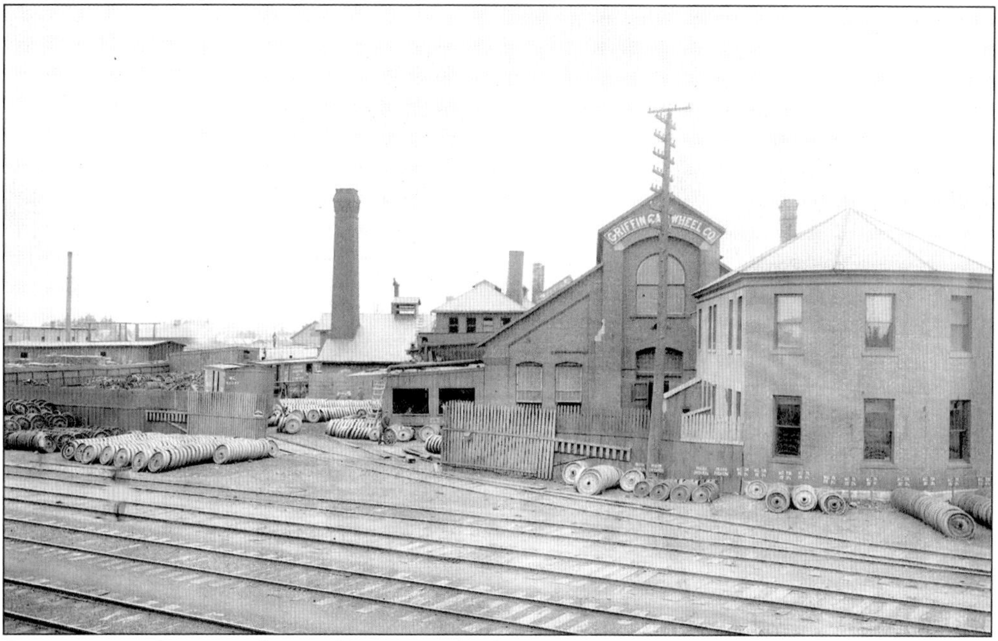

CAR WHEEL GIANT. The Griffin Car Wheel Company, originally organized in 1877, had grown to this size by 1881. Nowhere in the country were more railway cars and car wheels made than in Detroit, and Griffin was a leader in wheel manufacture. They furnished wheels and castings for six Michigan and Ohio railroad companies.

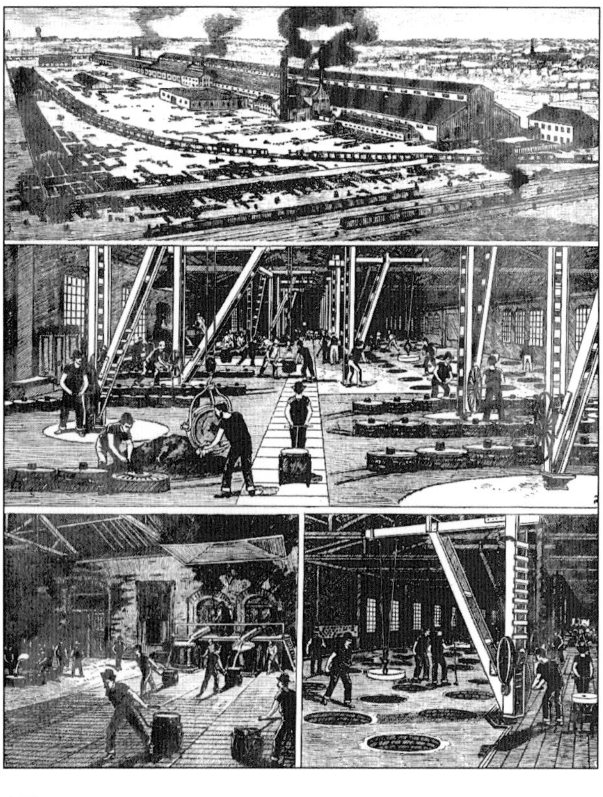

FRANK LESLIE'S VIEWS. Taken from Frank Leslie's Illustrated Newspaper in August of 1889. These are excellent views: the plant and its interior; the wheel foundry (middle); handling the molten iron (lower left); and depositing the finished wheels in the "pits." They could make 300 wheels per day.

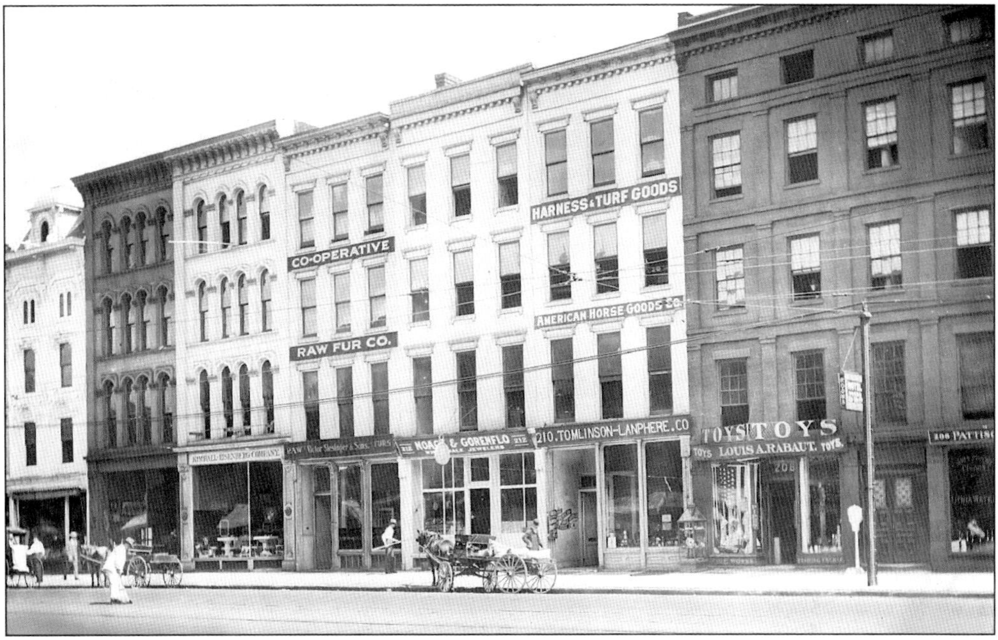

East Jefferson Avenue. The 210 block of East Jefferson Avenue just around the turn of the century reveals a typical mix of businesses. There was still a need for harness and turf goods and the Tomlinson-Lamphere Company were the agents. The appearance of a toy store signifies the specialization of some of the businesses.

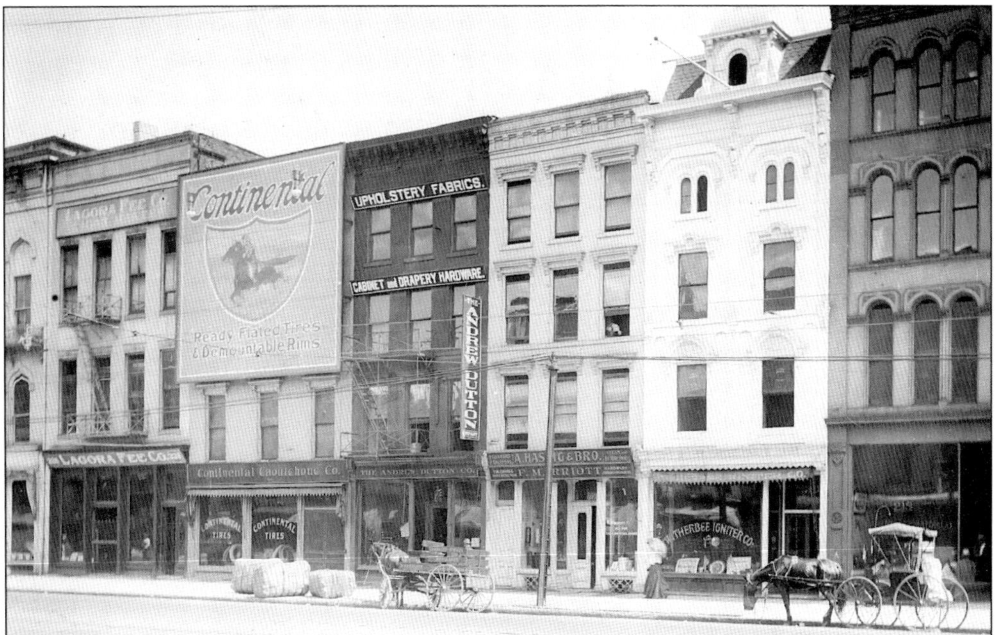

A Little Farther Down Jefferson. Older buildings with newer businesses in the next block of Jefferson were definitely here to stay. One sure sign of change to come is the large advertisement for Continental Tires with ready Flated Tires and Demountable Rims. Around the turn of the century, there were still more horses than automobiles in the city.

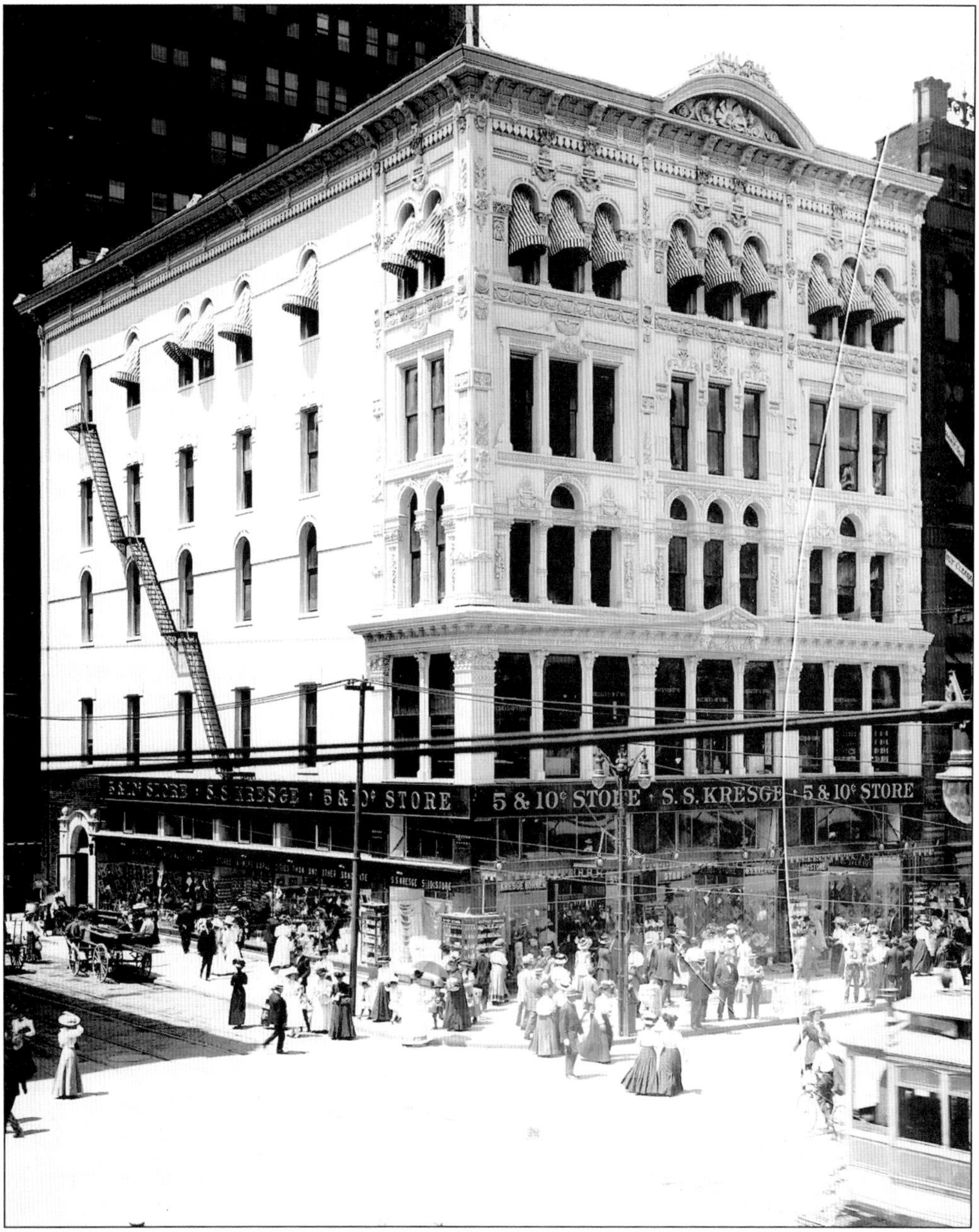

The Kresge Korner. The dime store originated in New York around 1870, and Detroit's first one was founded in 1899 by Sebastian S. Kresge. Store number 1 stood midway between State Street and Grand River Avenue on Woodward Avenue. On the front of that store hung a sign saying: "Nothing Over Ten Cents In Store", a policy that would prevail until the end of World War I when inflation forced prices up. 18 employees worked in the original store #1, which was divided into two sections: one for five cent items and the other for ten. Kresge moved store #1 to this location at the corner of State Street and Woodward Avenue in 1909. In 1899, Kresge also opened a store in Port Huron, Michigan, sharing interest with his brother-in-law Charles J. Wilson. By 1912, Kresge was operating 85 stores and doing $10,000,000 worth of business.

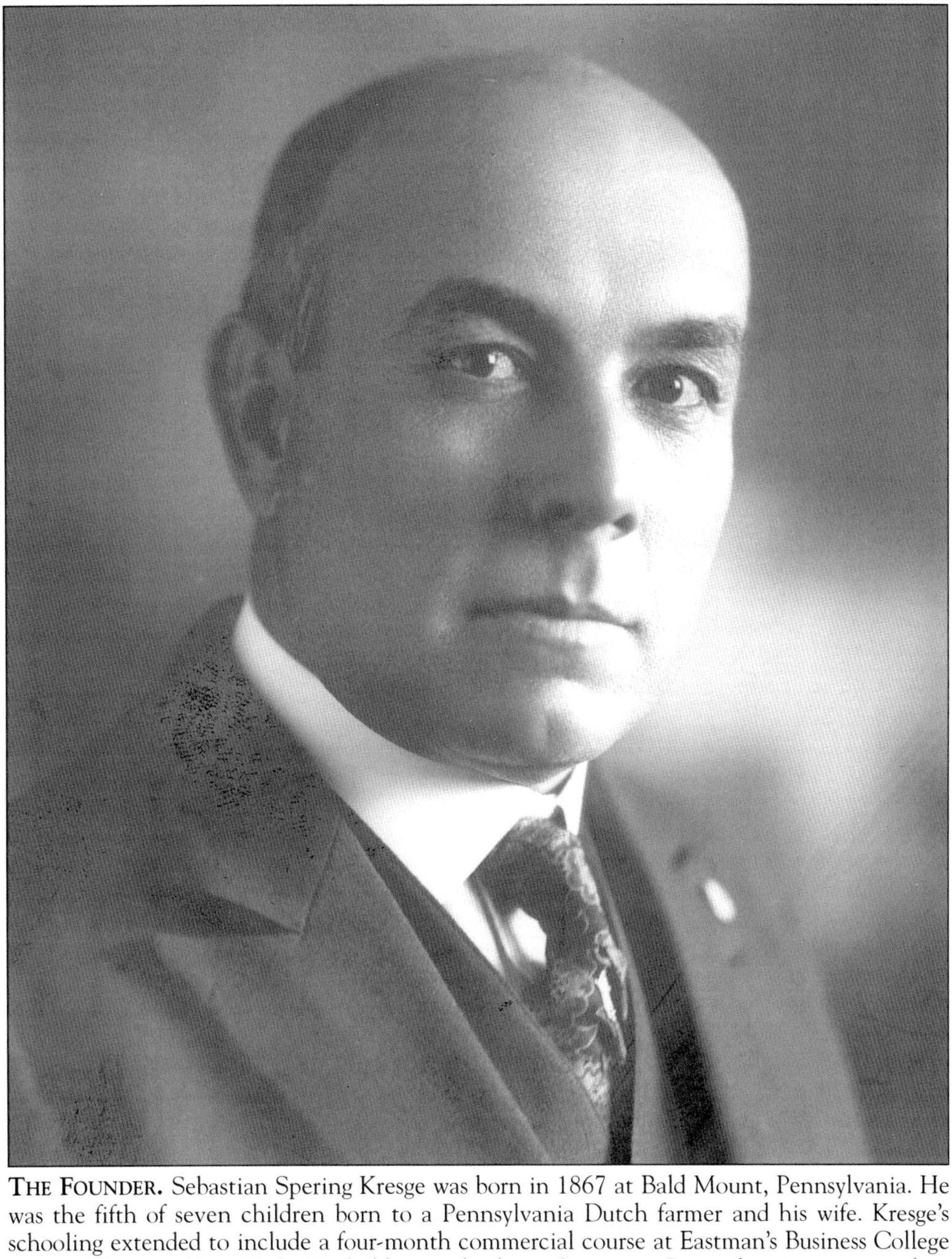

THE FOUNDER. Sebastian Spering Kresge was born in 1867 at Bald Mount, Pennsylvania. He was the fifth of seven children born to a Pennsylvania Dutch farmer and his wife. Kresge's schooling extended to include a four-month commercial course at Eastman's Business College in Poughkeepsie, New York. He held several jobs in Scranton, Pennsylvania, as a traveling salesman and bookkeeper, among others. He managed to save $8,000 by 1897 and Kresge made an offer to buy into the business of F.W. Woolworth. Woolworth turned him down and Kresge approached another of his customers, John McCrory, who agreed to share interest in his store in Detroit and Memphis, Tennessee. In 1899, the two agreed to split and Kresge had full ownership of the McCrory store Detroit, which would become Kresge store #1. S.S. Kresge, coming from a family blessed with longevity (he lived to be 99), was there to approve the $80,000,000 Kmart venture.

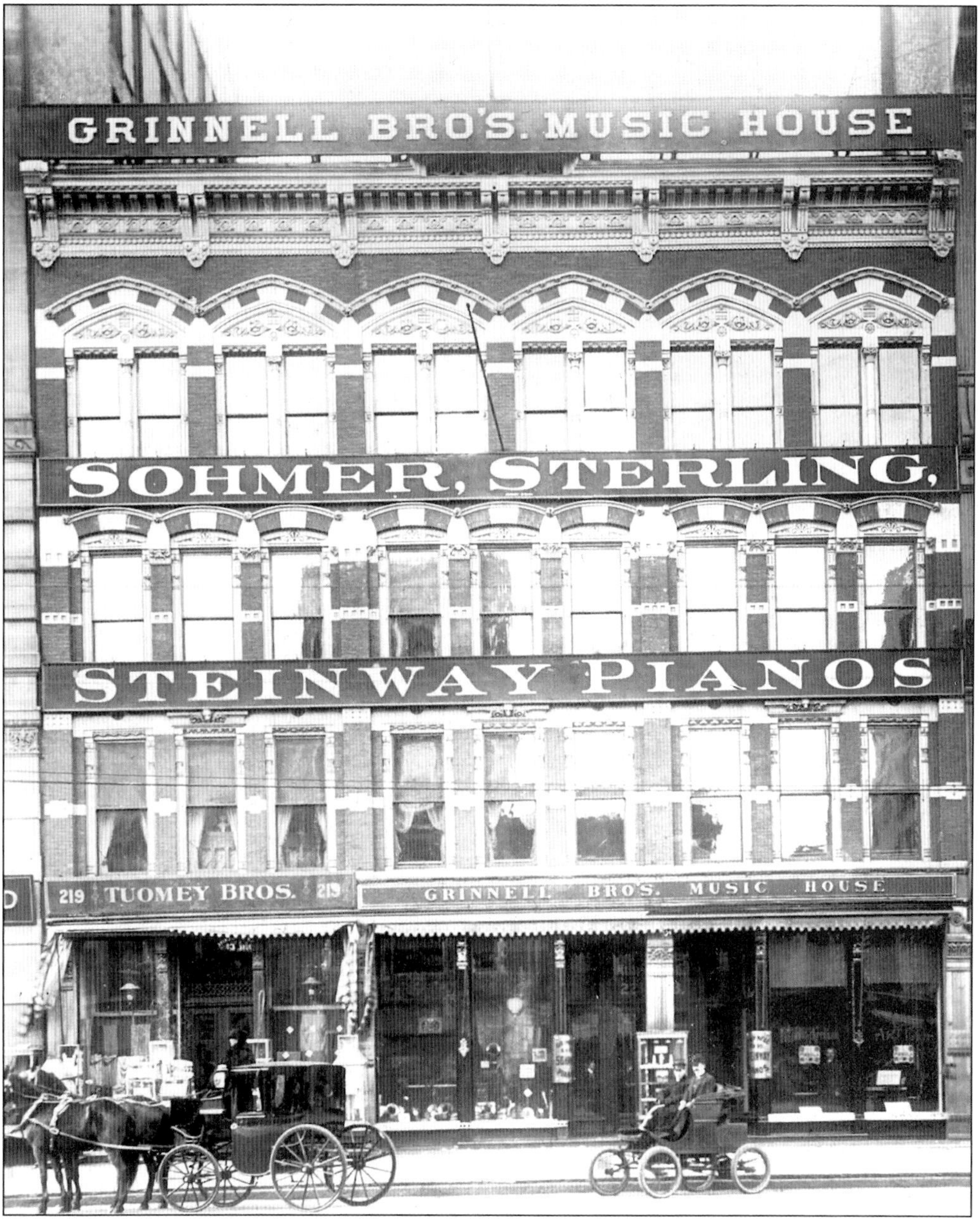

THE PLACE TO BUY A PIANO. The Grinnell Brothers Music House on Woodward Avenue occupied three lots in the 200 block (old numbers). The brothers opened this, their third store in 1896 and stayed here until 1908. Ira L. Grinnell came to Michigan in 1872 from New York, where he worked as a lumberjack and opened a small store in Ann Arbor, Michigan, dealing in sewing machines and sewing supplies. When they opened their first store in 1882, sewing machines and supplies were the lead item and only occasional piano sales were made. An ever increasing volume of business necessitated the move to larger quarters and music sales had become of major importance. The Grinnell Brothers turned to musical instruments and sheet music for the larger part of their sales.

Six

THE INTERNATIONAL FAIR AND EXPOSITION, 1889

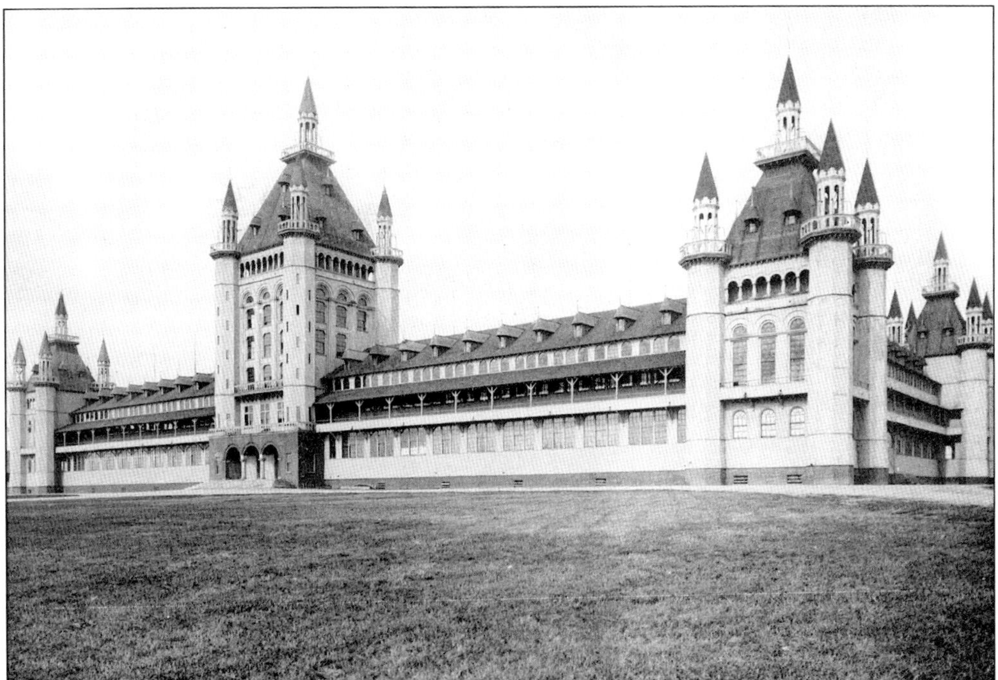

A CHANCE TO STRUT. Detroit had a chance to showcase itself and its many manufactures at an International Fair and Exposition held in 1889. The main exhibit building was located on the fairgrounds at the southern city limits where the Rouge River met the Detroit River. Looking like a king's palace, it was the largest exhibit building in the world.

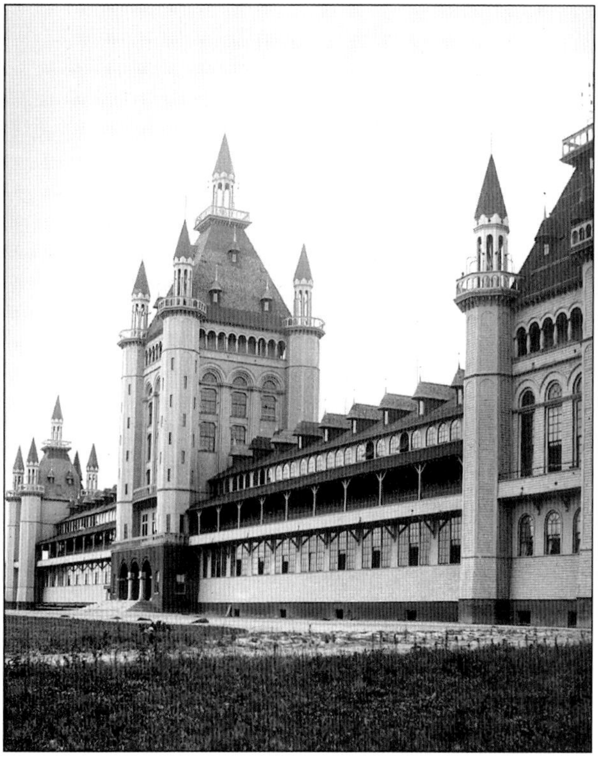

The Exposition Building. The central tower of the main building rose 200 feet in the air; there was a total of 200,000 square feet of exhibit space and 4.5 acres of glass in its walls. There were two boat landings at the grounds, one on each of the rivers.

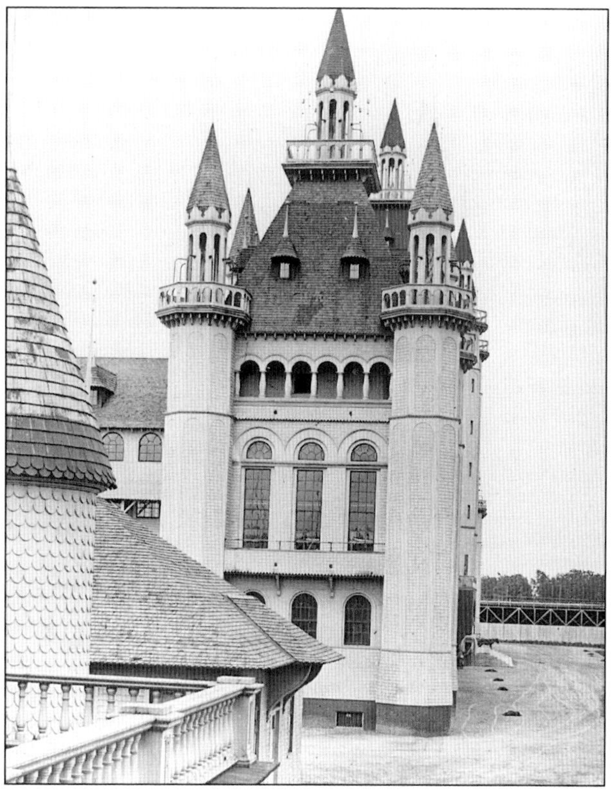

Fit For A Princess. The towers of the building each boasted five garrets, from which sightseers could see for miles. The Exposition sat on 14 acres and a committee raised a quarter of a million dollars to finance it, which was more than one dollar for each resident of the city.

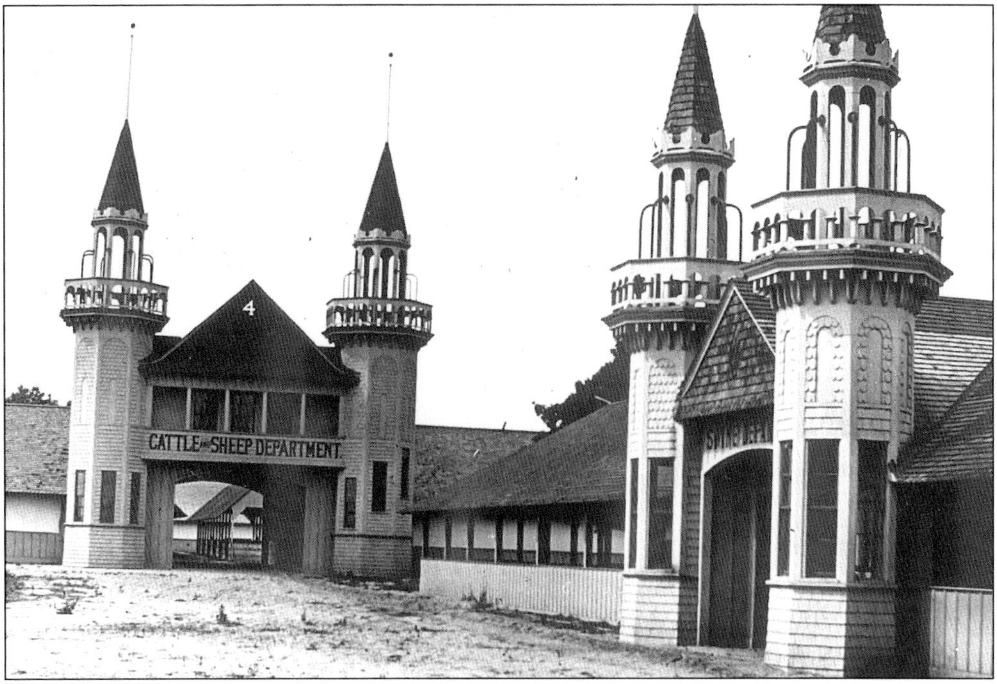

OUTSIDE EXHIBIT AREA. One of the four larger exhibit areas behind the main one contained the cattle and sheep department. There was a definite state-fair type of competition between farmers over their livestock. The Exposition offered $43,136.00 in premiums for competition.

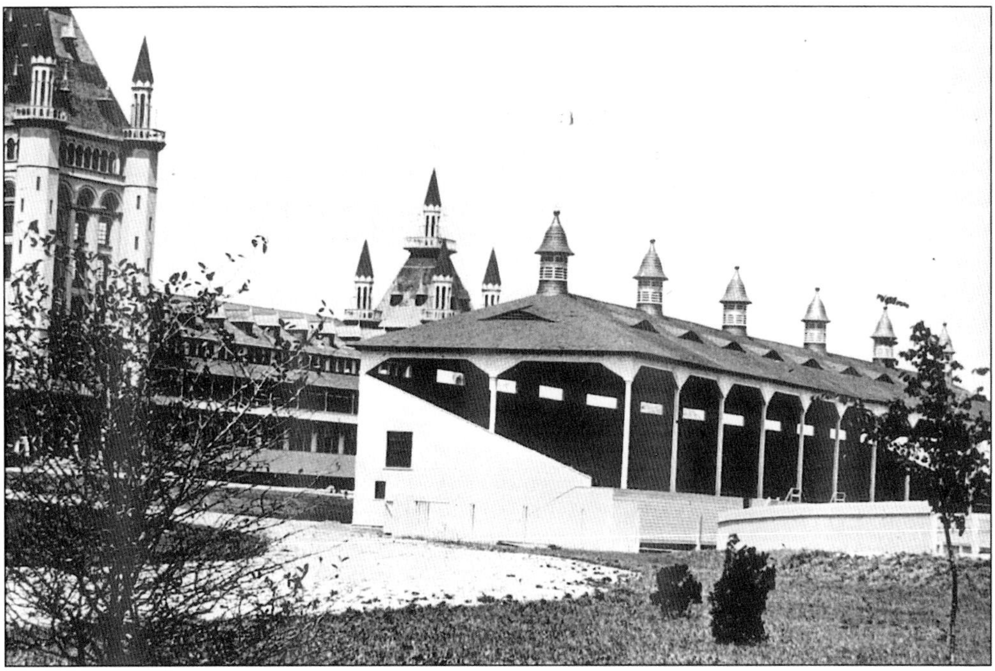

HORSE AND BOAT RACES. A huge oval track was used for horse races and a water basin just as large was used for sailboat races. These grandstands offered an excellent vantage point to see either race and out of the sun as well. Baseball games were also held here during the Fair.

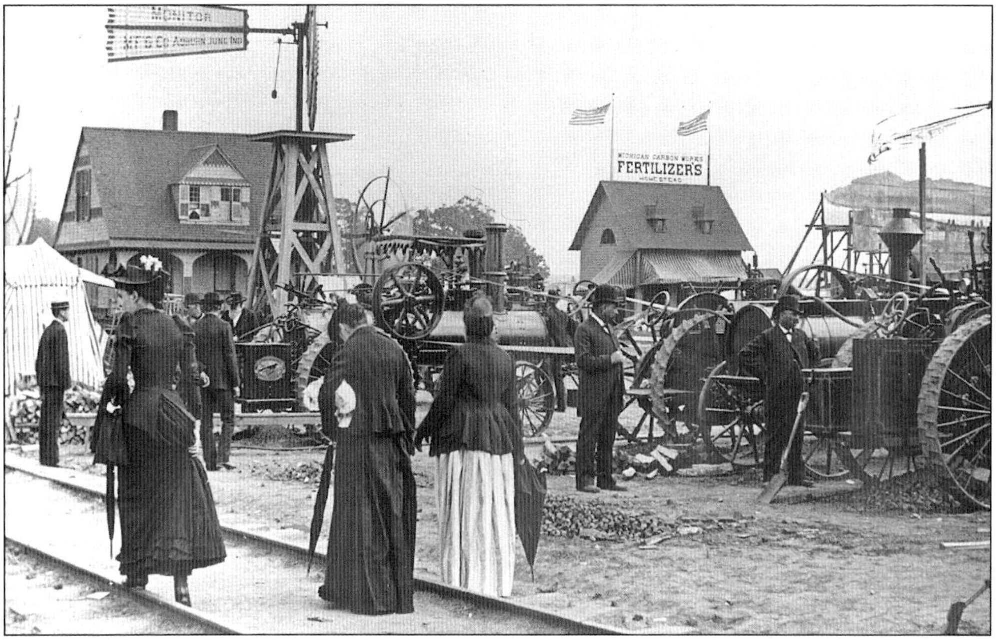

MACHINE EXHIBITS. These ladies wait patiently for their spouses who are eagerly inspecting the latest models in steam-powered tractors at the farm machinery exhibit. The "Monitor" brand windmill is also shown, and the Michigan Carbon Works stand can also be seen advertising their "Homestead" fertilizer.

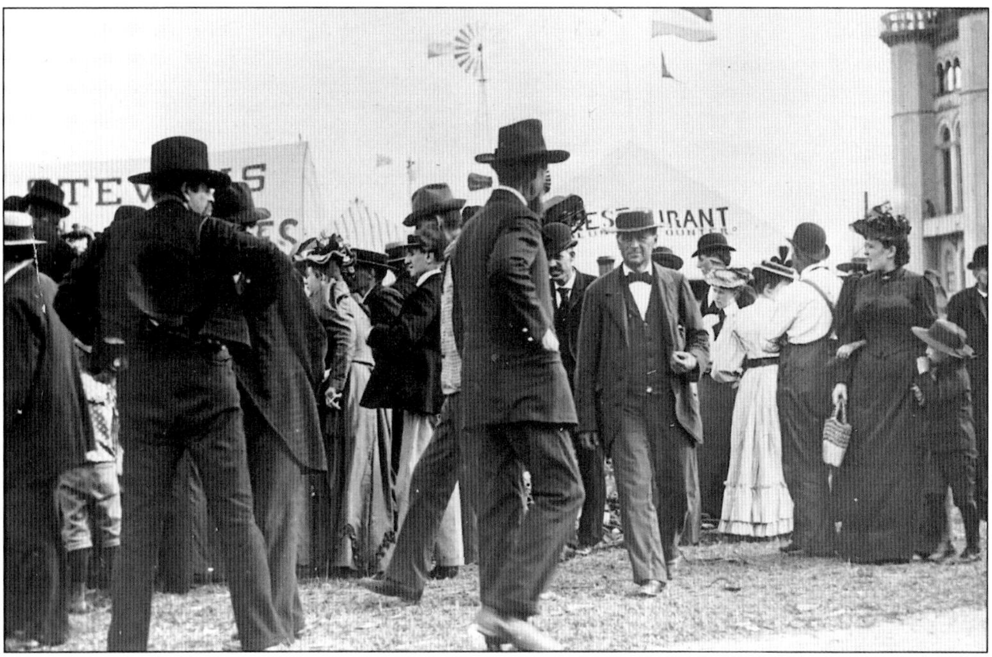

AT THE FAIR. The International Fair and Exposition drew tens of thousands of visitors from the United States and Canada during its ten-day run in September, 1889. There were plenty of things to see and do, including a midway-type portion of the fair where one could see trick shooters.

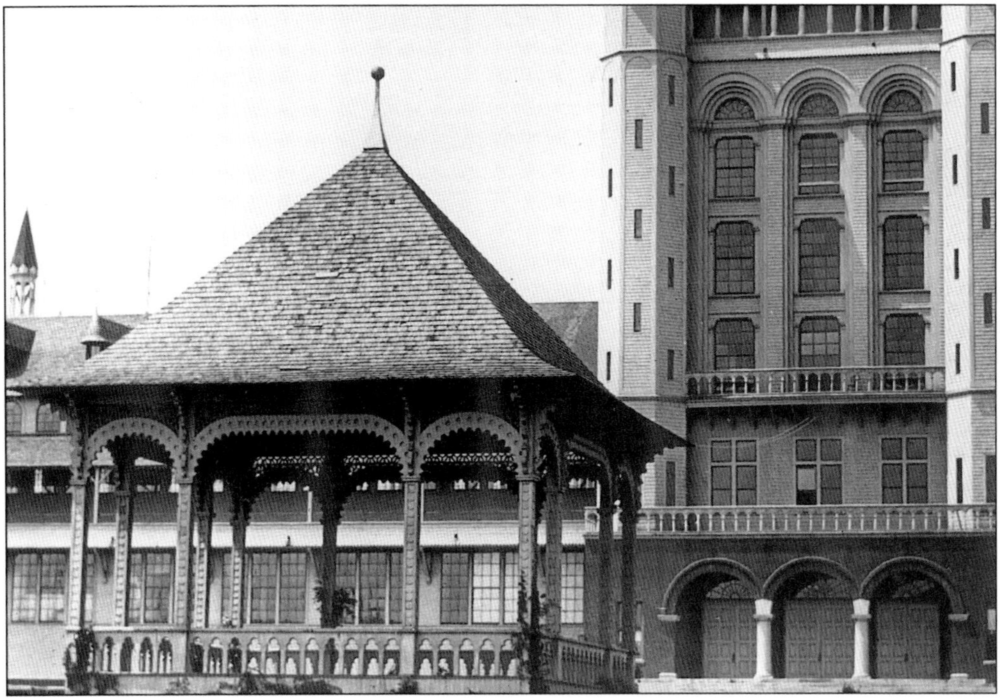

A BANDSTAND FOR CONCERTS. The city of Detroit pulled out all of the stops to make the Fair a success, including assembling the best musical talent in America. Considered one of the leading aesthetic features of the Fair, it included the matchless 7th Regiment Band, conducted by C.A. Cappa.

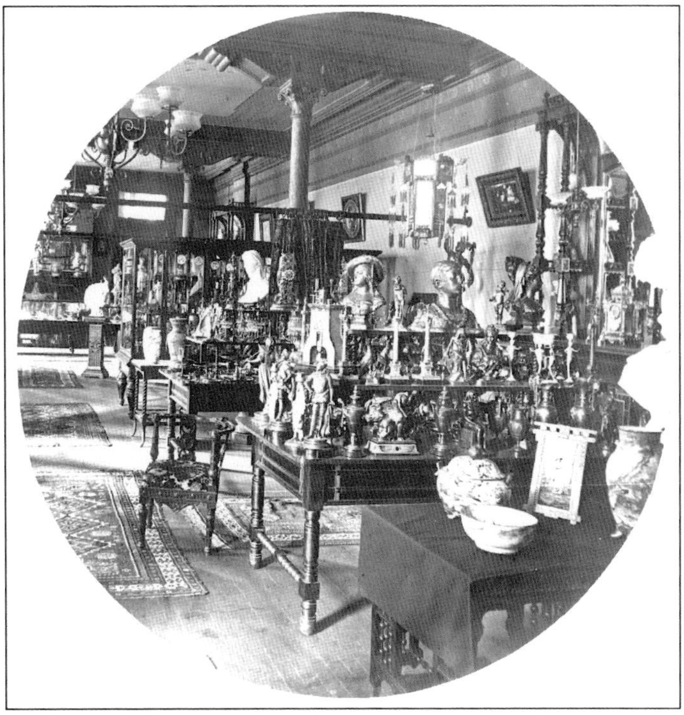

THE ART GALLERY. A glimpse of the exhibits in the art building reveals row upon row of attractions both typical and unusual. The building had a frontage of 150 feet filled with art treasures. Among the features was the American Prize Fund Collection, numbering 350 paintings by 200 of the country's leading artists.

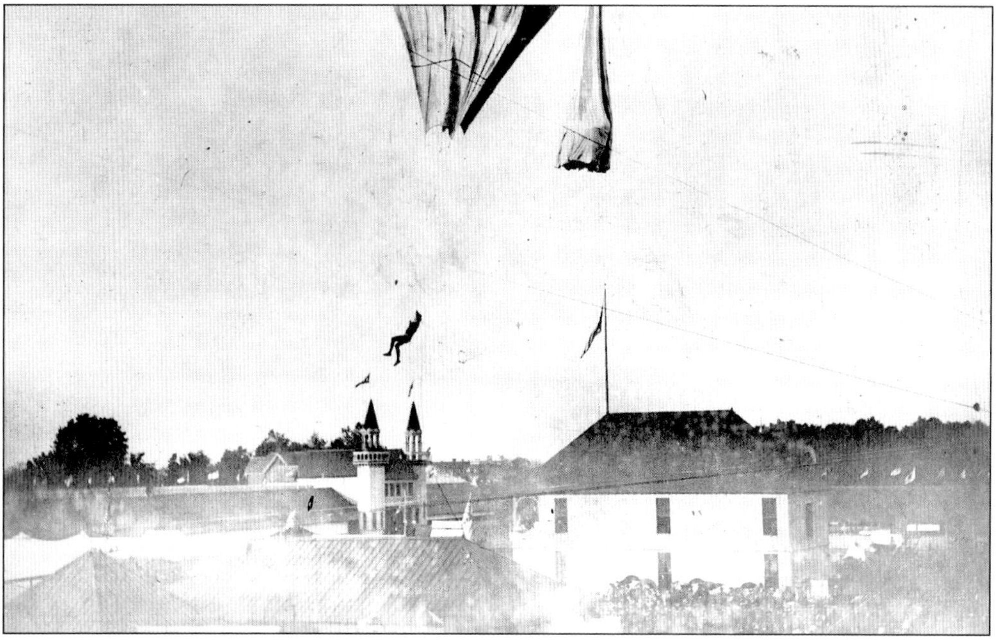

TRAGEDY. Balloon ascents were always a popular attraction of any state or county fair, and the Detroit Exposition was no different. During the 1891 version of the fair, aeronaut John Hogan fell to his death during a much-heralded balloon ascension.

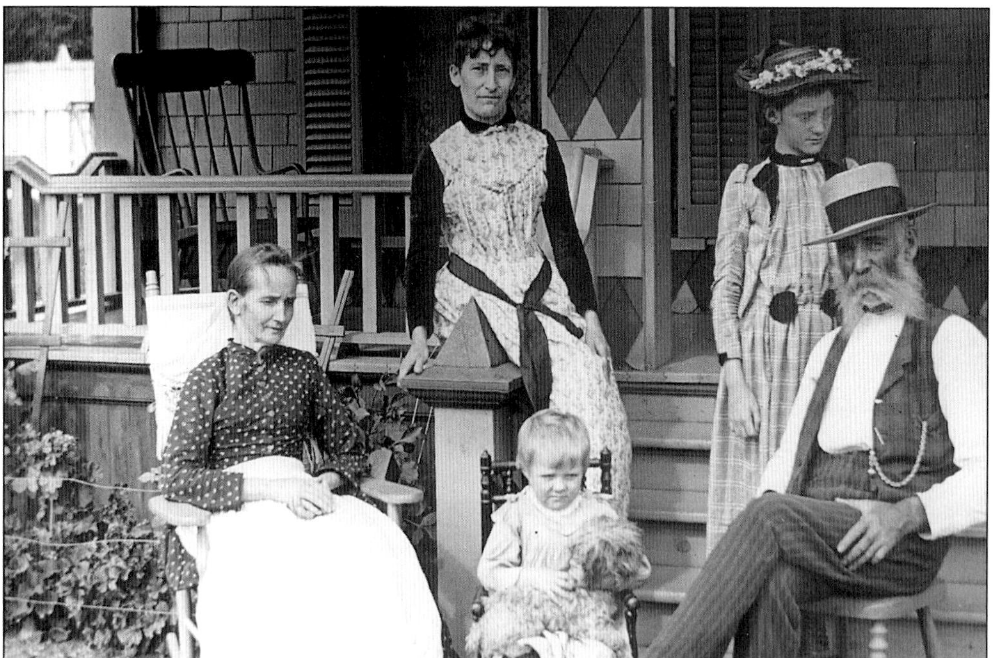

AFTER THE FAIR. The aftermath of the Fair finds this family relaxing in front of their wooden bungalow, looking fairly worn out by all of the excitement a ten-day long event can generate. But this family's work had just begun. This is the Park Superintendent and his family. The Fair would be held for four more years.